Philip Lewis's Science Book

Tell No:(01285, 860825)

I live in south cerney.

Year 2000.

THE NEW WORLD OF KNOWLEDGE

The encyclopedia of SCIENCE

7

ALADDIN BOOKS
LONDON

This edition produced in **1999** for
BOOKMART LIMITED
Desford Road
Enderby
Leicester
LE9 5AD

Created and produced by
Aladdin Books Ltd
28 Percy Street
London W1P 0LD

Design
David West Children's Book Design
Designers
Steve Woosnam-Savage, Flick Killerby and
Ed Simpkins
Series Director
Bibby Whittaker
Editors
Jen Green, Sarah Levete, Angela Travis, Jim Pipe,
Suzanne Melia, Elise Bradbury and Richard Green
Picture Research
Emma Krikler
Illustrator
Dave Burroughs, Simon Tegg, Karen Johnson
and Biz Hull

ISBN 1-85605-515-9

Printed in Singapore

Some of the material in this book was previously
published in the Focus On series.

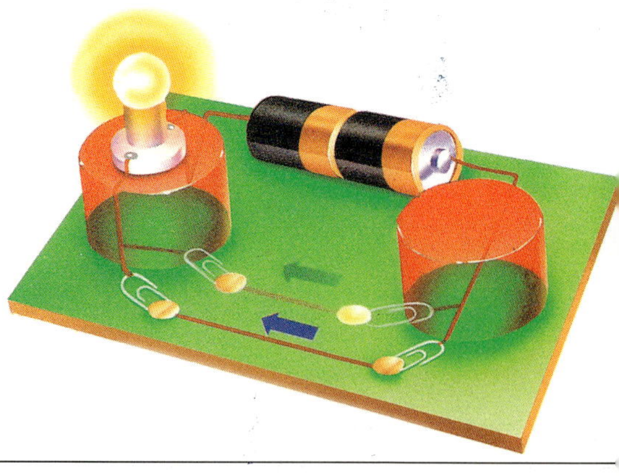

CONTENTS

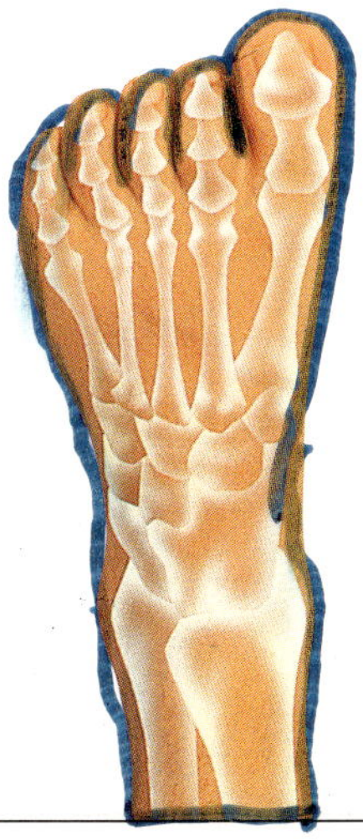

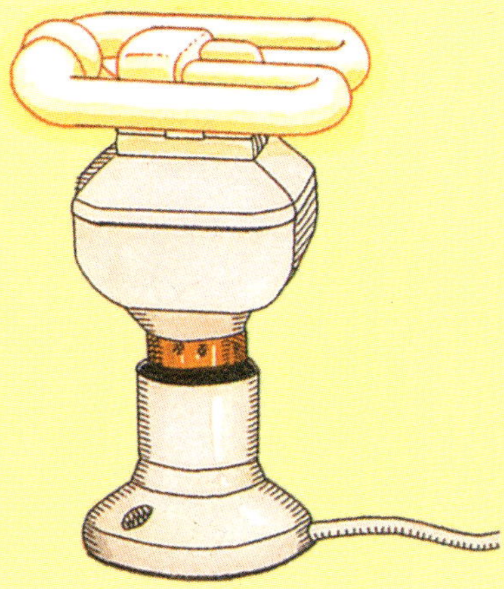

INTRODUCTION

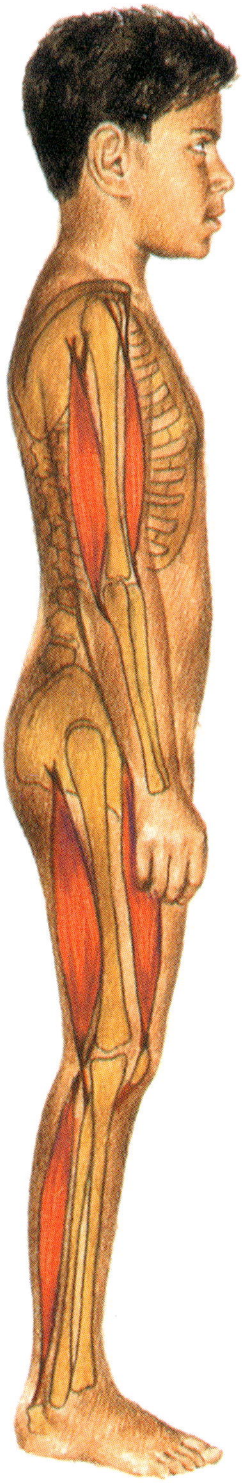

This encyclopedia introduces the ever-changing world of science. The first chapter covers sound, explaining how sound travels, how we hear sounds and how some animals like bats feel sounds instead. Did you know that light was a form of energy and is made up of a spectrum of colours? More properties of light are discussed in chapter two.

We breathe the same air, and drink the same water that dinosaurs did! In chapter three, learn how air is recycled and find out about the many properties of air. Water is one of the most common and unusual substances on earth – discover its many properties and uses.

Social History

The symbol of the family signals information about social history. Topics discussed include the significance of water in religious ceremonies, and ideas and medical beliefs that exist in different countries, or the effects of natural disasters caused by water.

Geography

The symbol of the planet Earth shows where geographical facts are used. Such facts include how water affects people's lives, and how different weather patterns create different living environments.

Language and Literature

An open book is the sign for activities which involve language. These sections discuss the influence science, realistic and imaginary, has on the literary world, and the development of communication.

The Sun is our main energy source. Chapter four looks at the ways in which this energy is used by all living things. Lightning is nature's form of electricity. Chapter five discusses the different ways we generate and use electricity. The human body is very complicated and truly amazing. Scientists are discovering more about the way it works and how it is made. This is discussed in the last chapter.

A glossary and an index are provided. Information on the arts, language and literature, maths, science and technology, history and geography is highlighted. The boxes (shown right and left) illustrate how the subjects are divided.

Science and Technology

The microscope symbol is used where a science or technology subject is included. These sections examine key significant discoveries such as hydro-electric power or equipment used for studying our solar system.

History

The sign of the scroll and hourglass indicates that historical facts are included. Sections explore the development of scientific discovery, such as apparatus and equipment used as well as the people involved.

Maths

A ruler and compass indicate maths information and activities. Topics include how the speed of sound through the air is used as a unit of speed, and how we have learned to measure and quantify intangible objects.

Arts, Crafts and Music

The symbol showing a sheet of music and art tools indicates arts, crafts or musical information. These sections discuss the importance of the elements of nature, such as water, as a source of inspiration to both artists and musicians.

CHAPTER 1

SOUND

Sound is a form of energy. Every sound that we hear is produced by the vibrations of an object. We use sound in so many different ways, from ships that gauge the depth of the ocean floor beneath them to leisure activities such as singing and dancing.

We use our ears to detect sounds, but some animals, like bats, sense sounds through the vibrations that cause the sound. Discover the many uses we have for sound, and how we can measure and store sound. How fast is the speed of sound – can you move that fast?

CONTENTS

SOUNDS ALL AROUND

From the ringing of a telephone to the sound of someone's heartbeat, sounds give us information about what is happening inside and outside our bodies. Unpleasant sounds, such as sirens, usually warn of danger, while musical sounds can be happy and relaxing. People and other animals use a variety of sound messages for communication. When people talk, they are able to learn from each other and pass on ideas, opinions, thoughts and feelings.

Sounds around the world

People have been making music for thousands of years, first from natural objects like shells, then crafting instruments from gourds, wood or metal. Around the world, groups of instruments, such as pipes, share similar features.

Latin American pipes
Traditional music in Latin America often features pipes. Pan-pipes have different length hollow reeds for each note.

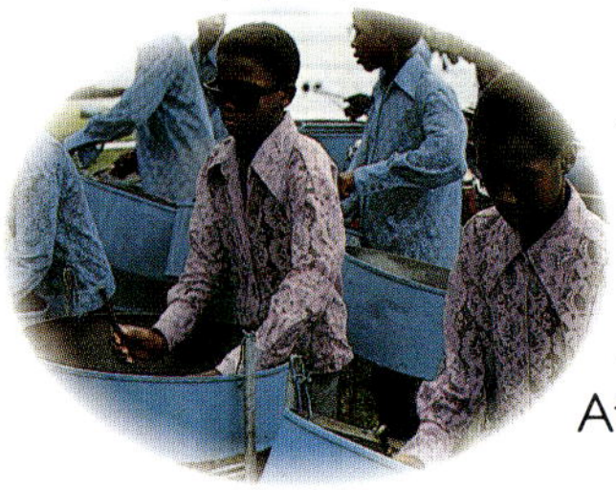

African influence
The importance of drums in African music has influenced the music of other cultures where African people live.

Strings of the world
From the Indian sitar to the Spanish guitar, nearly every culture has a stringed instrument.

Musical note

Human heartbeat

Making sound visual
Sound can be difficult to express in words. One method language uses to portray sound is called onomatopoeia, which means a word sounds like its meaning. Examples of this are "pop", "hoot", "crack" and "hiss". Cartoonists put visuals to sound. Loud noises like explosions are expressed with words like "BOOM", drawn in bright colours and big, bold letters. The star shape gives the impression of contact. Experiment with words and shapes to see how you can best express sounds.

Learning to discern
We hear so many sounds around us that we tend to block out the less important ones. A normal ear can identify up to 400,000 separate sounds. Try listing every sound that you hear during an active part of each day. After a few days divide the sounds into different categories, like mechanical, weather, human, animal and so on, and compile a bar chart. What are the most and least common noises you hear on an average day?

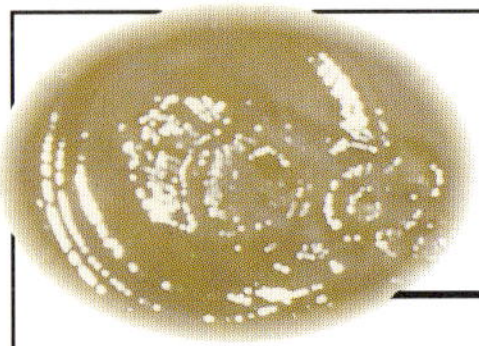

WHAT IS SOUND?

A sound is made by something moving. The something can be a solid, such as wood, a liquid such as water, or a gas such as air. We usually hear the sounds made by air moving. The sound compresses or squashes a little package of air, which soon stretches out again, squashing the air next to it and so on. Sound is sent through the air as squash- stretch-squash-stretch ... In other words, the sounds we hear are really very small changes in air pressure. People can hear sounds from about 20 to 20,000 squashes and stretches per second.

Sound waves

Sounds spread out in a regular pattern, like ripples on a pond. They are pressure waves rather than up and down waves, but when they are plotted on a graph, wave shapes are produced. Sound is a form of energy. Like the water in an ocean wave, the sound itself does not move. It passes on its moving energy to the piece of air, water or gas next to it, and this in turn passes on the sound. It's rather like a line of dominoes falling over, one after the other.

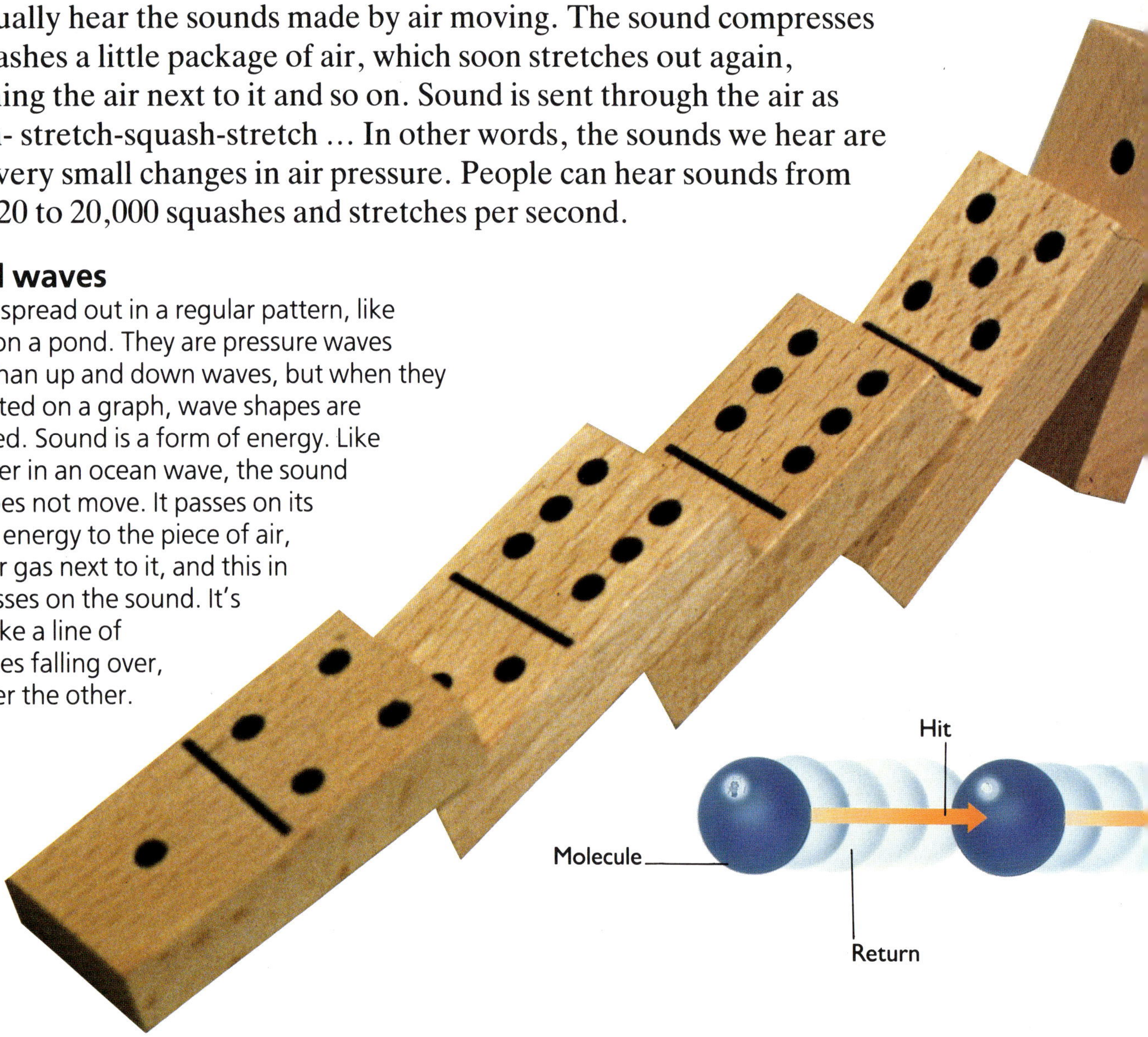

Feel the vibrations

You don't normally think of sound as something you can see or feel. However, this activity shows that sound is made up of vibrations. Blow up a balloon and hold it to your mouth. Have someone else touch the balloon while you speak. Then repeat this exercise with them holding the balloon next to their mouth. Can you "feel" the person speak?

Sound travels through materials when the particles – the molecules – move back and forth. Each molecule hits another and then returns to its original position. Sound travels fastest through dense materials, such as metals, because the molecules are close together.

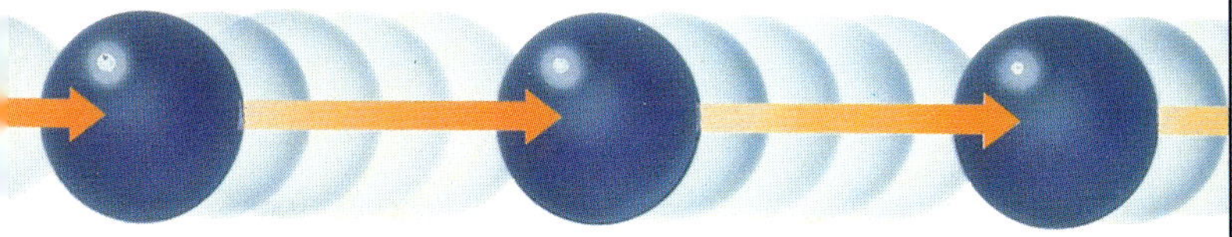

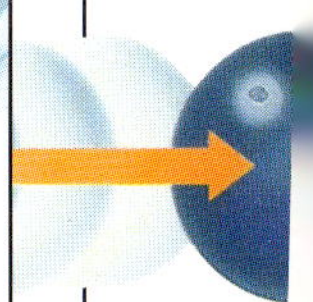

Sound in space

For sound to travel, there must be something to carry the vibrations along. On Earth, air molecules send and receive sound by bumping into one another and transmitting the vibrations. In space there is no air and no molecules so sound has no way to travel. Beyond the Earth's atmosphere there is complete silence. Astronauts in space must communicate either by radio (radio waves travel differently than sound waves) or by putting their helmets together and speaking. The sound can then travel through the helmets as vibrations and get the message across.

The loudest bang...

The loudest known explosion occurred in 1883 when a volcano called Krakatau erupted. Krakatau was a small, uninhabited island off the coast of Sumatra. On 27 August 1883, the volcano erupted, and the island collapsed into the sea. The massive explosion this caused was heard 3,000 km away on the island of Rodrigues in the Indian Ocean – the loudest sound ever recorded. A huge tidal wave washed over the shores of nearby islands, killing about 36,000 people. Volcanic dust remained in the air for about a year afterwards.

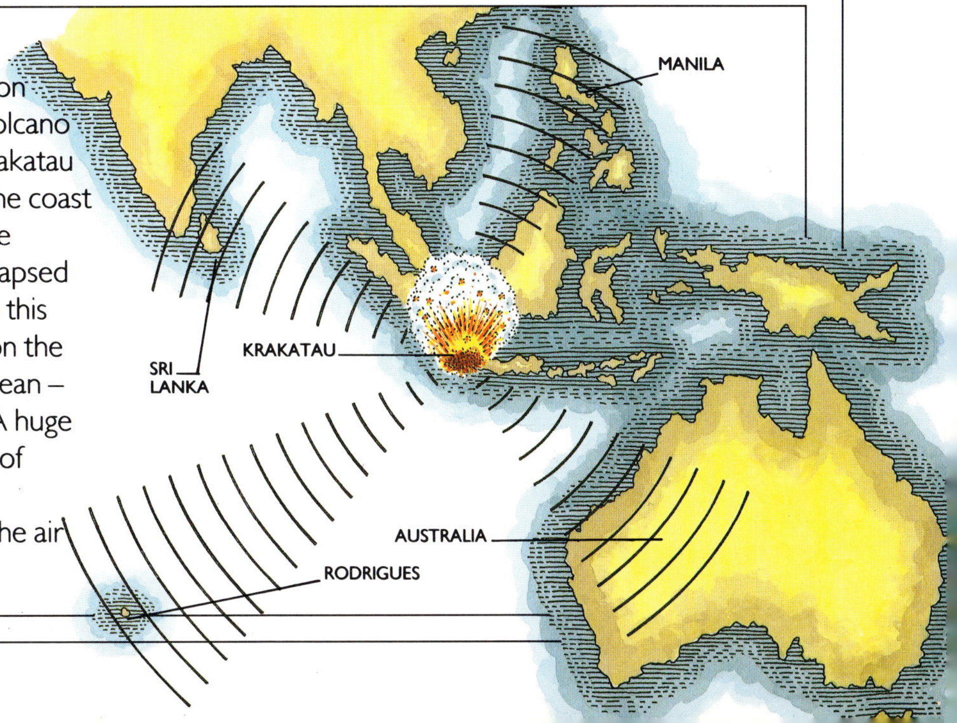

EARS AND HEARING

Many animals have special structures called ears to pick up sounds and send messages to the brain. Ears change sounds into electrical signals which are the language the brain "speaks". The brain tries to identify these signals by comparing them with the huge memory of sounds it has stored away since the animal was born. Most animals have two ears so they can tell which direction a sound is coming from. The sound will be louder in the ear nearest to the sound.

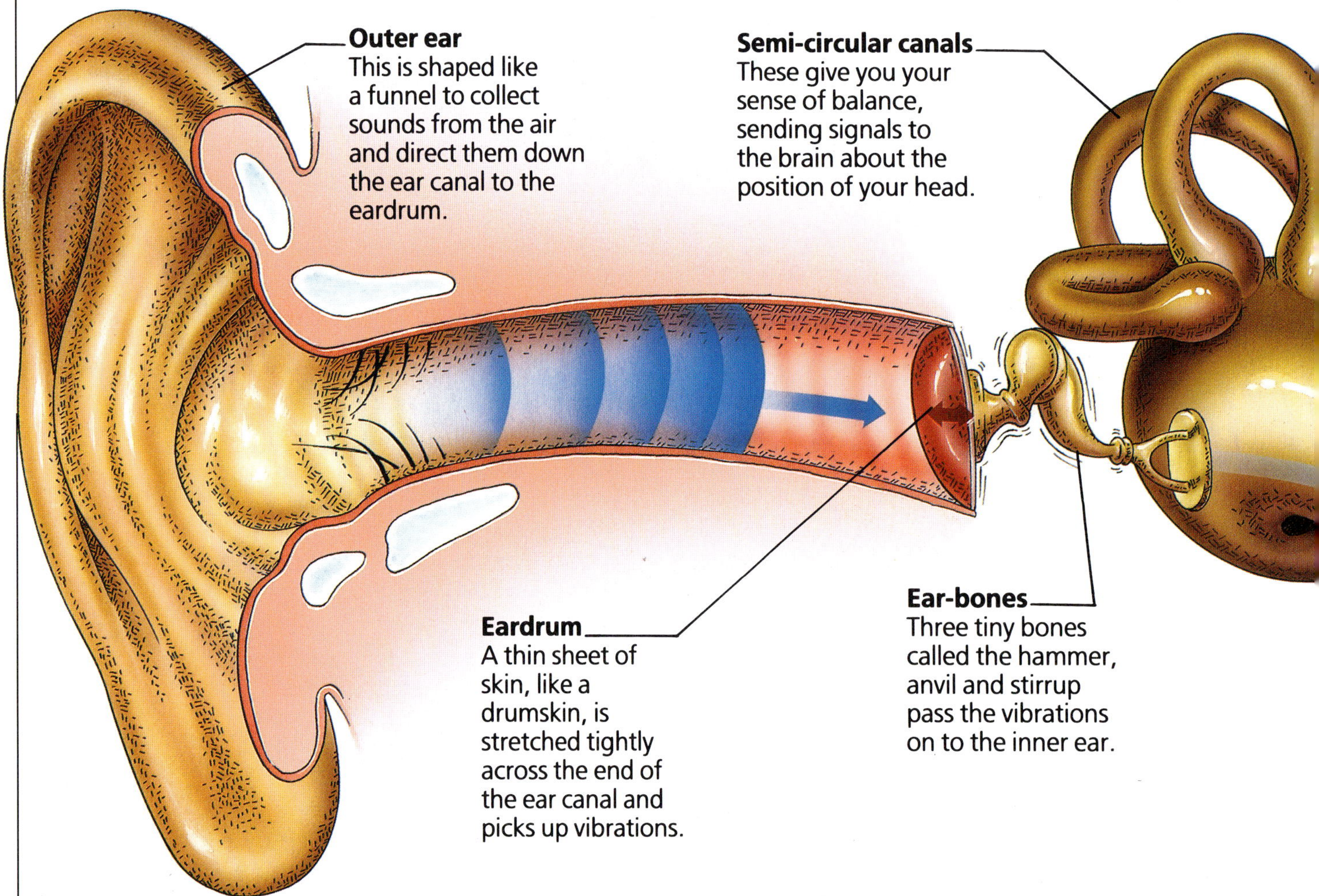

Drumming away

A simple drum can be made using a hollow container and a strong material such as plastic. Stretch the plastic over the top of the container and fix it tightly with tape or a rubber band. A hard drumskin can be made by using cloth or paper dipped in wallpaper paste. Improvise drumsticks from pencils or old toothbrushes.

Changing pitch

Experiment with the pitch of the drum by making the drumskin tighter or looser. The tighter the skin is stretched, the higher the pitch, because the skin vibrates faster.

Beethoven

Ludwig van Beethoven (1770-1827) is considered one of the greatest classical composers. His music is remarkable for the fact that his hearing faded early in his career. By 1824 he was completely deaf. However, he wrote some of his best work after this time.

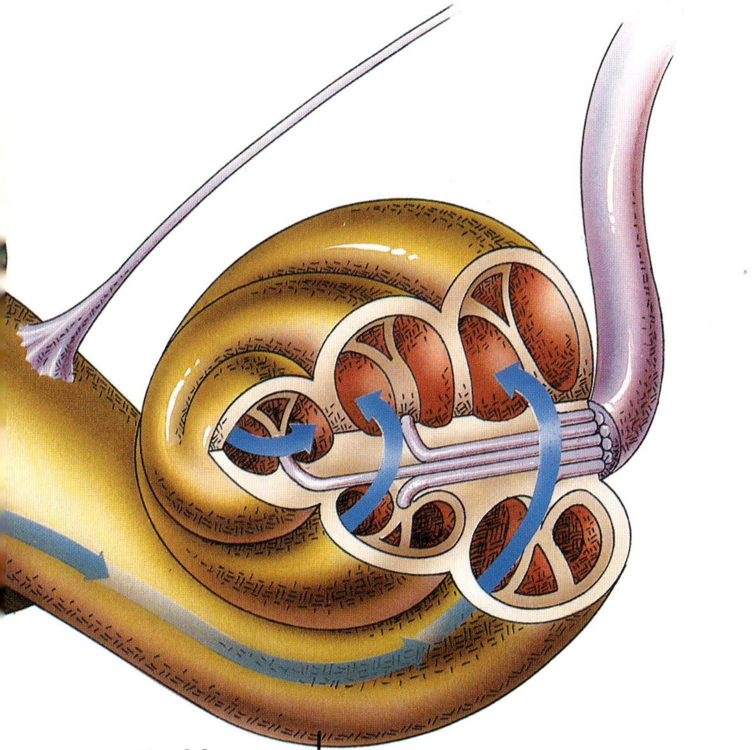

Cochlea
Inside this coiled tube, tiny hairs convert the vibrations into pulses of electrical signals.

Pellet drums

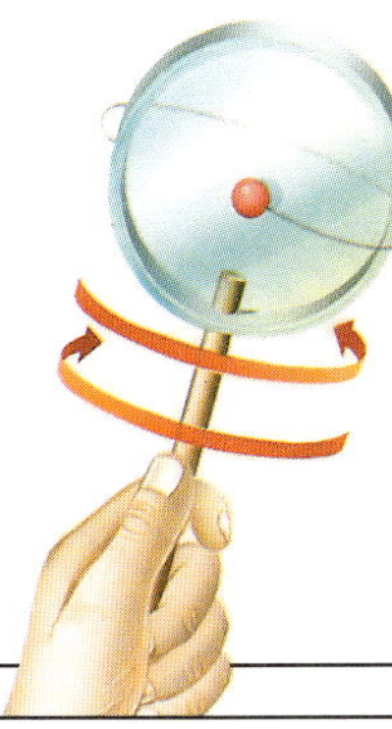

Cut off the bottom of a carton and stretch plastic over both open ends. Push a stick through the drum and thread a piece of string with a bead attached through each side. Twist the stick back and forth.

Animal ears

Biologists believe that ears developed from the balance organs of primeval fish. These were not likely to have been sensitive to sound, but detected vibrations in the water so that the fish could sense its surroundings. Ears for hearing probably did not come about until life emerged from the water and had to adapt to living on land. Most mammals then developed the funnel-shaped outer ear to collect sounds from the air.

Frogs
A frog's eardrum needs to be immersed in water frequently or it would dry out.

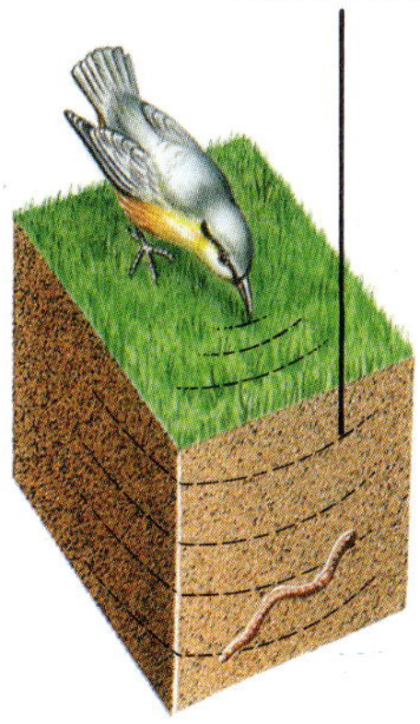

Cockroaches
Cockroaches detect sound with hairs on their bodies. These hairs are sensitive enough to respond to the slightest air movements caused by sound waves.

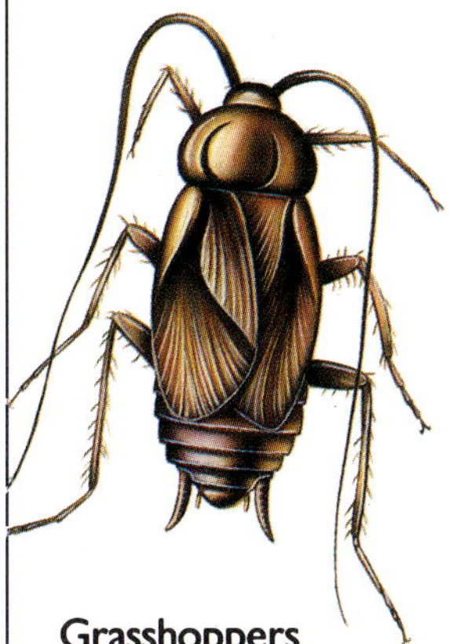

Worms
Worms do not have ears, but they can detect vibrations in the soil around them and react accordingly.

Vultures
Birds have exceptional hearing. They do not have an external ear, which would slow them down in flight.

Grasshoppers
A grasshopper's ears are located on the midsection of the body. Crickets have ears on their knees.

MAKING SOUNDS

Many of the sounds around us are produced as a result of natural forces in the environment. The wind happens when hot air rises and cool air rushes in. Thunder happens when air gets so hot that it expands rapidly, bumping into cooler air. People and other animals make sounds with their voices or with parts of their bodies. Many loud sounds can also be caused by machines such as lorries or electric drills.

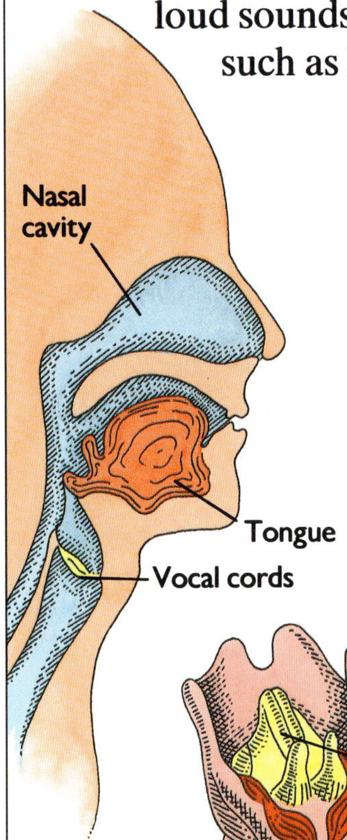

The lump you can feel on your throat – the Adam's apple – is also called the voice box or larynx. Inside it are flaps called vocal cords. When you speak or sing, these cords move closer together, producing a sound as you breath out. Our mouth and tongue shape the sounds into words.

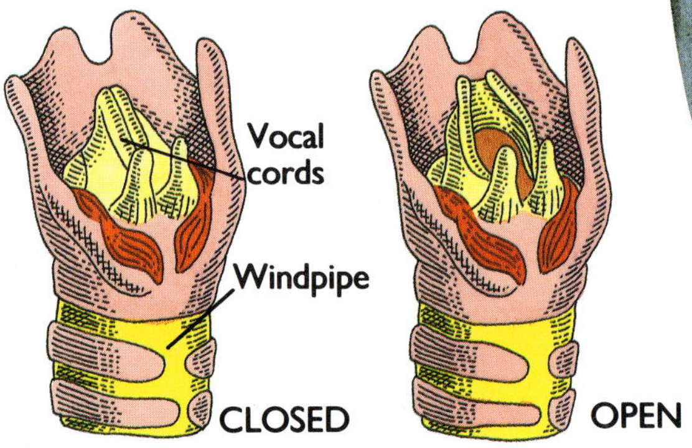

Variances in language

There are at least 5,000 languages spoken around the world. Every language has its own sounds with specific meanings. Some languages, like English and German, share certain words. Other languages are completely different. The African language Yoruba for example, shares no sounds with English. However, all languages suit the needs of the people who speak them – there are no inferior languages and any language can be translated relatively accurately into any other.

Xhosa

The Xhosa language is one of a group of southern African languages that contain their own unique sounds. Clicks (represented most closely in English by the written "tut-tut") are used as consonants.

Animals make sounds that carry messages such as "I live here, keep out" or "Here I am" or "I'm dangerous, don't attack me". Animals such as frogs and birds make a lot of sounds during the breeding season, when they want to find a mate. Some animals, such as wolves and monkeys, make sounds with their voices in a similar way to people. Other animals, especially insects, use different parts of their bodies. Grasshoppers "sing" by rubbing their legs against their wings. Death-watch beetles knock their heads against wood to make a tapping sound.

Making sound effects
You and your friends can improve the dramatic effect of a play by making sound effects offstage. Hitting two plastic cups together in rhythm produces a sound like horses' hooves. Swinging a piece of ribbed vacuum cleaner tube can make ghostly noises like howling wind. Scraping a grater with a metal fork makes a frightening din. Experiment with other objects to reproduce sounds.

Vacuum cleaner tube

Cheese grater

Arabic
Arabic languages contain gutteral noises which are difficult for non-native speakers to produce. They are made by constricting the pharynx in the throat.

Dialects
There are often variations in the way people of different areas speak. Different accents and words may be used in the same country, but they are not separate languages. A strong accent may reveal where a person comes from.

Sounds in nature
Although most of the sounds we hear are created by humans, there are also natural sounds. When the wind picks up, it can make all sorts of eerie noises, rustling leaves and rattling loose windows.

Wind rustles leaves

Wind
Wind rushes through the branches of trees and howls down chimneys.

Snow
Falling snow muffles sound which would otherwise reflect loudly off hard surfaces.

Crisp quiet snow

Rain
Rainstorms can be a soothing sound. The noise of rain falling on water or hard surfaces blocks out many other sounds.

Rain splashing in a puddle

HIGH AND LOW SOUNDS

The lowness or height of a sound is called its pitch. It depends on the speed at which the source of a sound is moving to and fro, or vibrating. High-pitched notes come from things that vibrate rapidly. A violin gives out a high note if a string vibrates at about 10,000 times a second. Low-pitched notes come from things that vibrate slowly. Pitch is affected by the size, weight and density (thickness) of the object making the sound. Some animals and insects can produce and hear extremely low-pitched or high-pitched sounds. These are often impossible for humans to hear.

The shorter bars on a xylophone vibrate faster, producing higher notes. The longer bars on a xylophone vibrate more slowly, producing lower notes.

Musical bottles

Measure out half a litre of water and pour this into a bottle. Then measure half this amount (one quarter of a litre) into an identical bottle. Continue, leaving your last bottle empty. Now blow across each bottle. Which had the highest and which the lowest sound?

Glass-breaking sounds

One common visualisation of a high-pitched sound is a female singer causing a glass to shatter. This occurs because objects naturally vibrate at a certain rate. If another sound near them is vibrating at the same frequency – like a voice at a certain pitch – then the vibrations increase and the glass can shatter. This is caused by resonance.

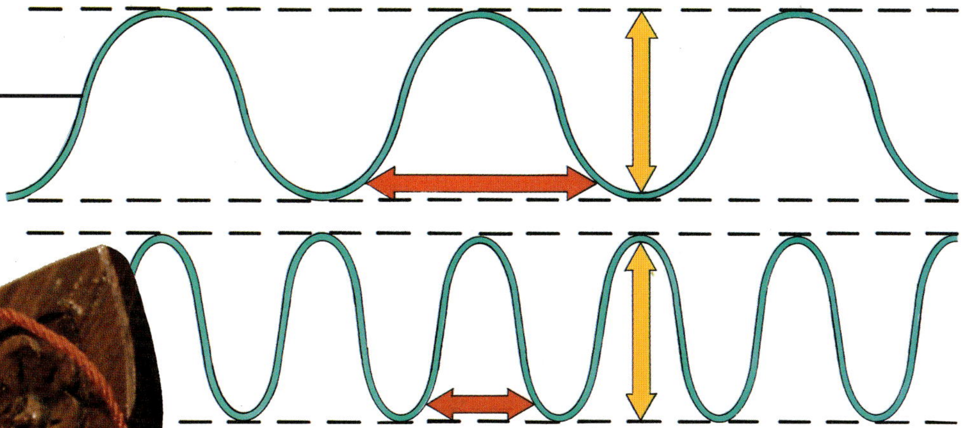

Fewer waves per second equal low frequency, resulting in a low-pitched sound.

More waves per second equal high frequency, resulting in a high-pitched sound.

The pitch of a sound depends on the number of sound waves passing a point in a second. This is called the frequency. High-pitched sounds have a high frequency, that is lots of waves per second. Low-pitched sounds have a low frequency. Pitch does not affect the speed of sound. You hear the high note of a flute at the same time as the low note of a drum. But higher frequency notes have a shorter wavelength – in other words, more packages of air are being squashed and stretched to produce sounds.

Range of hearing

Animals differ in the range of frequencies – high- or low-pitched sounds – that they make (emissions) and hear (receptions). Birds and humans have similar hearing ranges, whereas bats and dolphins communicate outside the human range of hearing. The chart below shows where various animals fit on the scale of frequencies.

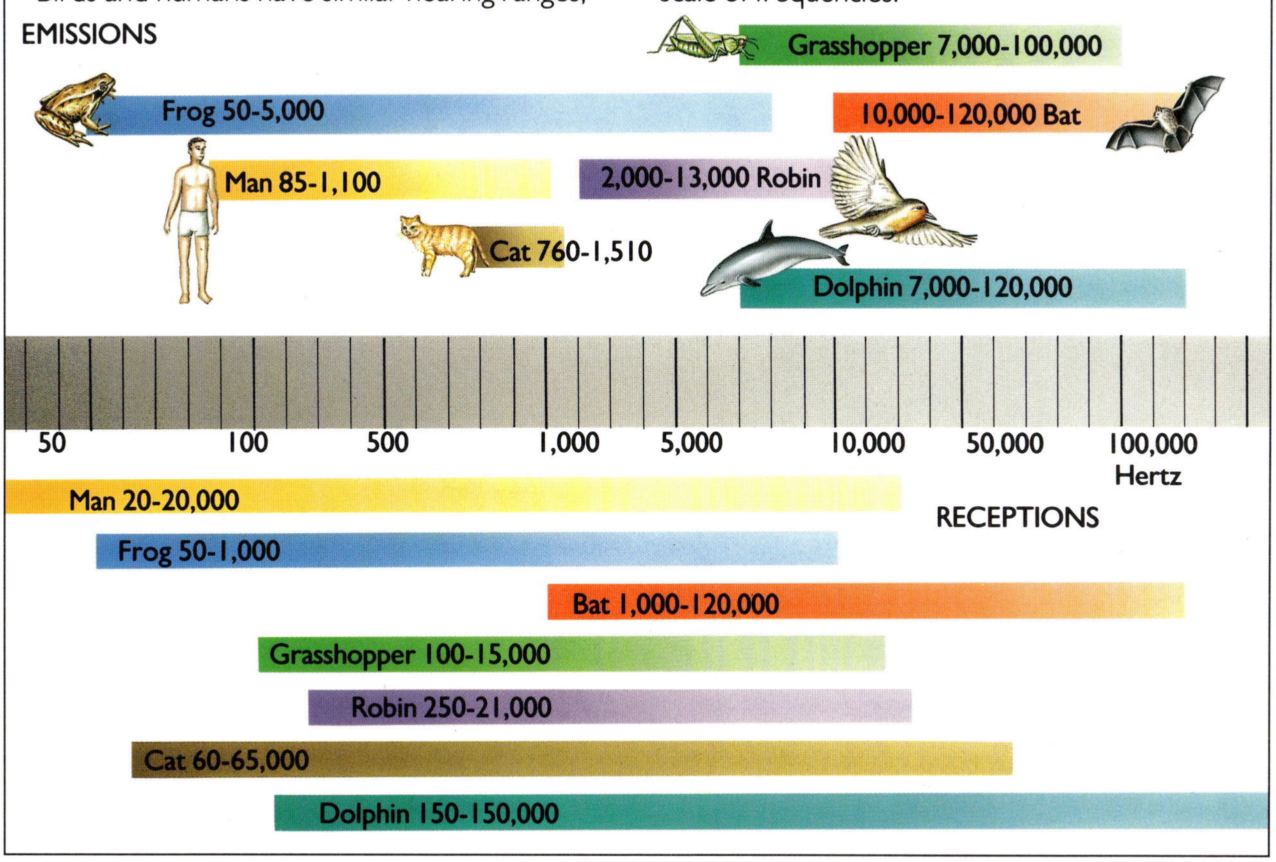

LOUD AND QUIET SOUNDS

Loud sounds cause large squashes and stretches of the particles in air or other substances because they have a lot of energy. Quiet sounds cause small squashes and stretches. Our ears are more sensitive to changes in quiet sounds than changes in loud ones. Sound waves spread out from a source in all directions, like ripples from a stone thrown into a pond. The more they spread out, the weaker they become. The cone shape of a megaphone keeps the sound of a person's voice from spreading out, and therefore makes it louder.

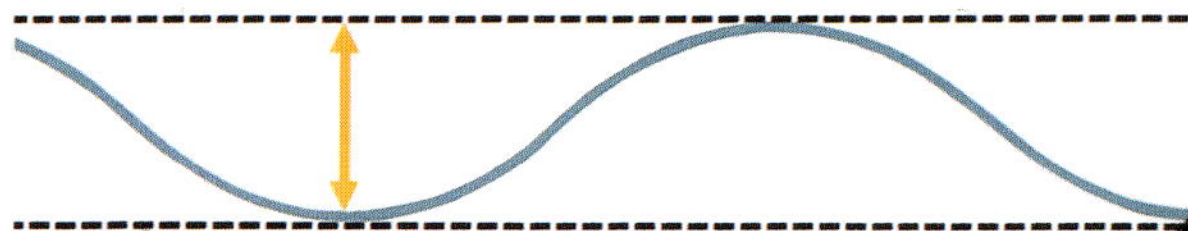

Short waves with a small amplitude produce a quiet sound

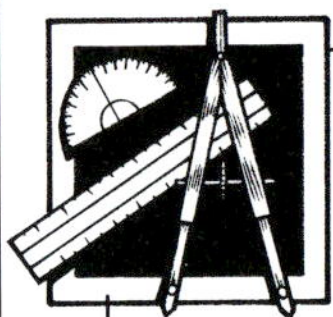

The decibel scale

A decibel (db) is a unit scientists developed to compare the intensity (or loudness) of sounds. The measurement refers to the amount of power hitting a certain area. The zero point usually refers to the faintest sound the human ear can pick up. When a volume doubles, the rating goes up by 6 decibels. Normal conversation usually takes place at about 60 decibels. Sounds become physically painful at above 130 decibels.

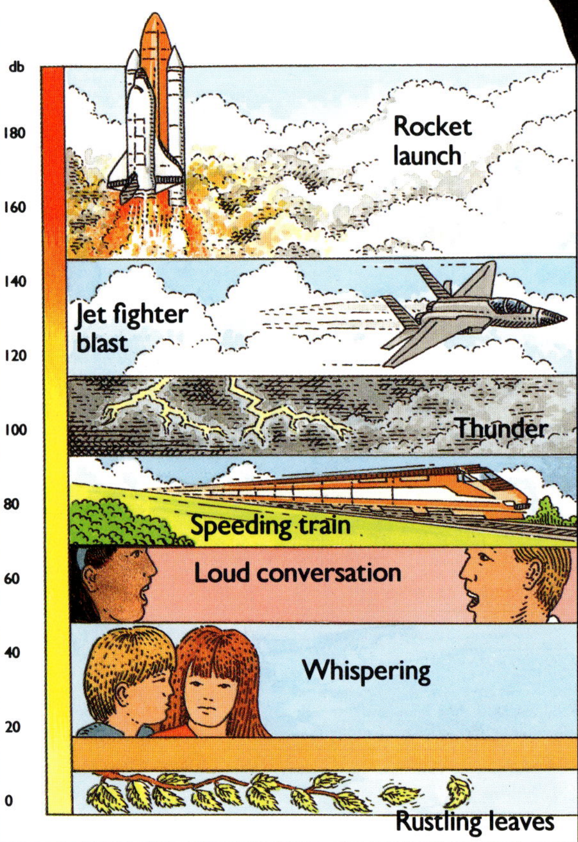

The sound of a jet aeroplane taking off can be very loud. But a butterfly flapping its wings makes hardly any sound at all. Owls have special fringes on their feathers to swoop silently down on their prey, taking it by surprise. Hummingbirds beat their wings so fast – at over 80 times a second – they make a humming sound as they fly. Animals are usually quieter than machines, but a humpback whale can make a sound louder than Concorde on take-off.

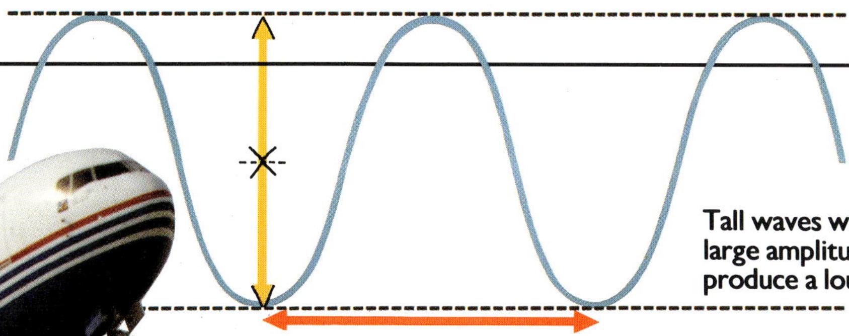

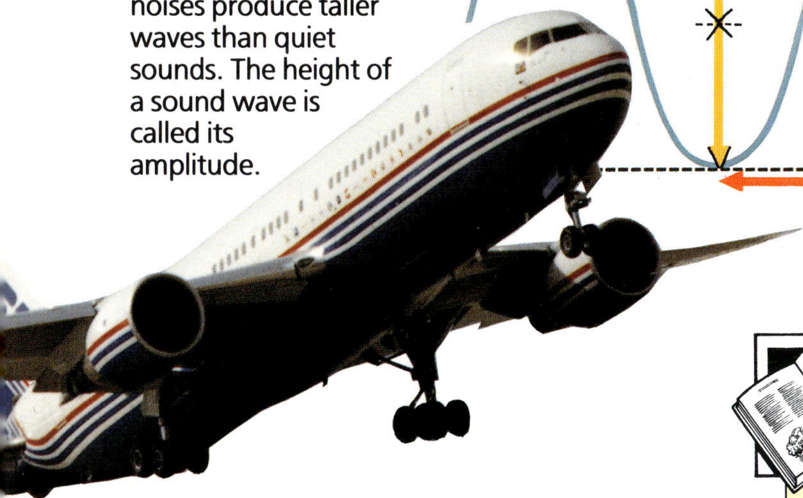

When recorded, loud noises produce taller waves than quiet sounds. The height of a sound wave is called its amplitude.

Sounds good

Poets use words to create specific effects. They express loud and quiet, slow and fast, and other sensations by using devices like onomatopoeia. Words with soft consonants and vowels sound quiet, like the words murmuring and rustling. Harder consonants and short words such as crash and giggle, all give the impression of loudness. How words are set out on a page can also emphasise the effect of the words. Write a poem in which you try to express loudness and strength. Think about the quality of the words and how they are displayed on the page.

Sounds of silence

Among the quietest places where people live are monasteries. These are communities set apart from the rest of society where monks committed to a purely religious life live. The first Christian monasteries began in Egypt and Syria in the 4th century, spreading into Western Europe throughout the 5th and 6th centuries.

Monasteries have always been places of learning, prayer, meditation and a quiet, spiritual life. Trappist monks, an order set up by a French monk in Normandy in the 17th century, take vows of silence. Other religions, like Buddhism, also have monasteries. The largest monasteries in the world are in Tibet. Similar places for women are called convents.

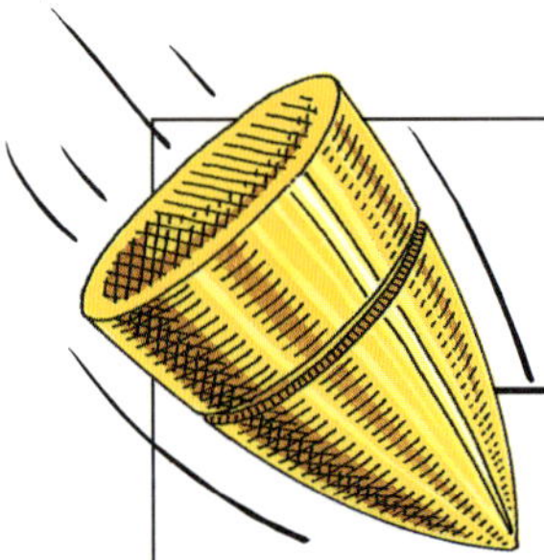

THE SPEED OF SOUND

The speed of sound – how far it moves in a particular time – depends on the substance through which the sound is moving. In a gas, such as air, sound takes about three seconds to travel a kilometre. Sound, however, travels faster in warm air than cold air. This is because the molecules in warm air are moving faster and bump into each other more frequently, passing on the sound. In solids or liquids, the molecules are closer together than they are in a gas, so sounds travel even faster.

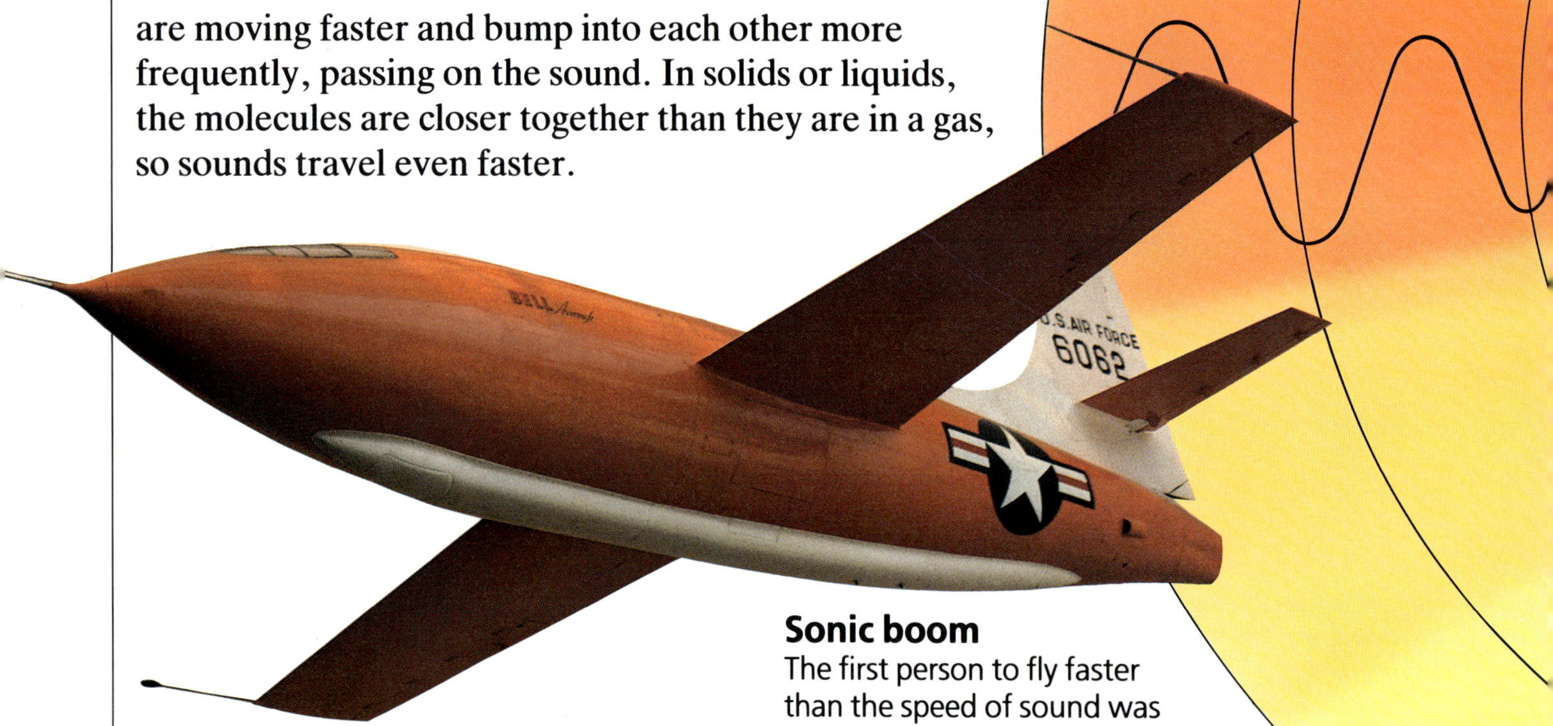

Sonic boom

The first person to fly faster than the speed of sound was Captain "Chuck" Yaeger in a rocket plane called Bell X-1. He blasted through the sound barrier at a speed of 1126kph on October 14th, 1947. Jet aircraft that fly through air faster than sound are called supersonic. These aircraft fly so fast that the sound is compressed by the nose of the plane. As the plane (A) overtakes its own sound (B), it spreads out behind in a shock wave (C) we hear as a loud bang or sonic boom. The higher a plane flies, the less speed it needs to break the sound barrier. This is because the air higher up is colder and sound travels more slowly.

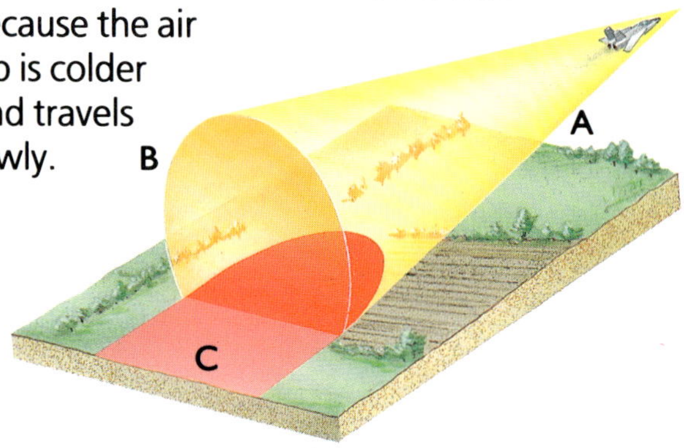

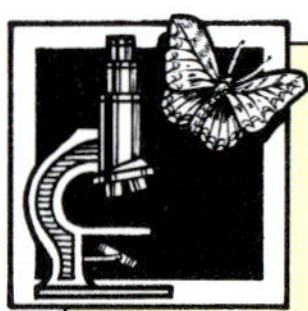

Thunder and lightning

Light travels a million times faster than sound. Thunder is produced when lightning heats the air and causes a shock wave. They occur at exactly the same time. However. we see the flash before we hear the rumble, and the time between the two increases the farther away the lightning is. Measure how far away lightning is by counting the seconds between the flash and the thunder. Sound takes about three seconds to travel one kilometre.

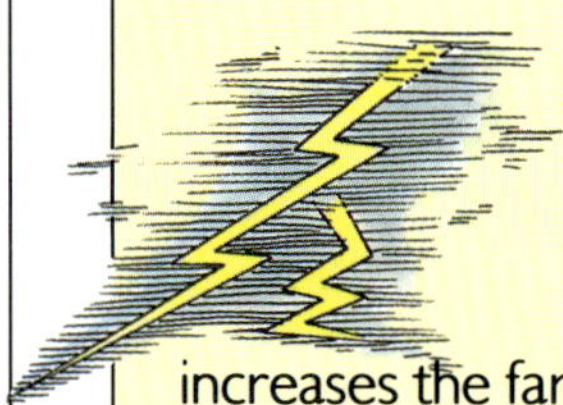

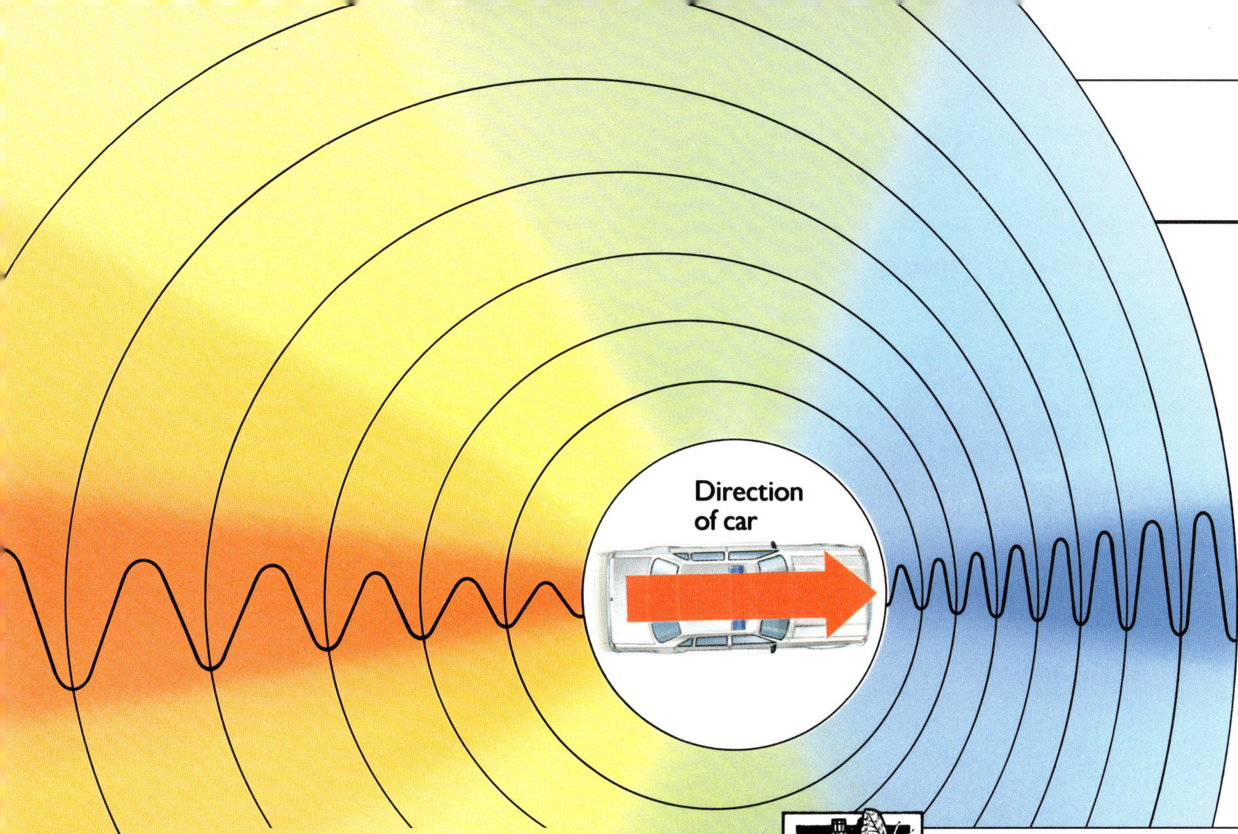

The Doppler effect

When a vehicle with sirens blaring speeds past you, the sound of the siren drops from a high-pitched to a low-pitched sound. The sound waves produced by the siren travel at a constant speed. As the vehicle comes towards you, however, the sound waves are squashed up, making more waves per second and a high-pitched sound. As the vehicle moves away, the sound waves are more spread out and take longer to reach your ears. There are less waves per second, creating a low-pitched sound. This effect is named after the Austrian scientist Christian Doppler, who first worked out the theory.

Whale song

Sound travels four times faster through water than through air.

Humpback whales communicate by means of complex "songs". The songs are made up of low frequency waves that travel long distances and high frequency waves that lose energy as they hit the surface and the bottom of the ocean.

Ear to the ground

If you are a fan of Western films you may have seen a bandit put his ear to the railway track. In real life as well, railway workers can use this method to check for approaching trains. This is because the sound is trapped in the rails and travels much faster through the steel than through the air. The molecules that make up metals are packed very tightly together and can therefore transmit the vibrations caused by the sound very quickly. You may also have seen a cowboy put his ear to the ground and listen for the sound of horses' hooves.

ECHOES AND ACOUSTICS

When sound hits a hard surface, such as a wall or a cliff, it may bounce back like a rubber ball. If the surface is far enough away from the source of the sound, we hear the reflected sound after the original sound as an echo. Echoes usually occur when sound in air meets a solid, but can be caused when sound in a liquid hits a solid. Most bats find their way in the dark and catch their food by giving out very high-pitched squeaks and listening for the echoes. This is called echo-location.

Bats have large ears to pick up echoes. These tell the bat where things are, how far away they are and if they are moving. Bats' ears are movable. This helps to channel sounds towards them.

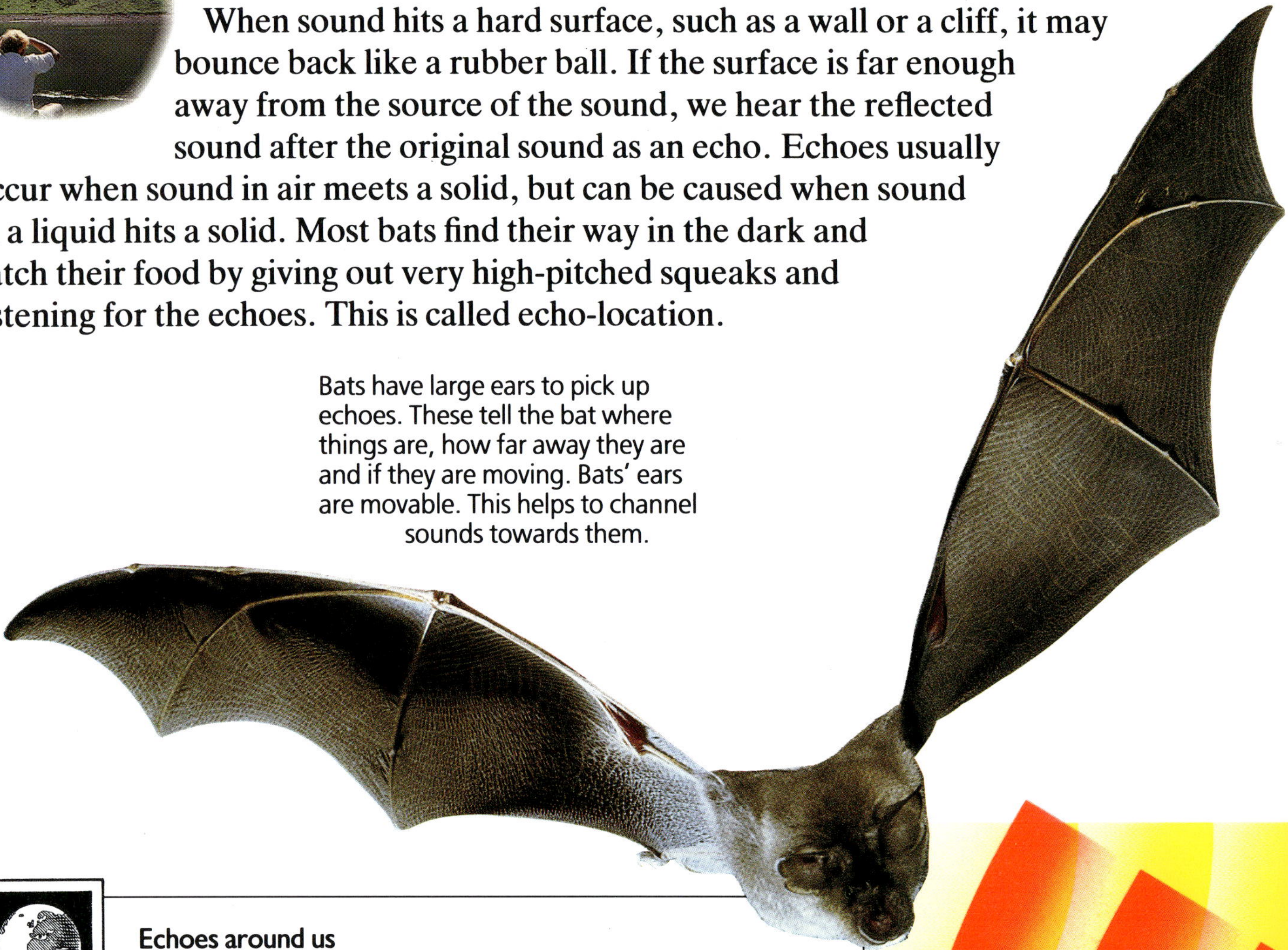

Echoes around us

Many blind people have a highly developed sense of hearing to compensate for their lack of sight. Their ears can perceive the slightest echoes that are reflected off the objects around them. For the rest of us, echoes usually only become noticeable in places like tunnels, caves, valleys or natural amphitheatres, which are large areas in cliff faces that have been hollowed out by erosion.

Some of the largest caves in the world are found in Borneo.

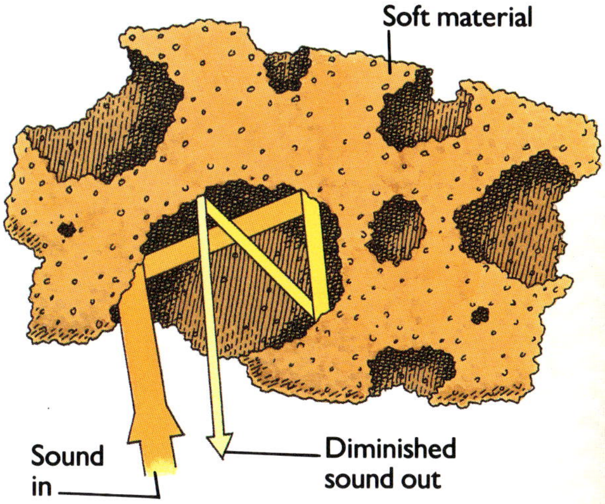

CONCERT HALL ACOUSTICS

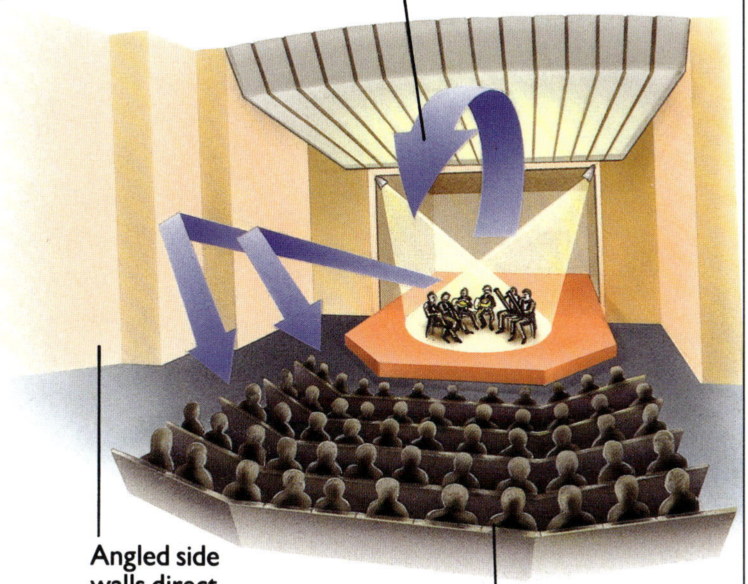

Soundproofing

Hard surfaces reflect sound well, while soft surfaces, such as cloth, carpets, or wood, soak up or absorb sound – rather like a sponge soaks up water. Sound is trapped inside holes within soft materials, and less is reflected to give an echo. Soft materials may be used to soundproof a recording studio. Specially designed shapes in a concert hall direct the music to the audience and cut down unwanted echoes. The study of controlling sounds is called acoustics.

Amphitheatres

The Ancient Greeks were the first to use the principles of echoes and acoustics in their theatres. They began building amphitheatres to stage their dramas around the 5th century BC. These theatres were always open-air and usually built in a semi-circle around a small circular stage. The terraced seats sloped upwards, forming a chamber that contained the sounds from the stage below. The Colosseum was the largest in Rome, and once sat 50,000 people.

Amphitheatre

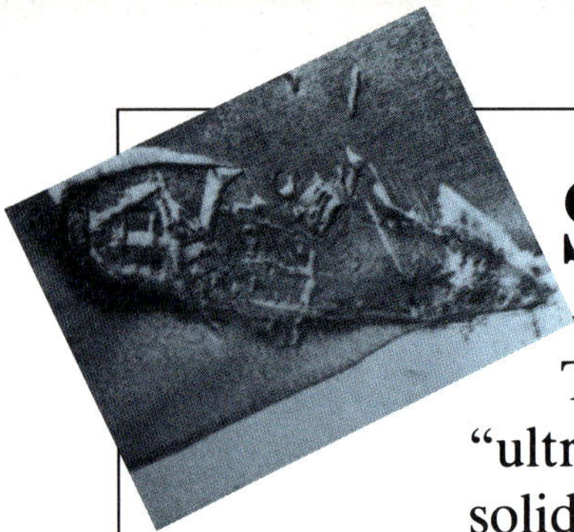

SEEING WITH SOUND

The echoes of very high-pitched sounds we cannot hear – "ultra" sounds – can be used to "see" through liquids and solids, such as under the sea, under the ground or inside the human body. Ultrasounds can also be used to detect faults in the metal of factory machines or aircraft. There are even microscopes that use reflected ultrasounds instead of reflected light. We know how fast sound travels, so the time it takes ultrasound to bounce back from a surface can be used to calculate how far away things are.

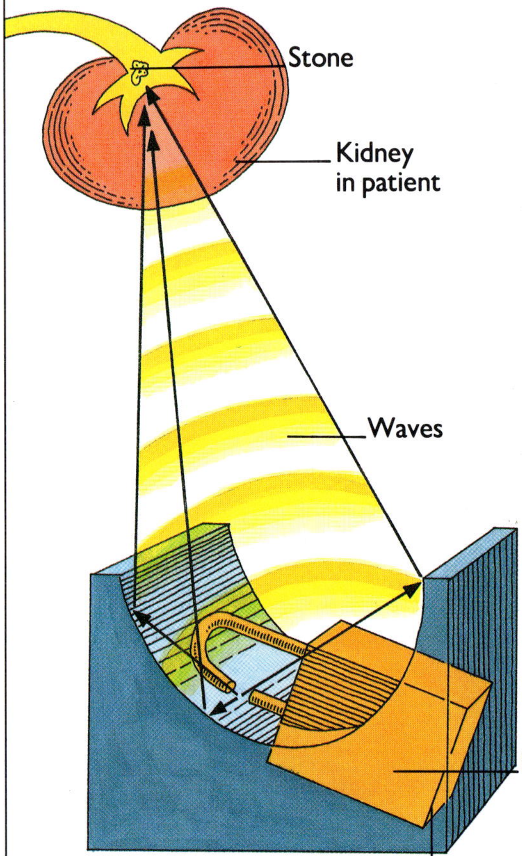

Surgeons can use pulses of ultrasound to destroy kidney stones without having to cut the patient open. A reflector focuses the sound so it can be aimed at a particular point. The sound shakes the stones apart and the smaller pieces can be passed out of the body without any pain.

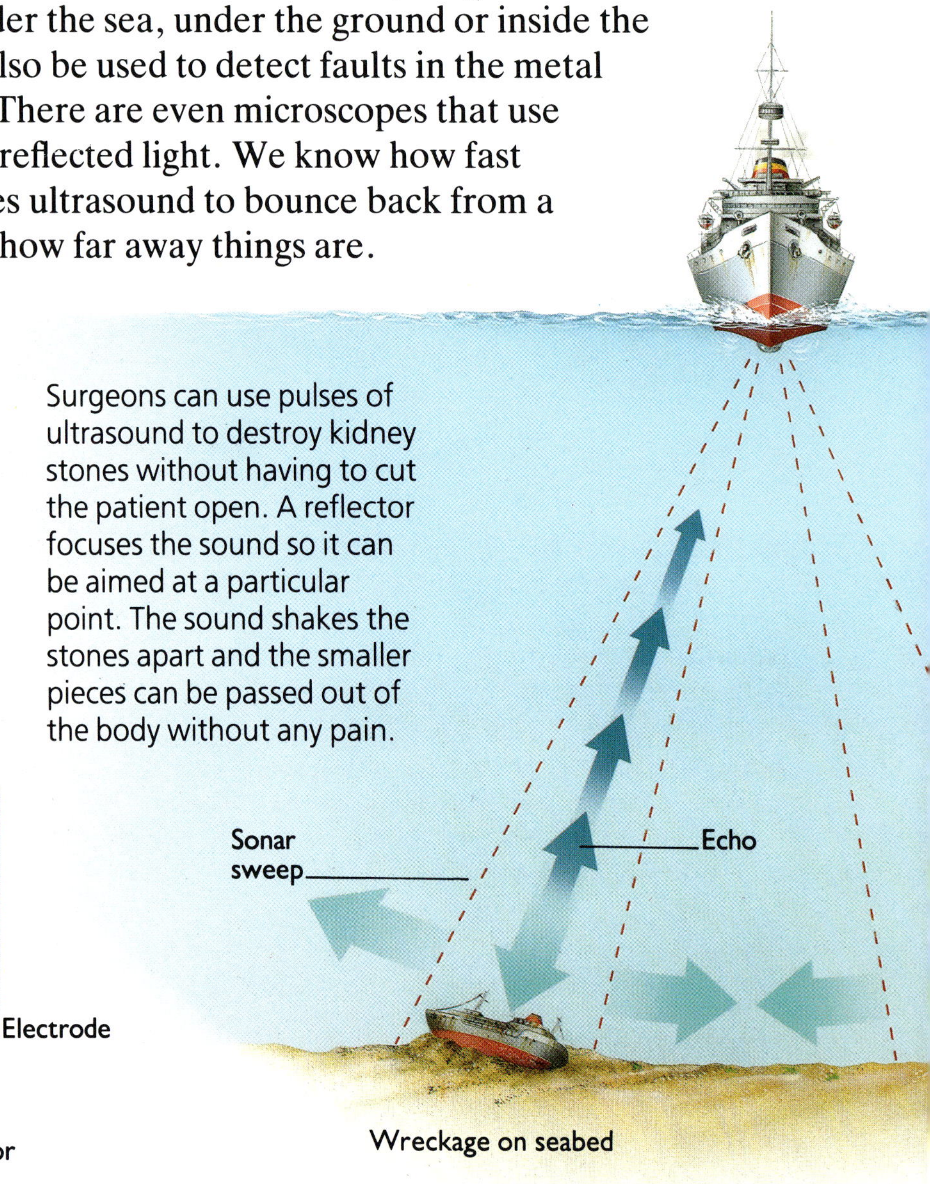

Wreckage on seabed

The start of sonar

Sonar stands for SOund Navigation And Ranging. It was developed in the 1920s as a response to the need to detect enemy submarines during World War I. The British and Americans kept sonar a secret, surprising the Germans with its use during World War II. Sonar units of that time only had short ranges. They also had to be rotated by hand. Sound was used rather than other forms of measurable energy like light because sound is not absorbed by water.

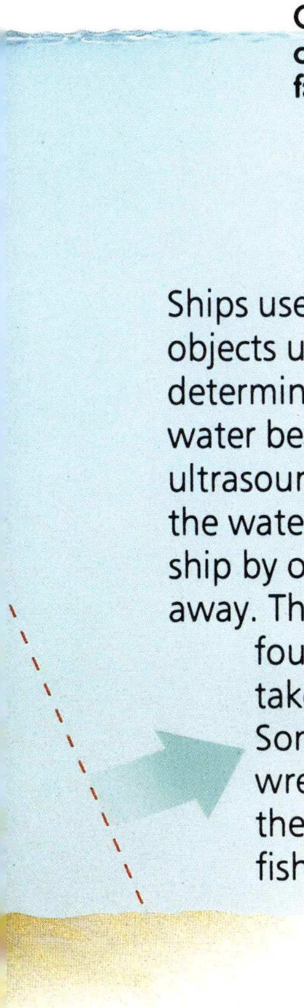

Ships use sonar to search for objects under the sea and to determine the depth of the water beneath them. Pulses of ultrasound are sent down through the water and reflected back to the ship by objects up to 10 kilometres away. The distance to the object is found by measuring the time taken for the sound to return. Sonar can be used to find wrecks and submarines, map the seabed and spot shoals of fish.

Ultrasonic scanners can be used to form pictures of the inside of the human body. Unlike X-rays, quiet sound waves are not known to have any harmful effects so they can be used to examine pregnant women. The echoes are recorded as a series of spots where the brightness varies according to the strength of the echo received. A computer converts this information into a picture of the baby. A scan shows if the baby is developing properly.

Sounding out dangers
Ultrasound is not only used in medicine. The technique has been adapted to industry as well. Ultrasound detectors can be used to find internal cracks in aircraft by bouncing sound off the metal. The fault may then be repaired by using an ultrasonic welding machine. The sound waves vibrate so quickly that they heat the material up and weld the cracks together. Ultrasonic machines can also cut holes in very hard metal.

MUSICAL SOUNDS

Musical sounds are usually a series of notes with a smooth, regular pattern of sound waves. They are produced by instruments that contain something which vibrates or wobbles to squash the air and make the sound. Nearly all musical instruments also have something to amplify the sound. Amplifying sound makes it louder. A violin has a thin soundboard of springy wood under the strings which vibrates strongly when the strings vibrate. The air inside the hollow body of the violin also vibrates.

Japanese bamboo flute

Wind instruments make a sound when air is blown into them. Woodwind instruments have holes which can be covered to change the notes.

Percussion instruments produce sound when they are hit, scraped or shaken with the correct amount of force.

Chinese wind gong

Chinese mandoline

Junk orchestra

Even if you do not have access to many instruments, it is still possible to make your own band with things you find around the home. Invite some friends over and look around for materials you can use to make music. Be creative!

Bind two lids from jars together with tape to make your own castanets.

Stick tacks into a wood block at increasing lengths as shown. Stretch rubber bands between pairs of tacks and pluck away.

Turn some empty tins bottom up and hit them with something that serves as a drumstick.

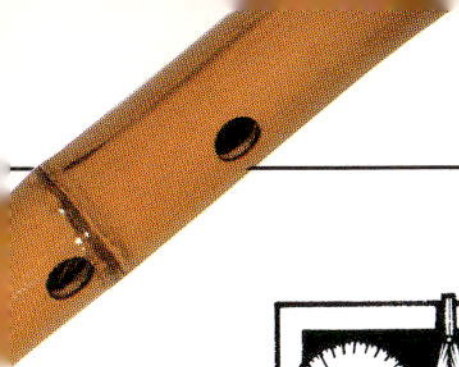

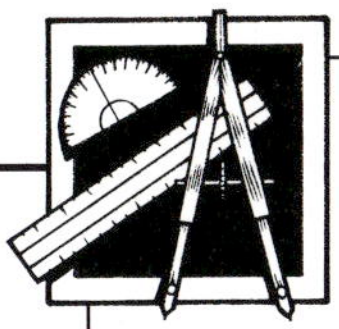

Counting time

Music is a sequence of melodic sounds built around a rhythm, or pattern of beats. In a piece of music, the rhythms are organised into groups of beats, called bars. Musical notes have different values which stand for varying lengths of time. These values are given below. The notes in each bar of 4/4 time (below) add up to the value of four quarter notes. Try writing some more bars of four beats using the notes provided.

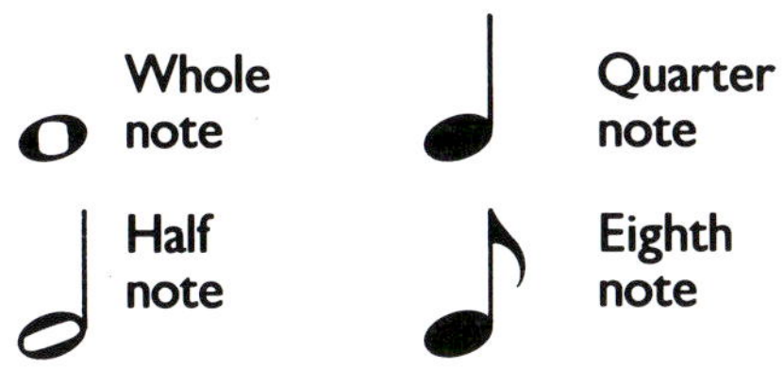

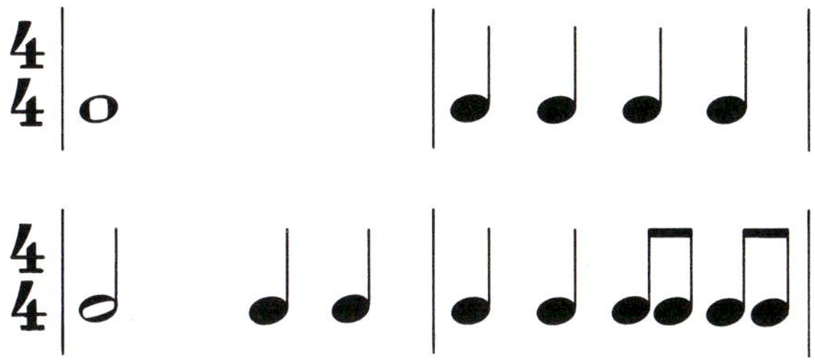

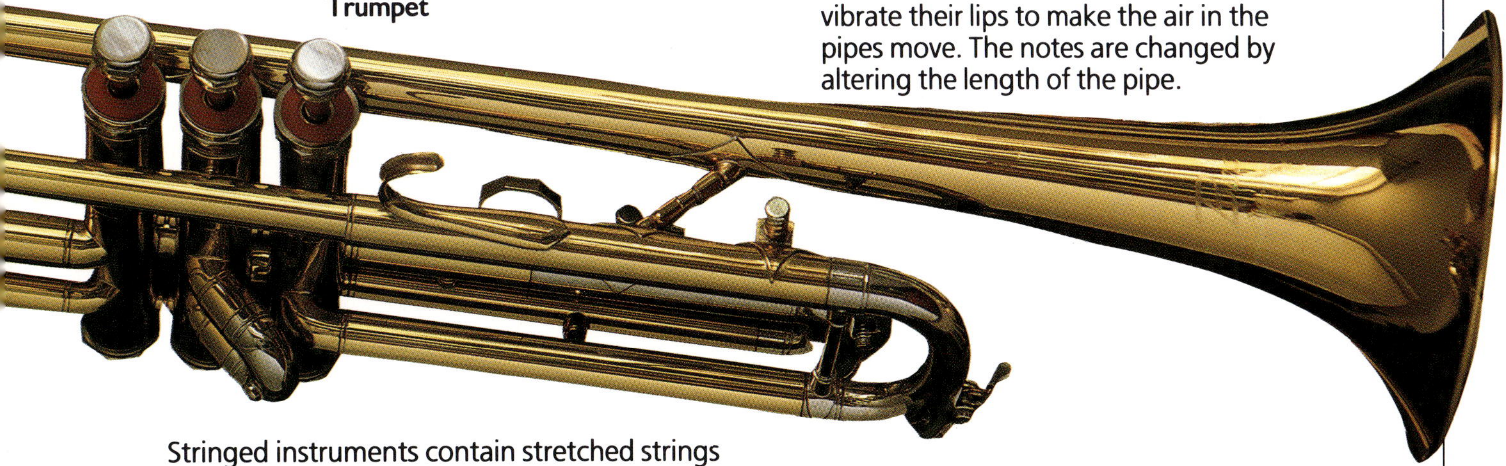

Trumpet

In a brass instrument, musicians vibrate their lips to make the air in the pipes move. The notes are changed by altering the length of the pipe.

Stringed instruments contain stretched strings which are plucked or scraped to produce musical notes. Shorter strings, tighter strings, or lighter strings have a higher pitch.

Keyboard instruments have a series of keys which activate small hammers to strike or pluck strings. Pipe organ keys activate columns of air.

Piano

The story so far...

We can roughly date the beginnings of the musical styles we listen to today. Some folk music dates back hundreds of years. Classical music began during the 18th century and jazz sprung out of the American South in the early 1900s, with blues developing from slave spirituals around the same time. Rock music dates from the 1950s, with its offspring soul arising in the 1960s. Reggae developed in the West Indies during the 1970s, and in the 1980s rap became popular worldwide. Popular music often influences dance styles.

Jazz

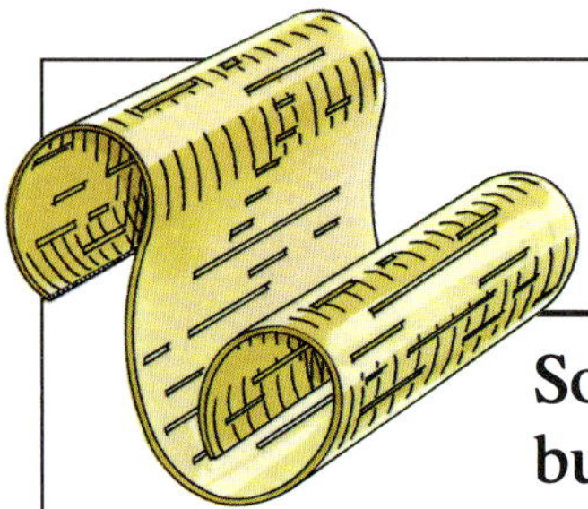

STORING SOUND

Sounds can be written down on paper and stored as musical notes but the actual sounds can be stored as magnetic patterns on tapes, as grooves on records, or as patterns of pits on compact discs.

Sound is captured and stored in the form of electrical signals. Storing sound means we can still listen to musical recordings, famous speeches and historic events many years later.

Famous words have been captured on tape for several generations.

Sir Winston Churchill

Martin Luther King

Neil Armstrong

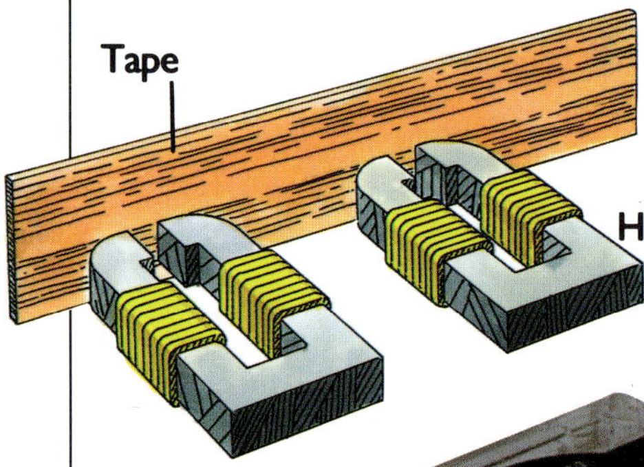

TAPE CASSETTE

RECORD

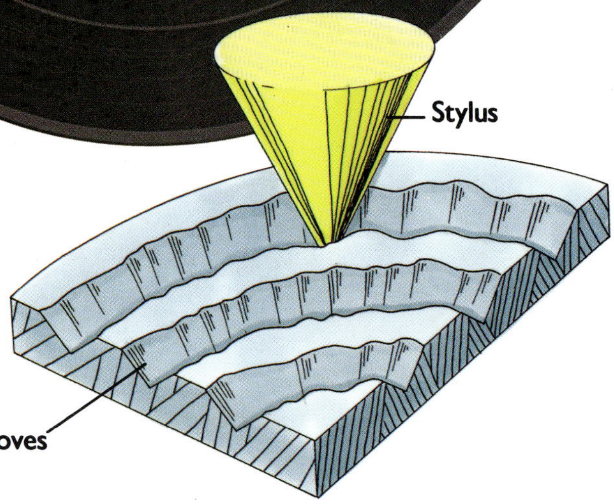

Tapes and records

Tapes and records store sounds in two different ways. Tapes feed electrical signals from a microphone or other sound source to an electromagnet in the recording head. The electricity produces a magnetic field which turns the metal particles on the tape into little magnets. These group together in coded patterns that stand for the original sounds. When you play a tape, these patterns produce electrical signals which go to a loudspeaker. Records store sounds as a spiral groove in a flat piece of plastic. Loud sounds make the grooves deeper and high sounds make them more frequent. When you play a record, the needle or stylus vibrates along the groove, setting up electrical signals in the pick-up head.

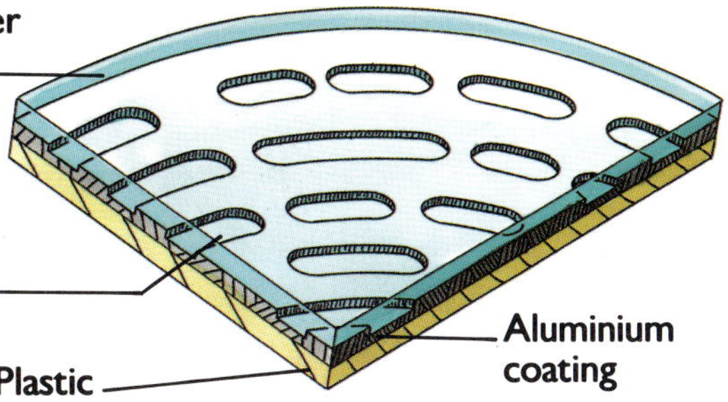

COMPACT DISC

Compact discs

On a compact disc or CD, sound is stored on a spiral track made up of a series of microscopic pits and flats. The track is thinner than a human hair and about 5 km long. The pits and flats are in the form of a code made up of the numbers 0 and 1, which can be "read" by a laser beam. The laser converts the code to on and off flashes of light, which are then converted into electric current. This is fed into loudspeakers which turn the electric signals back into sound again. CDs give the most accurate reproduction of the original sound. They do not get scratched or wear out as they are played because no needle or stylus touches the surface.

History of recording

The technology to record and play back sounds has been around for over 100 years. Thomas Edison (1847-1931) invented the phonograph in 1877. Flat discs like the modern LP were developed in 1888; before that phonographs played wax cylinders. The first electrically recorded gramophone records appeared in 1925. In 1898, the Danish inventor Valdemar Poulsen devised the first tape recorder. Compact cassettes like the ones on sale today were developed in 1963. Digital recording was developed in the 1970s, with compact discs appearing on the market in 1983.

Design to music

A record company has to attract the customer's attention with the cover artwork. Record companies hire artists to design eye-catching sleeves for records and CDs. Imagine you are a record cover designer. Listen to a record you like. Draw the images which the music brings to mind. For instance, if the music seems tropical, try a tropical setting for your cover. If the music is loud and energetic, use lots of bright colours.

SENDING SOUND

Our ears can only hear sounds over a short distance, but sounds can be sent around the world by changing them into different forms of energy and then back to sound again. Telephones change sounds into electrical signals or light rays which are sent down cables. Radios change sounds into radio waves which can then be sent through the air. Synthesizers produce electrical sound signals which are turned into sounds through amplifiers and loudspeakers. Computers can store, process or even compose electronic music.

Animal amplifiers

Many animals rely on sound to send signals to one another – to warn of trespassers for example or to attract mates. Certain species have evolved ways to send sounds over long distances. Many frogs have membrane sacs in their mouths that fill with air when they croak. The sacs amplify the sound – a bullfrog's croak can be heard a kilometre away, ten times farther than a frog without an air sac. Howler monkeys, named after their ability to produce sound, have one of the loudest of animal calls. They have a resonating chamber made of bone under their lower jaw. A howler monkey's call is a claim of territorial rights, and can travel up to 3 km.

Bullfrog

Howler monkey

Synthesizers can produce musical sounds electronically. Most are played by means of a keyboard, and performers can use them to imitate the sounds of other instruments.

CONTENTS

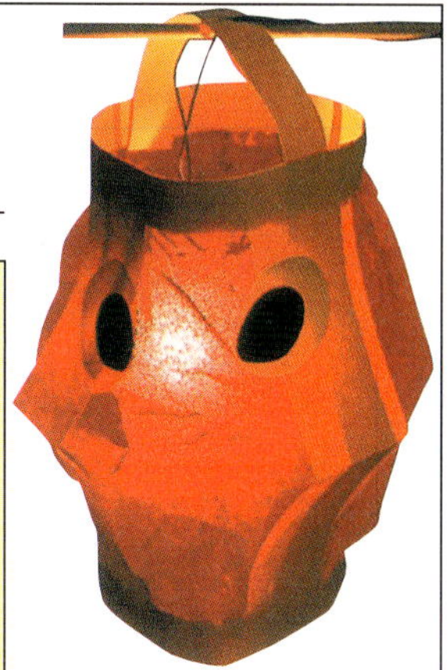

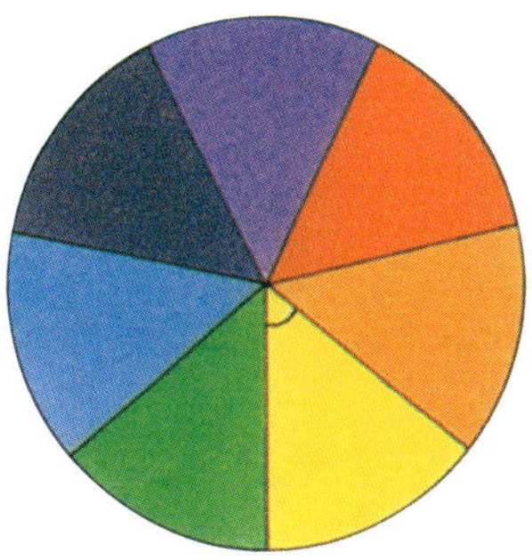

LIGHT ALL AROUND

Nearly all the Earth's light comes from our nearest star, the Sun, which is a whirling cloud of very hot gases. These gases glow very brightly, emitting (giving out) light. All hot things give out light – even people, who emit invisible infra-red light. Other natural sources of light on Earth come from lightning, fire and the rest of the stars. Insects, such as fireflies, and some deep-sea fish glow as a result of chemical reactions that release light. We can create artificial light by burning fuels in lamps, and by producing electricity for light bulbs.

Celebrations with light

Light has a special significance in cultures around the world, because it has long played an important role in human life. When people gather together to mark certain occasions, they might burn a bonfire or light candles.

Diwali

Diwali is the Hindu festival of light. It is celebrated at the end of the year as a victory of good over evil. Hindus light divas (lamps) for the occasion.

Independence Day

On 4th July in the United States, people celebrate their country's independence from British colonial rule by holding great firework displays.

Christmas

Millions of people around the world celebrate Christmas. Some decorate trees with strings of electric lights. Others light candles, and may set fire to a traditional Christmas pudding.

Seeing in the Stone Age

One of the most important things that sets human beings apart from other animals is their ability to make and use tools. At the point when humans found they could make fire by rubbing sticks or flint stones together, they began to control their environment. There is evidence of humans using fire hundreds of thousands of years ago. Fire was used for cooking, for heat, for making tools, and was also used for illumination. Cave dwellers made lamps of burning animal fat in order to see inside dark caves. These lamps enabled them to paint pictures on the cave walls.

Shedding light on language

Words often carry meanings which are more than just their literal definition. "Light" has come to mean more than just visible brightness. Our language uses it to describe happiness, someone's "face lit up"; and to symbolise truth, they "saw the light". Sunlight and daylight are often considered to be inspirational, hence the phrase "It dawned on me". "Dark", on the other hand, is often associated with the night, and all things bad and sinister. See if you can compose a story or poem using the symbolic meanings of light and dark.

WHAT IS LIGHT?

Light is a mixture of electrical and magnetic energy which travels faster than anything else in the universe. It takes less than one tenth of a second for light to travel from New York to London. Light is made up of tiny particles of energy called photons. The light moves along in very small waves that travel forwards in straight lines, called rays. Light can travel through air and transparent substances, but can also travel through empty space. This is how sunlight reaches the Earth. Light is similar to other forms of electro-magnetic energy which have different wavelengths.

Radio waves
These have the longest wavelength. They are used for satellite communication and to carry TV and radio signals.

Visible light
Appears white or colourless, but is made up of colours, each with a different wavelength.

Electro-magnetic spectrum
This shows different kinds of electro-magnetic energy arranged in order of their wavelengths. Wavelength is the distance between two consecutive waves.

Microwaves
Very short radio waves used in microwave ovens. They are also used in radar.

Infra-red rays
Invisible, but we can feel the heat from them. They can be used to detect cancer and arthritis, or to take photographs in the dark.

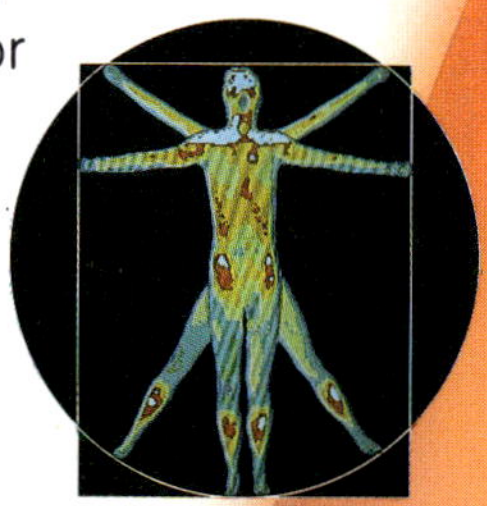

Different ways of seeing
Most animals see visible light like we do. However, others have evolved sight which detects different wavelengths along the spectrum. Some insects see in ultraviolet light, which is invisible to most mammals and birds (except pigeons). Insect-pollinated flowers have lines which guide insects to their nectar. These lines only appear in ultraviolet light. The insects follow the guide lines to the nectar, scattering pollen on the way. This process helps the flowers to reproduce.

Bees cannot see the colour red. They are strongly attracted by yellow and blue flowers which usually have strong ultraviolet markings. These markings attract bees to the flowers, and even pinpoint the location of the nectaries.

Ultraviolet rays
These cause us to tan and help the skin to produce vitamin D. Large amounts are dangerous and may cause skin cancer, although most ultraviolet light from the Sun is absorbed by the ozone layer.

Gamma rays
These have the shortest wavelength. They are given off by naturally radioactive materials, such as uranium, and are part of the fall-out after a nuclear explosion. They can travel through lead and cement, and damage living tissue.

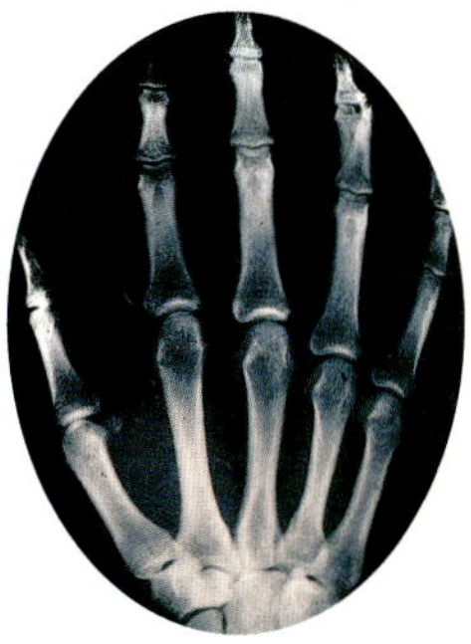

X-Rays
Called "X" by their discoverer because he was unsure of their nature. They pass through flesh, but are absorbed by bones and teeth, causing them to show up on X-ray film. Small doses are safe but large amounts are harmful to living tissue.

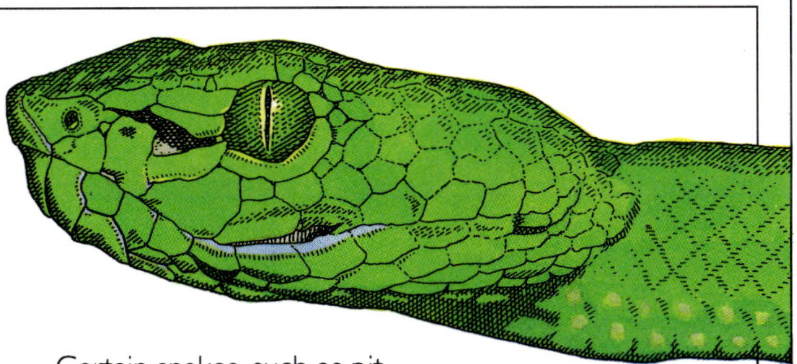

Certain snakes, such as pit vipers and pythons, detect prey by sensing the infra-red light or "heat" they give out. They have special heat sensors which form an image from the infra-red emissions. This helps them to hunt at night.

Taking the straight path
Try this experiment to prove for yourself that light travels in straight lines. Cut out two pieces of card, about 20 cm square. Make a hole in the centre of each card, and stick a knitting needle through both holes, ensuring that they are aligned. Stand the cards on a flat surface, fixing them with plasticine. Turn off the light and shine a torch through the holes. What happens? Try putting certain materials between the two cards when the torch is on. Try cellophane, paper, a book and so on. Describe what happens to the ray of light.

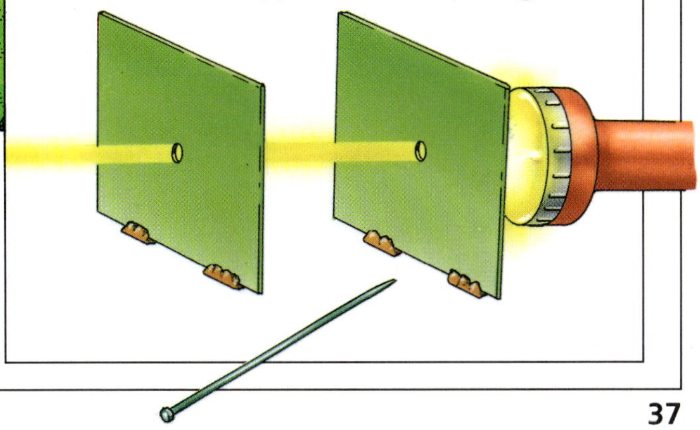

COLOURS

Can you imagine a world without colour? Some animals, such as horses and dogs, cannot see the colours we can. Their world is full of shades of black, white and grey. We can only see all the colours of visible light when they have been separated out into their different wavelengths. Drops of water, raindrops, or specially shaped pieces of transparent material called prisms, can do this. As light passes through these things, each colour is bent by a slightly different amount, emerging at the other side as a band of rainbow colours. This is called a spectrum. The colours always appear in the same order.

Primary colours

Most colours of light can be made by mixing together the three main colours. These are red, blue and green. You can see these colours if you take a close look at the tiny dots of light on a television screen. These are called the primary colours of light, and are different from the primary colours of paint, which are red, yellow and blue.

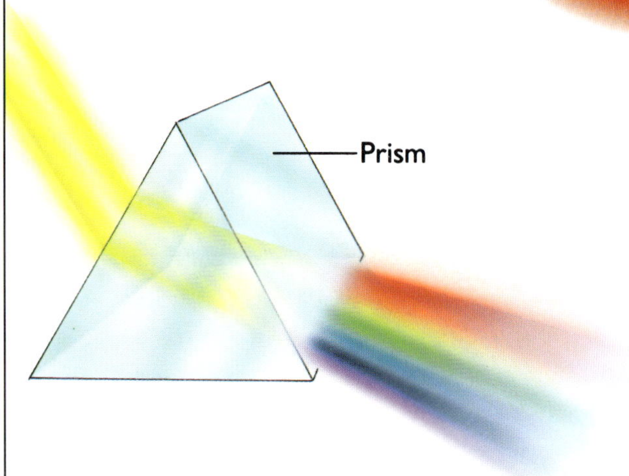

Violet light is bent the most.

Colours of the spectrum

"White light" can be separated into the colours of the spectrum. Make your own spectrum by putting a glass of water on a piece of white paper. Place this near a window in the morning or evening. Make a 1 cm slit in a piece of card and tape it to the glass. The spectrum will appear on the paper.

Experimenting with paint
When coloured paints are mixed together, they form a dark, black shade. This is because paint contains pigments which reflect certain colours when light shines on it. Try painting a picture using small dots of red, yellow and blue. This technique is called pointillism. Look at the picture from a distance. Do the dots merge to form new colours?

Use a fine paint brush to create the dots. Crayons and felt-tip pens are just as good.

Reflecting colour

The colour you see when you look at an object is the colour it reflects, or bounces back into your eyes. A red object reflects red light, and absorbs the other colours. An object looks white if it reflects all the different wavelengths of visible light. A black object absorbs all the colours, and hardly reflects any light.

Having illusions
A common saying about rainbows is that a pot of gold sits at the end, where it meets the ground. However, do not be allured by this trick – a rainbow can only be seen at a distance. If you try to reach it, it will disappear from your sight. You may have heard the song "Over The Rainbow" from the film *The Wizard of Oz*. Based on L. Frank Baum's book *The Wonderful Wizard of Oz*, the story follows Dorothy's adventures in a fantasy land beyond the rainbow.

Lost to history
Sir Isaac Newton (1642-1727) was an English mathematician and physicist, best known for his laws of motion and gravity. However, he also studied light, and was the first to prove light is made up of different colours. Ironically, a lit candle on Newton's desk burned 20 years' worth of his research papers on light and optics.

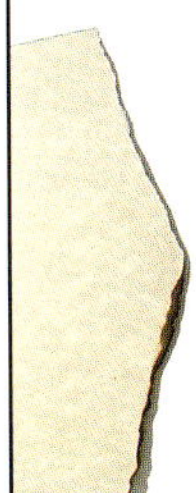

THE SUN AND STARS

For many millions of years, the Sun has been giving out visible light and all the other forms of electro-magnetic energy. The Sun is 150 million kilometres from the Earth, but its electro-magnetic energy travels so fast, it reaches us in only eight minutes. It moves at an amazing 300 million metres per second! Other stars are so far from the Earth that their light takes millions of years to reach us. The planets and their moons do not produce light of their own like the stars. They appear to shine only when sunlight bounces off them.

How the Sun makes light

The Sun is incredibly hot, which makes the atoms in its gases move about a lot, crashing into each other. When hydrogen gas (A) bumps into more hydrogen gas (B), another gas called helium (C) is produced. This process is called nuclear fusion, and it releases huge amounts of electro-magnetic energy (D), including light.

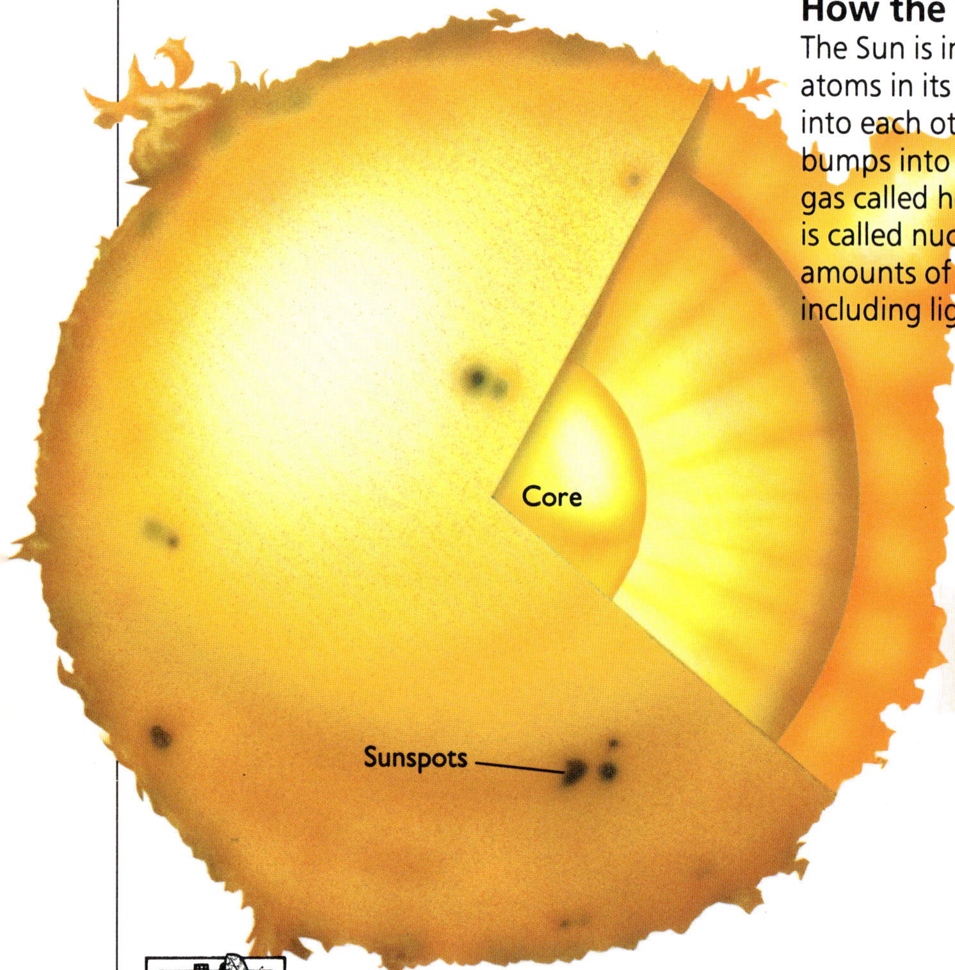

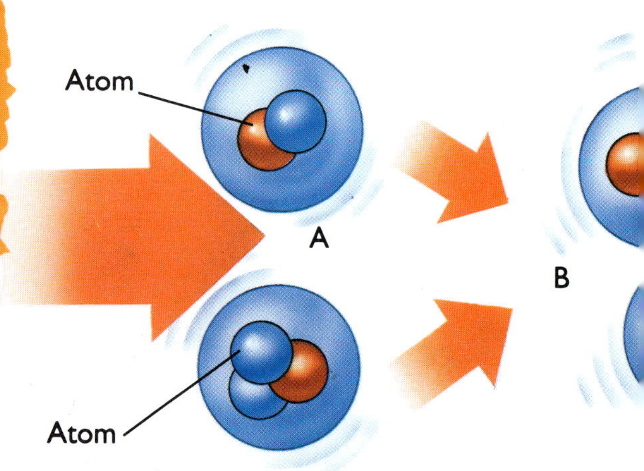

Food chains

Plants are the only living things that can make their own food. So animals have to eat plants – or other animals that have already eaten plants. A simple series of feeding links, such as grass-rabbit-fox, is called a food chain. The Sun's energy is passed on at each link in the chain. Food chains join, forming a food web which can easily be upset if one link changes.

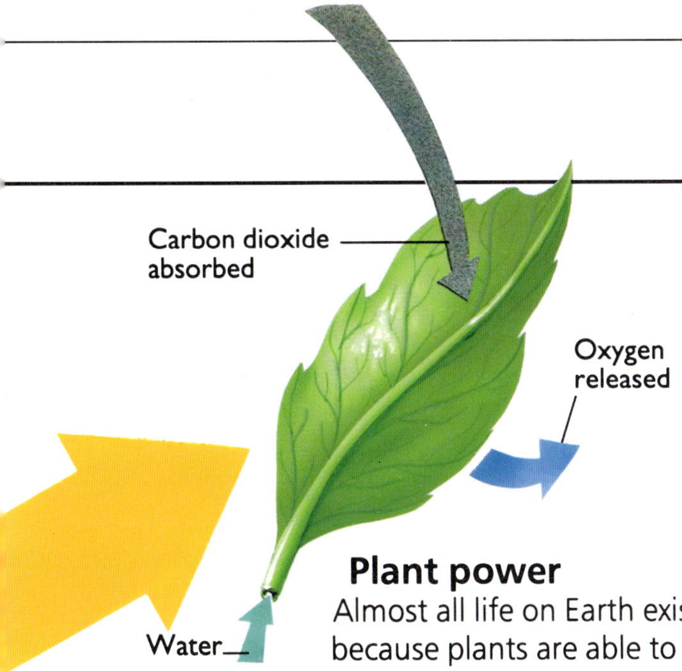

Plant power

Almost all life on Earth exists because plants are able to use the Sun's energy to make their own food. This process is called photosynthesis, which means "making things with light". It takes place mainly in a plant's leaves. The Sun's energy is trapped by a green pigment called chlorophyll, and used to join carbon dioxide and water to make sugars. Oxygen is released into the air as a waste product.

Reaching for the light

The Sun's light is essential for plants to grow. When seeds germinate under the ground, they look for the light in a process known as geotropism. Plant a sprouting potato in a pot of moist soil, and put it at one end of a box. Place partitions along the box, as shown, and then make a hole at the opposite end from the plant. Put a lid on the box and place it somewhere sunny. After several days, the sprout will emerge from the hole. What conclusions can you draw from this?

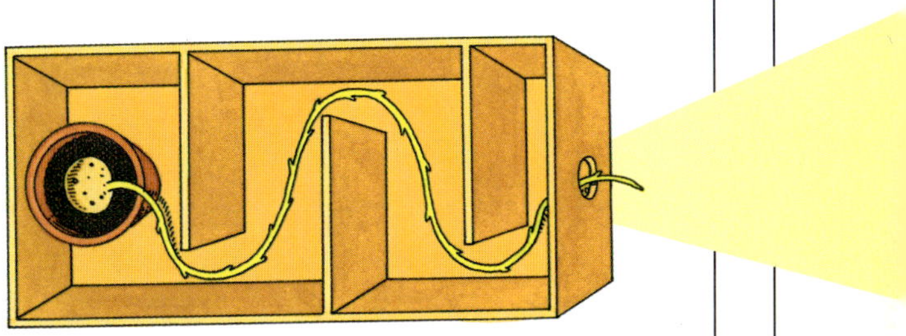

Sun worshippers

Most ancient cultures had a way of explaining phenomena we now understand in scientific terms. These explanations are known as myths. Many ancient peoples worshipped the Sun as a god. Some thought that an eclipse of the Sun was the Sun god's way of expressing anger.

Re

The ancient Egyptians worshipped the Sun god Re, who carried the Sun across the sky in a barge.

Helios

In ancient Greek mythology the Sun was driven from east to west in a flaming chariot, guided by the Sun god Helios. Can you think of any other myths about the Sun?

Solar power

Modern society relies on energy to function. It powers our cars, runs our factories, heats our homes and cooks our food. At the moment we burn oil and gas to get much of our energy. However, the Sun's rays carry enough energy to our planet to supply more than our present needs. Solar power can be used to heat water in our homes, or large solar power stations can be set up to provide electricity for towns and cities.

OTHER SOURCES OF LIGHT

Apart from nuclear fusion, there are several other ways of making light. In light bulbs, electricity is passed through a thin coil of metal, which gets so hot it glows with a bright light. Sodium lights (yellow street lamps) or the neon lights used in advertising, give out light when electricity is passed through a gas. Some plants and animals, such as fungi and fireflies, use chemical reactions to glow with light. This is called cold light, as it is emitted without high temperatures. Some rocks also glow with a cold light.

Life before the light bulb
Before the American inventor Thomas Edison developed the light bulb in 1879, people had to find other ways to light up their homes and workplaces. During the Middle Ages in Europe (1200-1500), most people had to manage with natural light. A fire for cooking would produce some light, but not enough to work by. By the 1800s, candlelight was far more widespread. People also made use of oil lamps. In European cities, like London, gas street-lights were used, which had to be lit each evening and extinguished each morning. By the 1880s, electric light was in general use by the majority of the public.

Electric light

In a light bulb, electricity has to push very hard to move through an extremely long, thin wire. This pushing makes the wire so hot, it gives out light. Fluorescent lights are filled with mercury gas, which gives out invisible ultraviolet rays when electricity flows through it. These ultraviolet rays strike a coating of chemicals, called phosphors, on the inside of the tube, which then give out visible light. This is called fluorescence.

Fireflies

Chemical lights

Fireflies and glow-worms flash their lights at night, like a sort of Morse Code, to find a mate of the right species. Some deep-sea fish glow, or carry groups of light-producing bacteria. These help the fish to find food, to defend themselves or to attract mates.

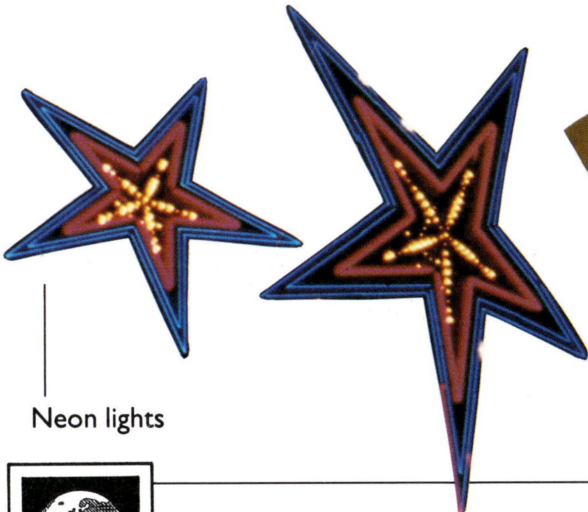

Neon lights

Glow-worm lantern

Glow-worms are whose larvae and females are luminous. They can glow or give out flashing light. You can make your own glow-worm lantern using coloured tissue paper, card and glue.

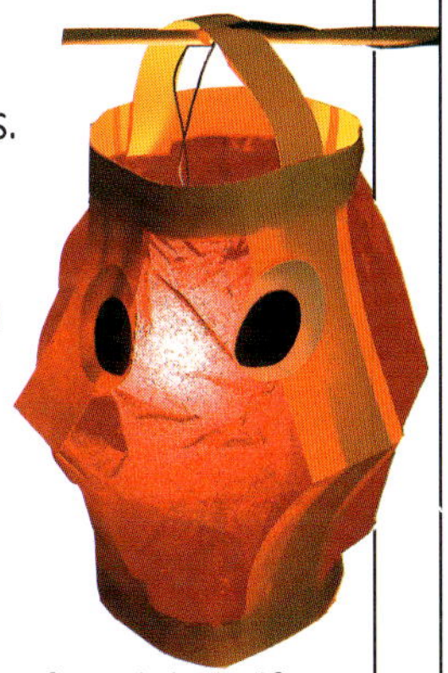

Fold a large piece of card in half lengthwise, and cut out some wide slits at regular intervals. Now roll one edge round to meet the other and glue in place. Line the lantern with tissue, and use a strip of card for a handle.

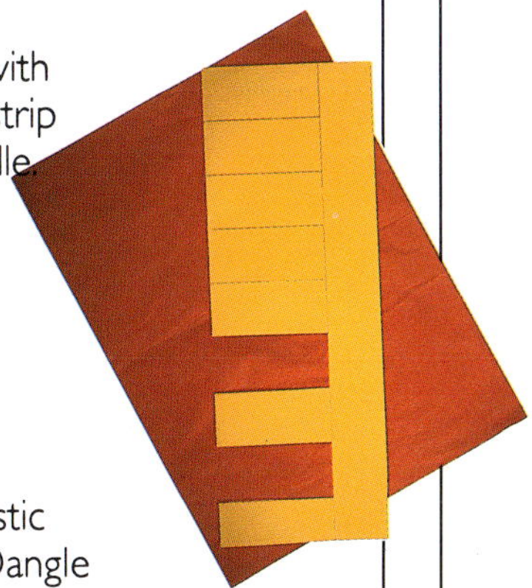

Make the worm glow by using a battery, a small bulb and two pieces of long plastic covered wire. Dangle the bulb inside the lantern from one end of a stick.

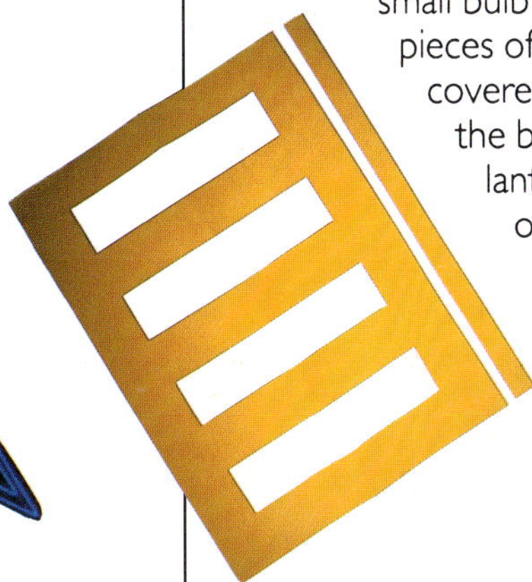

Northern lights

Far from the Equator, near the north and south poles, curtains of coloured lights appear in the sky at certain times of the year. These are caused by collisions between particles which are sent out from huge flares on the Sun's surface. The lights called *aurora borealis* are best seen from the northern parts of Canada, Scotland or Scandinavia. Similar lights in the southern hemisphere are called *aurora australis*.

LIGHT, DARK & SHADOWS

The amount of sunlight reaching a place on Earth, depends partly on the position of the Earth in space, and its relation to the Sun and the Moon. It also depends on the curved surface of the Earth and the way the whole planet tilts to one side. When the Sun, Moon and the Earth are all in a straight line, the Moon prevents some sunlight from reaching the Earth. The shadow the Moon causes makes some places on Earth dark during the day. This is called a solar eclipse. An eclipse of the Moon occurs when the Earth stops sunlight from reaching the Moon.

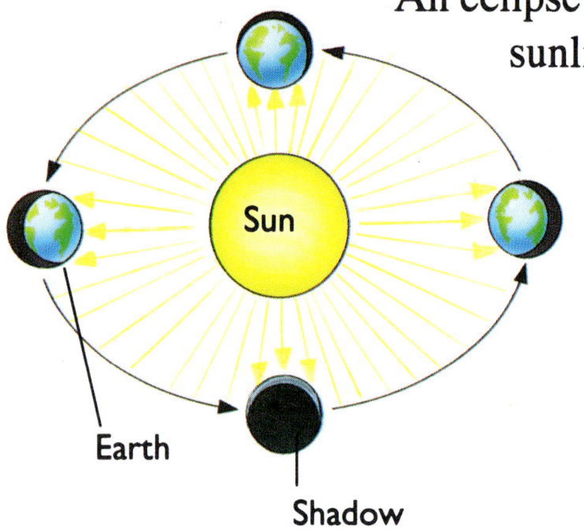

The Earth spins round (rotates) once every 24 hours. At night, your part of the Earth is turned away from the Sun, and is in shadow. The seasons happen because the Earth is tilted at an angle. As it moves around the Sun once a year, some places receive more light and heat.

Shadows form when objects block out light. Light cannot bend around the object because it travels in straight lines. The size of a shadow depends on the distance between the light and the object and the surface it falls on.

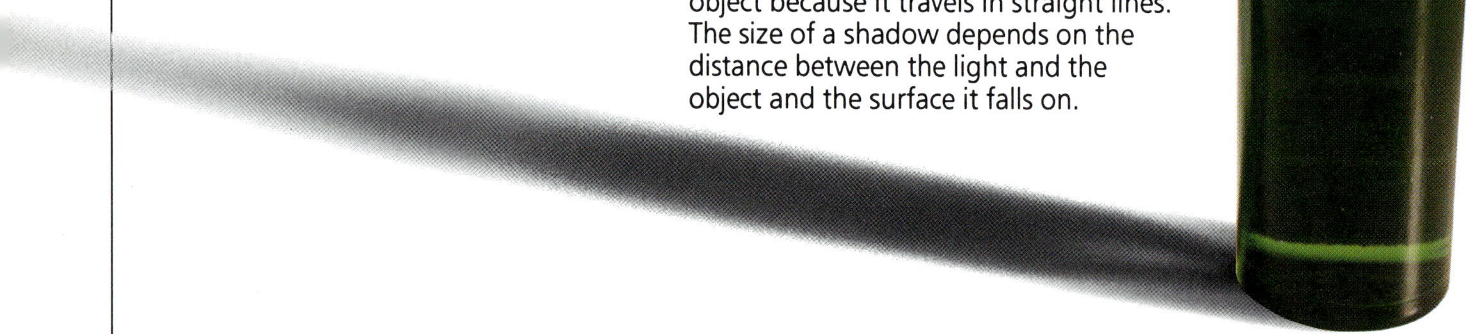

Measuring time from shadows

To make your own sundial you will need a piece of thin card, a protractor, a compass and a piece of thick card. Cut out a triangle, as shown, from the thin card. Make one angle a right angle (90°). Fold along the dotted line. With your compass, draw a semi-circle on the thick card. Fix the folded edge of the triangle to the card, as shown, and place the sundial outside so that the triangle points north-south. Every hour mark the position of the shadow on the base. Every day the shadow will travel the same distance, so you should be able to tell the time this way.

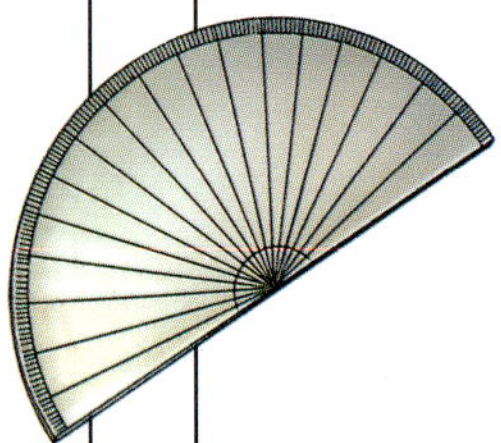

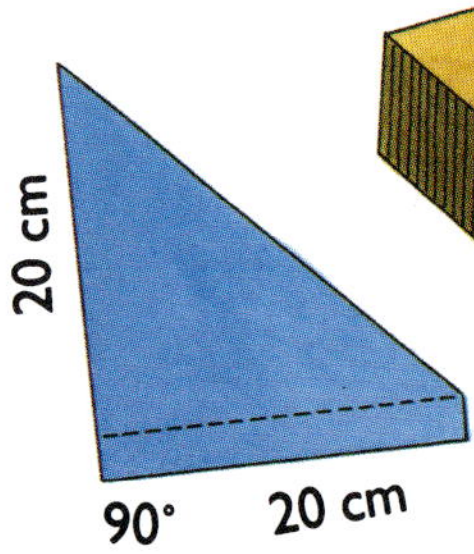

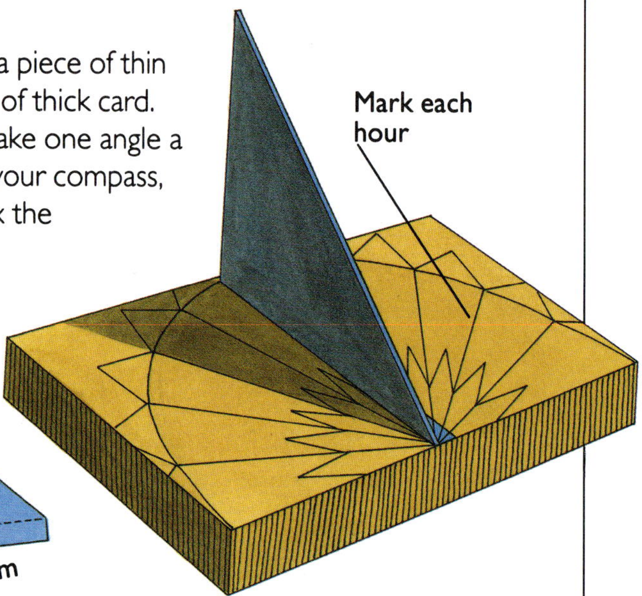

Opaque materials, like card, act as a barrier to light, and will not let light pass through. Shadows form behind them.

Transparent materials, like glass, let light pass through. We can see through these materials, and they do not cast shadows.

Translucent materials, like tissue, let some light through. We cannot see clearly through these materials, and objects look blurred – they form faint shadows.

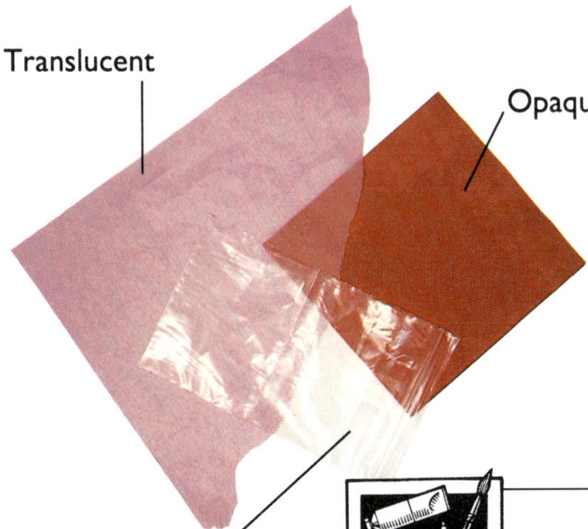

Darkness during day

Before scientists explained solar eclipses, some people thought they indicated the end of the world. Over 4,000 years ago, ancient Chinese myths held that an eclipse was a dragon trying to eat the Sun. Their solution was to make as much noise as possible to scare the monster away, and the whole population would scream, bang gongs and make a general uproar. However, they knew that eclipses followed certain patterns and were able to predict when they would occur.

Shadow theatre

Shadow theatre began in the Far East, in India and China. It is one of the oldest forms of theatre in the world. All you need to put on your own shadow show is a light source directed at a flat, white surface. Using a white wall or a sheet of white paper as a backdrop, place a torch on a chair or table. For the characters of your show, use your hands to make different shapes, or cut out shapes and attach them to sticks. Use black paper or coloured cellophane for a variety of results. For the best effect, make the room dark before you begin your show.

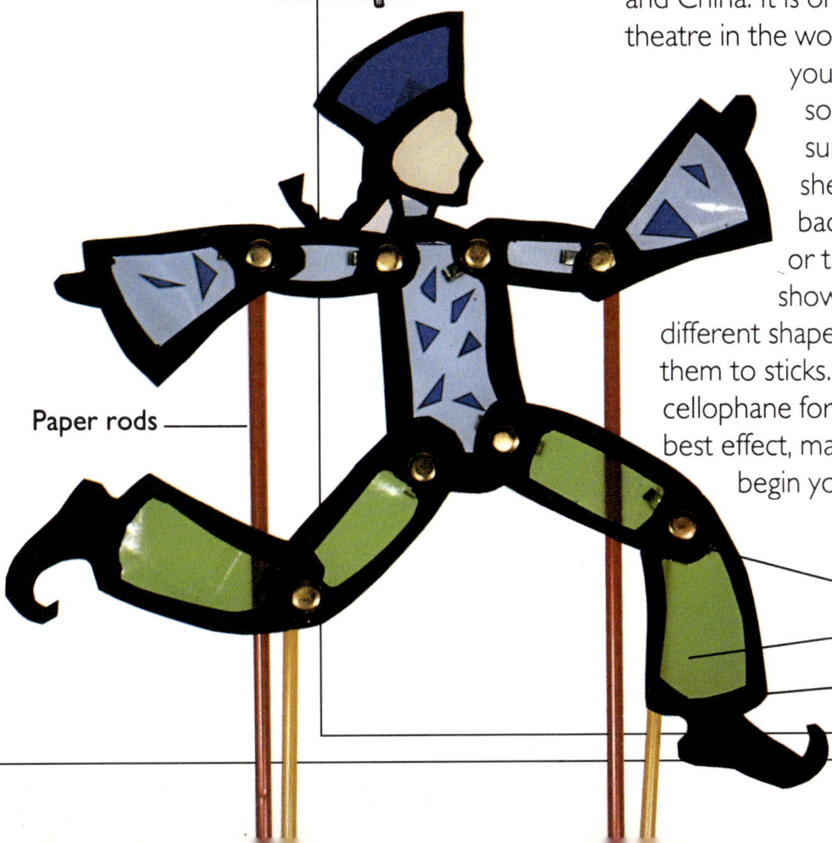

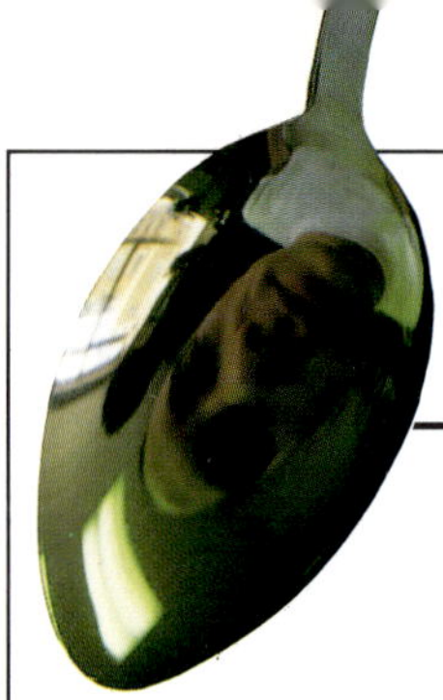

REFLECTION

When light hits a surface, it bounces off again – rather like a ball bouncing off a wall. This is called reflection. Reflected light makes things sparkle and shine. Mirrors produce the best reflections, because they are smooth and flat, and reflect most of the light that strikes them. The image in a mirror is different to real life, because it is inverted (or reversed). You don't see yourself in a mirror as other people see you. Curved (or convex) mirrors can change the size of images, and concave mirrors (which curve inwards) can turn images upside down.

Brilliant reflection
Birds' feathers vary from the dull-coloured tones of a sparrow, to the bright plumage of a parrot. Blacks, greys and browns result from pigments (colourings) in the feather itself. Yellow, orange and red plumage, however, come from pigments obtained in the bird's diet. A flamingo is only pink because of the red brineshrimp it feeds on. Green, blue and violet coloured feathers are produced as light reflects off the structure of the feather. A peacock's iridescent plumage is created by light reflecting off microscopic fringes, called barbules, on each feather.

Peacock's feather

Make a kaleidoscope
Kaleidoscopes form beautiful coloured patterns which are always changing. To make one, tape together three small mirrors of the same size (A). Make sure they are facing each other. Stand the mirrors upright on a piece of card, and draw around the end with a pencil. Cut out this shape and tape it onto the mirrors. Now poke a hole through the card (B). Tape a piece of tracing paper over the other end (C), and drop some coloured beads or bits of paper through the hole. Look through the hole and point the other end towards the light. Move the kaleidoscope, and you will see a different pattern.

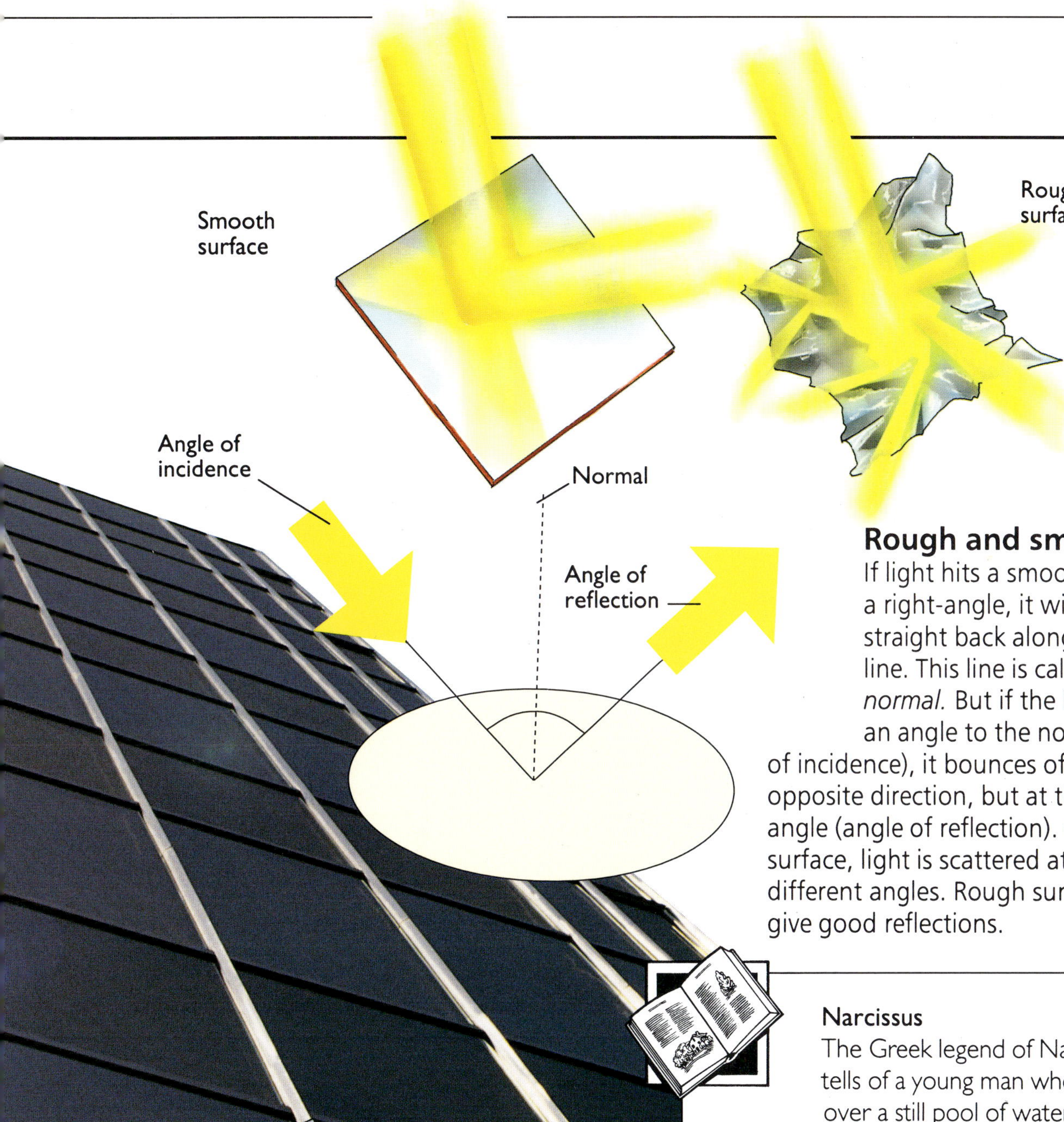

Rough and smooth

If light hits a smooth surface at a right-angle, it will bounce straight back along the same line. This line is called the *normal.* But if the light hits at an angle to the normal (angle of incidence), it bounces off in the opposite direction, but at the same angle (angle of reflection). On a rough surface, light is scattered at many different angles. Rough surfaces do not give good reflections.

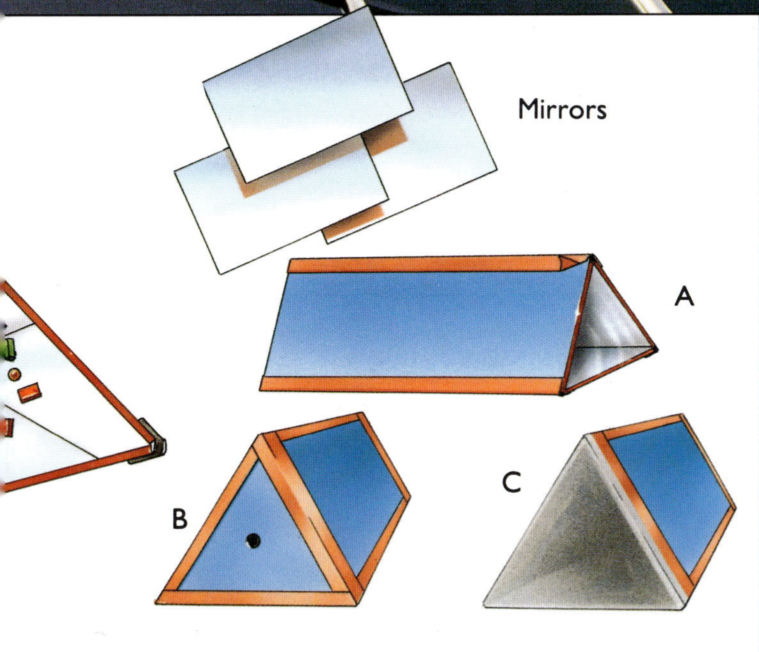

Narcissus

The Greek legend of Narcissus tells of a young man who leaned over a still pool of water for a drink. As his face neared the water, he caught a glimpse of a beautiful youth staring back at him. He was so entranced by this image that he would not leave the side of the pool, and he pined away. A Narcissus flower grew on the spot where he died. His name has given us the term narcissism, which means love of oneself.

REFRACTION

Light travels fastest through space, and moves more slowly through air. Water then slows light down further, by about 25 per cent, and glass slows it down even more, by about 35 per cent. When light passes from air to water or from air to glass, it slows down, causing it to change direction. This "bending" effect is called refraction. Swimming pools look shallower than they really are, because of the way the light from the bottom of the pool is refracted as it moves from the water into the air. Lenses refract light, and can make objects appear larger or smaller than they really are.

Convex lenses

Lenses are pieces of transparent material with a curved surface. Convex lenses curve outwards on both sides. They bend the light rays inwards, where they meet at the focus of the lens. They magnify (enlarge) things, and are used in spectacles to correct long-sightedness.

Bending light

Take a cardboard shoe box and cut two narrow slits, 2 cm apart, at one end. Put a sheet of white paper in the bottom of the box, placing a jar of water on top. Now line up the jar with the slits. Turn off the light in the room, and shine a torch through the slits. Can you see the light bending through the water and meeting on the other side?

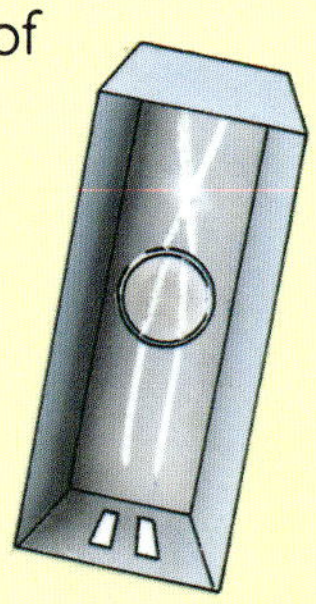

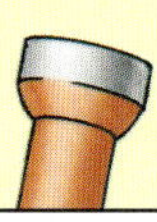

The power of light

Sunlight is extremely powerful. If concentrated onto one spot, it can cause fires. For centuries it has been known that light bending through a magnifying glass can set fire to wood. In the ruins of a city in ancient Mesopotamia (now Iraq), burning glasses have been found, dating back to the 7th century BC. And in 1774, the scientist Lavoisier, used this knowledge to build "the great burning lens" with which he roasted a mixture of metal and charcoal. However, it's not just magnifying glasses that can concentrate light. Pieces of ordinary glass are also able to do this. If you go for a walk in a forest or wood, you may see signs that warn against the hazards of fire. Glass bottles are dangerous things to leave behind if you have a picnic. On a hot day, sunbeams passing through glass bottles may cause a fire to start.

Mirages

In a desert, people sometimes think they can see objects or a pool of water in the distance. But this is really a refracted image, called a mirage. It happens when air near the ground is much hotter than air higher up. As light from the Sun passes from cooler to warmer air (A), it speeds up and is refracted (or bent) upwards (B).

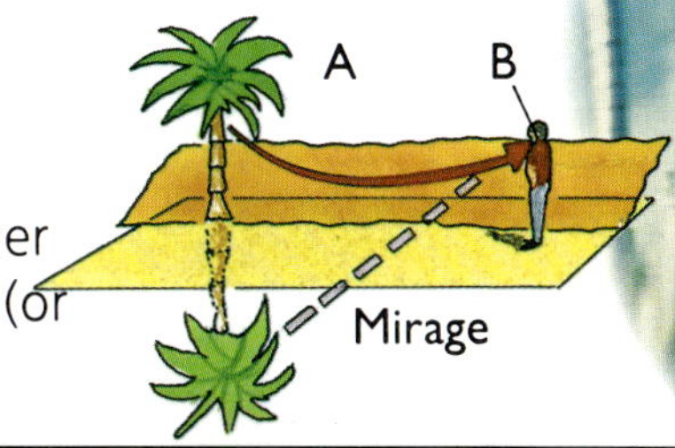

The rays that produce mirages are real, and can be photographed.

Concave lenses

Concave lenses curve inwards on both sides. They make light rays bend outwards or spread out. Concave lenses make things look smaller, and are used in the spectacles of short-sighted people, to correct their sight.

Lavoisier's burning glass was 132 cm in diameter. It comprised two sheets of glass, with the lens-shaped space between them filled with wine vinegar. Lavoisier is regarded as the founder of modern chemistry, and in 1772 he began a series of experiments that demonstrated the nature of combustion (burning).

Seeing things

At the north and south poles, the arctic cold creates mirages. A warmer layer of air (A) over a cold one, bends light rays (B) so that images appear where there is nothing. From a distance, ships can appear to be floating metres above the ocean's surface (C). At the end of the winter, after the long absence of the Sun, a reflection of the Sun can appear in a mirage days before it actually rises.

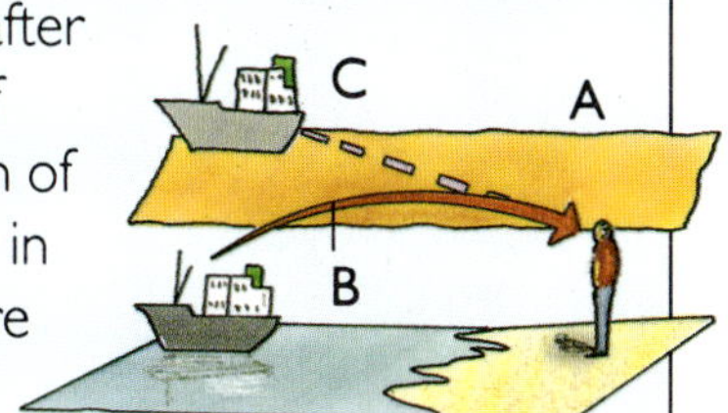

USING LENSES

Lenses are used to bend light in many instruments, from magnifying glasses and microscopes, to telescopes and binoculars. They also help us to see things that are too small or too far away for us to see with our eyes alone. Instruments that help us to see are called *optical*, from the Greek word for eye. The lenses in spectacles help people to see clearly when their eyes are not working properly. The lens in a camera brings the rays of light to a focus on the film, so a clear image is recorded. The lenses in microscopes, telescopes and binoculars make things look much larger than they really are.

The camera

A camera is a lightproof box with a hole at the front, called the aperture. A circular shutter usually stops light from getting inside. But when a photograph is being taken, the shutter opens for a split second to let light reach the film at the back. The film is coated with chemicals that are sensitive to light. The lens focuses the light to form an upside-down image on the film. The amount of light hitting the film can be controlled by changing the aperture size or the shutter speed.

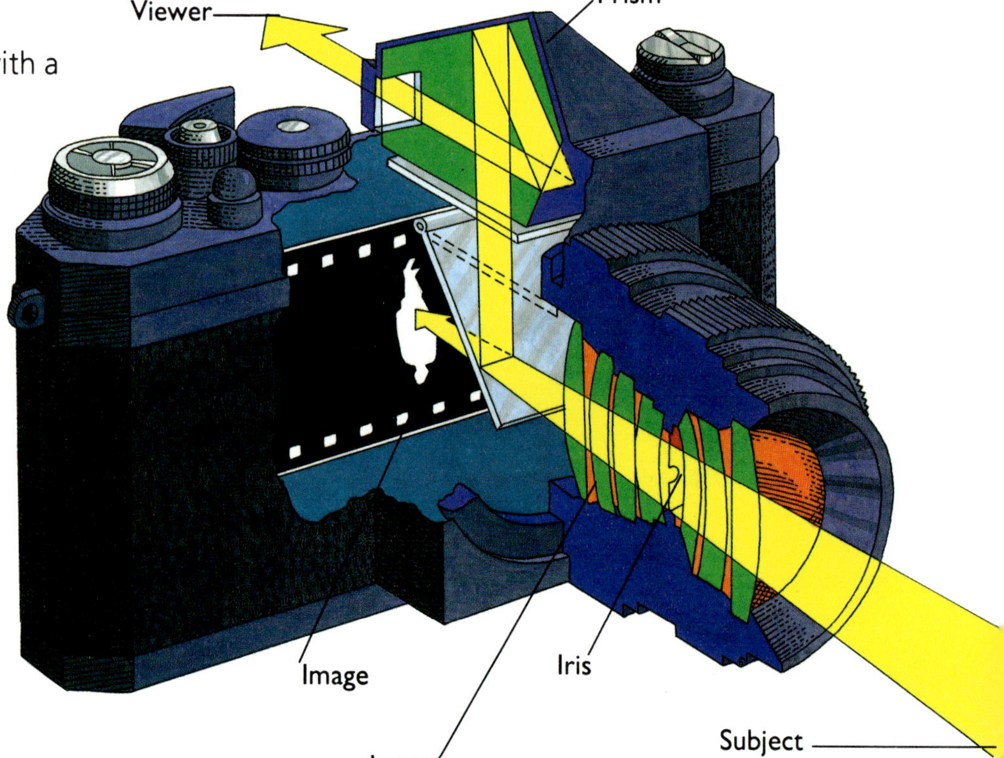

Correcting vision

Sight is one of our most valuable senses. In the past if you had less than perfect vision you would probably have had to be cared for by others. You could not hunt or keep an eye out for danger with blurry vision. As science progressed, people began to develop ways of correcting such problems as short- or long-sightedness. Marco Polo, an Italian explorer, reported seeing people wearing glasses in China, in about 1275. The earliest known picture of spectacles was painted in Italy in 1352. Demand for reading glasses increased after printed books started to become available in the late 1400s. Since then, spectacles have become commonplace in modern society, with contact lenses becoming widely available in the 1960s.

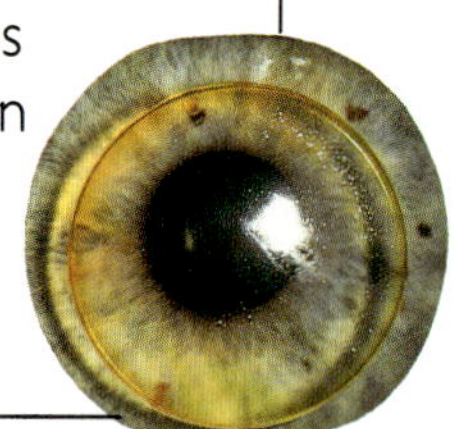

Contact lens

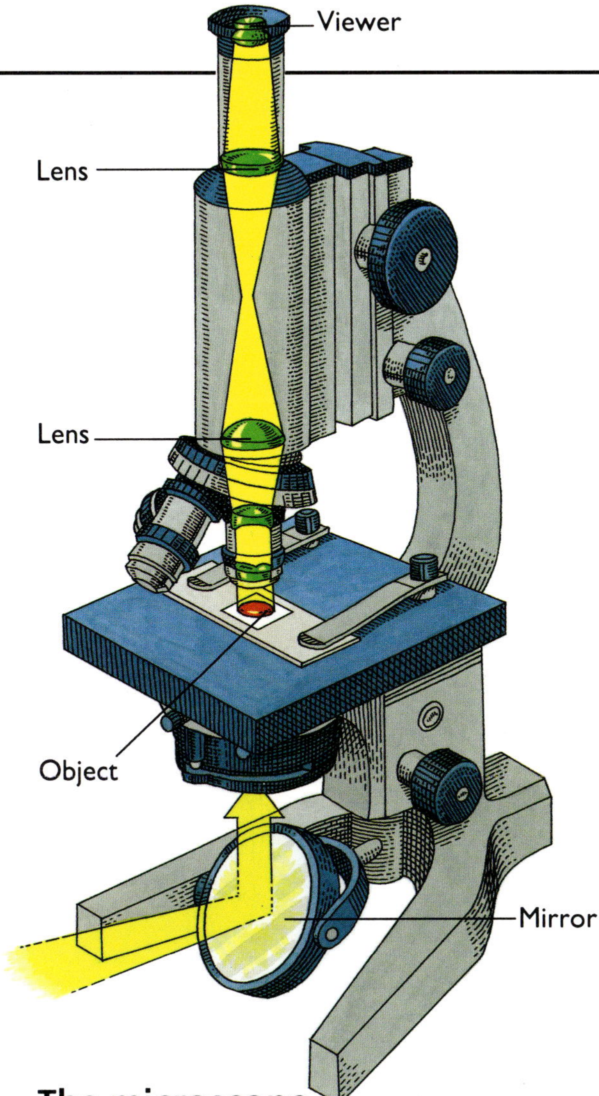

The microscope

A light microscope is used to make very small things, such as minerals in rocks or cells from living things, look hundreds of times bigger than they really are. This allows us to find out more about them. The objects are viewed from a very close distance. A mirror reflects light through the object, and convex lenses in the eyepiece and the body of the microscope magnify the image.

Do-it-yourself microscope

Microscope translates from Greek as "little watcher". You can make a basic microscope quite easily. You will need to place a thin glass upside down on a table, with a small mirror fixed at an angle inside it. Then take a thin strip of foil that has been folded several times, and punch a small hole in its centre. Bend the edges of the foil so that it will fit over the base of the glass – use tape to stick it firmly. Insert a drop of water into the hole, and place a small insect on the base of the glass beneath it. The water will magnify this object up to 50 times its life size.

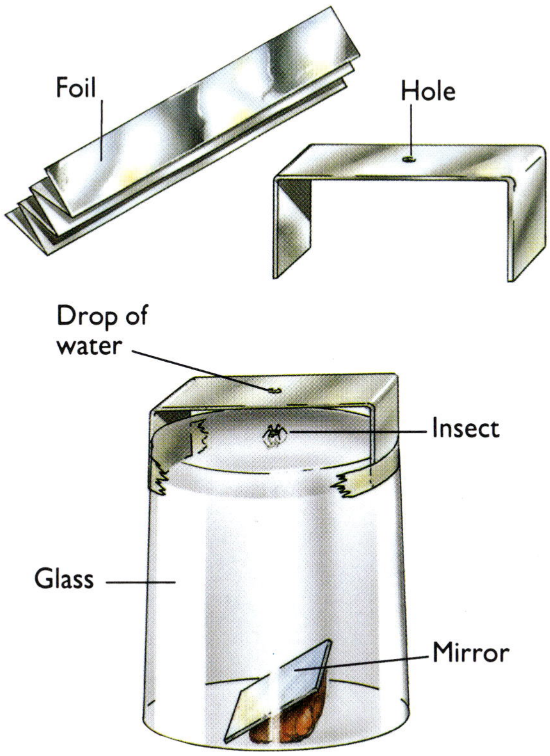

Mirror, mirror on the wall...

Mirrors and lenses appear in literature in a variety of ways. The English writer, Lewis Carroll (1832-98), sends his heroine, Alice, to a fantastical location on the other side of her mirror in *Through the Looking-Glass*. Sherlock Holmes carries a magnifying glass at all times. Can you think of other examples of stories featuring mirrors or lenses?

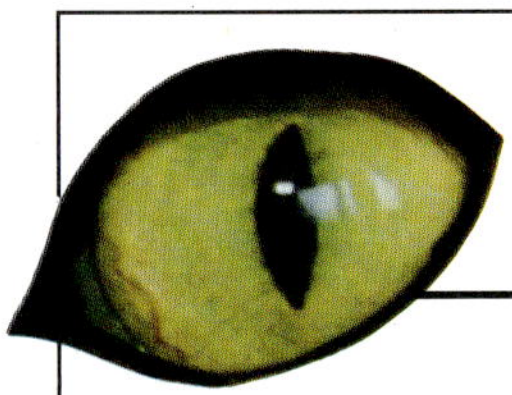

EYES AND SEEING

Animals can see things when light is reflected into their eyes. Without light, it's impossible to see. The sense of sight is very important to animals, helping them to move about, find food and mates, and to detect danger. Some animals, such as worms, can only see patches of light and dark. Others, such as humans and birds, have very good eyesight. The eye can see objects as far away as a star, and as small as a grain of sand. We can judge how far away things are from us and we can see in colour. About four-fifths of the information our brain receives about our surroundings comes through our eyes.

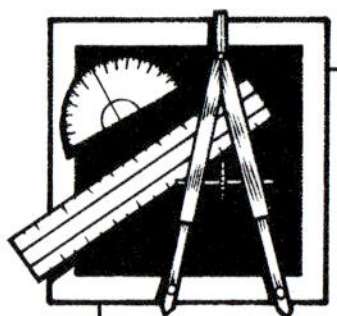

Estimating distance with one eye
Test whether you need both eyes to judge distance properly with the following experiment. Close one eye, and estimate how far away from you an object is. Write down your guess. Now try again with both eyes open. Write this guess down as well. Then measure the distance accurately to see which guess was closer to the truth. If you try this experiment several times with a variety of objects, does your brain begin to make allowances for the loss of sight in one eye?

The human eye

The eye is shaped like a ball, with a lens inside about the size of a pea. Light enters the eye through a hole called the pupil. The pupil is situated in the coloured part of the eye called the iris. Behind the iris is the soft, rubbery lens which focuses the light on to a layer, called the retina, at the back of the eye. The image on the retina is upside-down, because the lens bends the light rays towards each other where they eventually cross over. This cross-over point must fall exactly on the retina if we are to see a clear image. The retina contains light-sensitive chemicals which transform light into electrical messages. These messages are sent to the brain along the optic nerve, where they are turned the right way up and "decoded".

In short-sighted people, the light rays cross over in front of the retina.

In long-sighted people, the light rays cross over behind the retina.

Iris expands and contracts to change the size of the pupil and control the amount of light entering the eye.

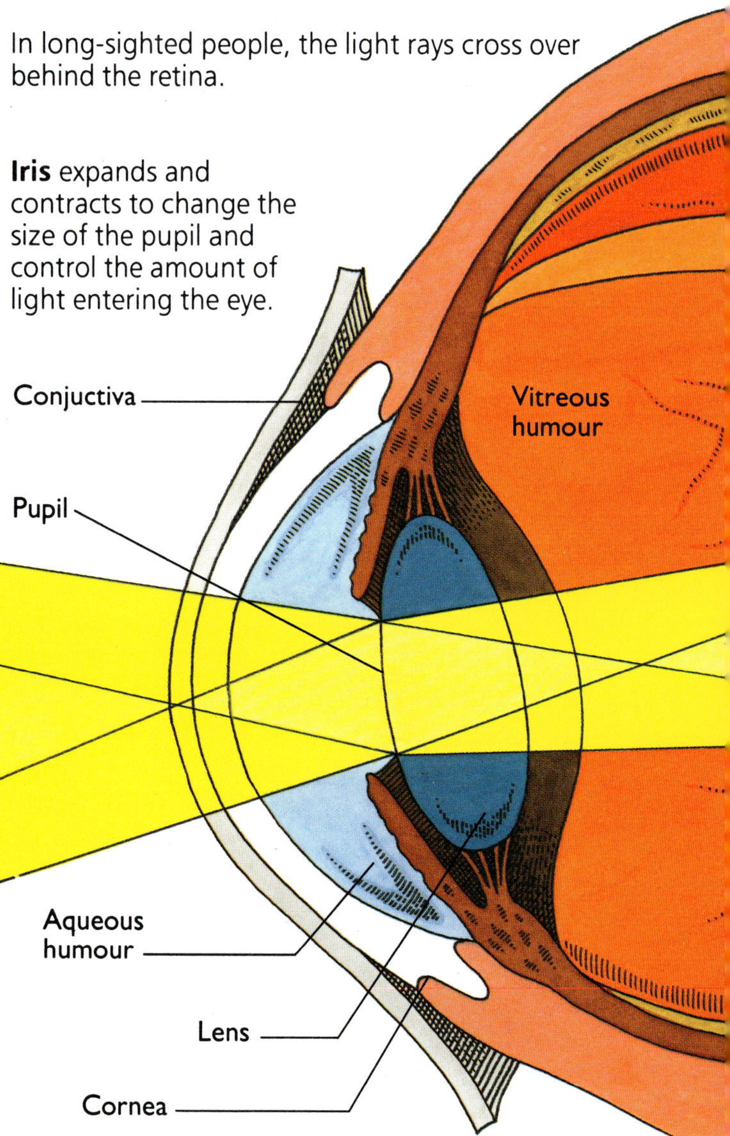

Muscles around the lens pull it into different shapes.

Other eyes

Not all animals have eyes which work like ours. Some invertebrates (animals without a backbone) have eyespots, which are small areas sensitive to light. Many fish and animals that hunt at night have large eyes and pupils. The tuatara of New Zealand, the oldest reptile in the world, has a third eye underneath a flap of skin on its forehead.

A chameleon's eyes stand out from its head and can move completely independently of each other. Spiders have 6-8 eyes to give them all round vision.

Insects and crustaceans have compound eyes which receive images in fragments, like a mosaic. These eyes are made up of many tiny lenses that see one bit of the total scene. All the bits combine to form an image.

Vertebrates can operate in a range of light intensities by adjusting the amount of light admitted through a pupil. A gecko's pupil can close to leave just a few pinhole-like openings.

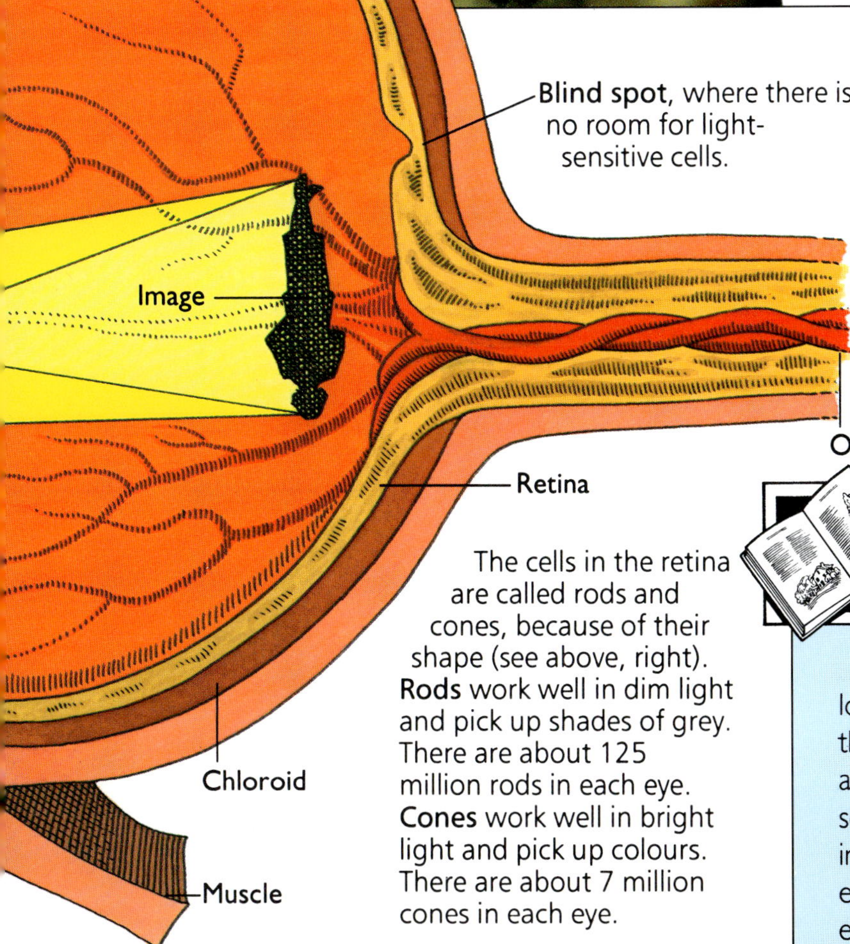

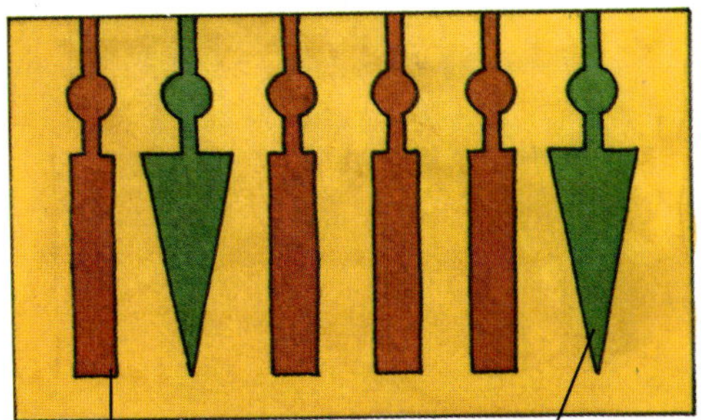

The cells in the retina are called rods and cones, because of their shape (see above, right). **Rods** work well in dim light and pick up shades of grey. There are about 125 million rods in each eye. **Cones** work well in bright light and pick up colours. There are about 7 million cones in each eye.

Up to the eyeballs

We use many expressions which contain references to the eyes. To "keep your eyes peeled" is to keep a look-out. If two people "see eye to eye" then they agree with each other. If a person "turns a blind eye", it means they are ignoring something. "In the mind's eye" refers to the imagination. Can you think of some other expressions, stories or songs which use the eyes to convey meaning? Perhaps you could invent some new ones?

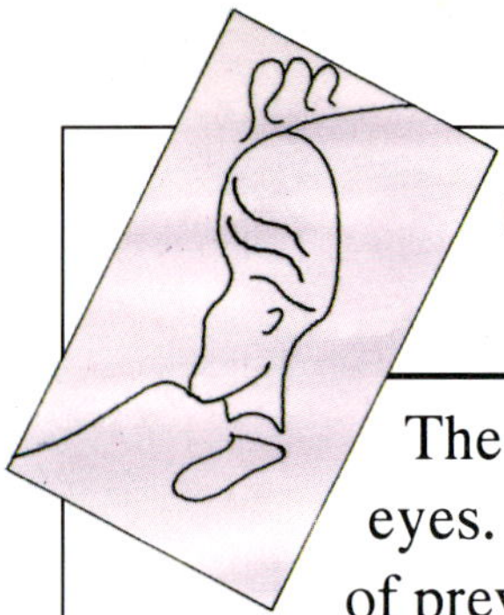

TRICK OF THE LIGHT

The human brain tries to make sense of the information detected by our eyes. To do this, it compares the information with its memory banks of previous experiences, using clues such as colours, shadows, shapes and perspective. But the brain can be tricked by "puzzle pictures". These may have two or more possible meanings. The brain cannot decide which to choose, and we "see" first one interpretation and then another. The brain cannot make sense of these artificial pictures.

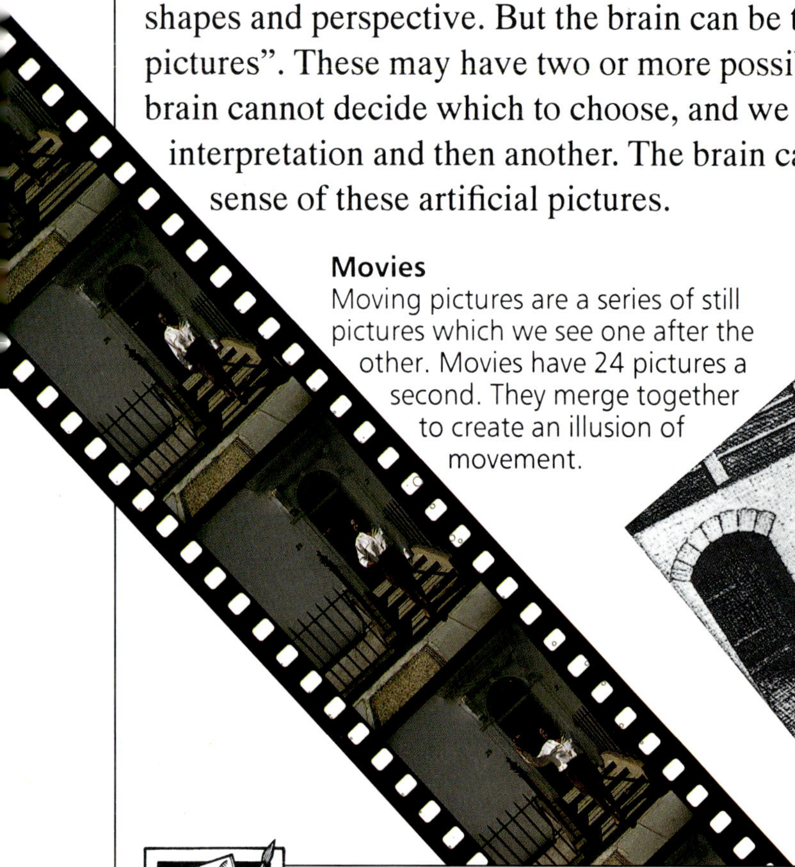

Movies

Moving pictures are a series of still pictures which we see one after the other. Movies have 24 pictures a second. They merge together to create an illusion of movement.

The first "movies"

The first moving picture is credited to Edward Muybridge in 1877. He set up 12 cameras along intervals at a racetrack. As the racehorse passed by, it triggered the cameras, setting off each one in turn. The Victorians invented a device, called a praxinoscope, to show these sequences of photographs. It was basically a cylinder of photographs which was spun quickly. By looking through a slit, the spectator could see the pictures "move".

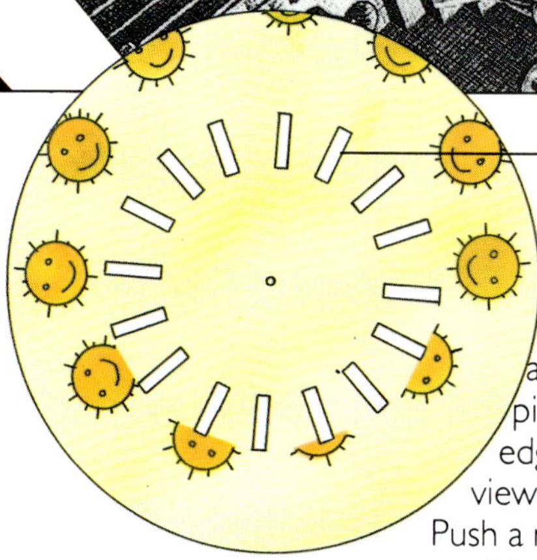

Cut out a disc of card about 21 cm across. Draw your pictures around the edge, and cut out the viewing slits as shown. Push a nail through the centre of the disc and into a cork. Put a bead either side of the disc to make it run smoothly. Now hold the disc up to a mirror with a good light behind you. Twirl the disc by gently striking the edge, and look through the slits. Watch the moving pictures in the mirror.

Muybridge's strip

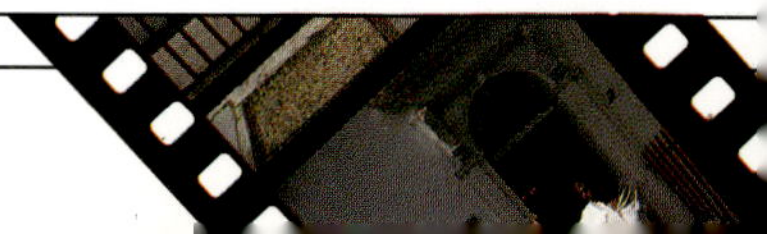

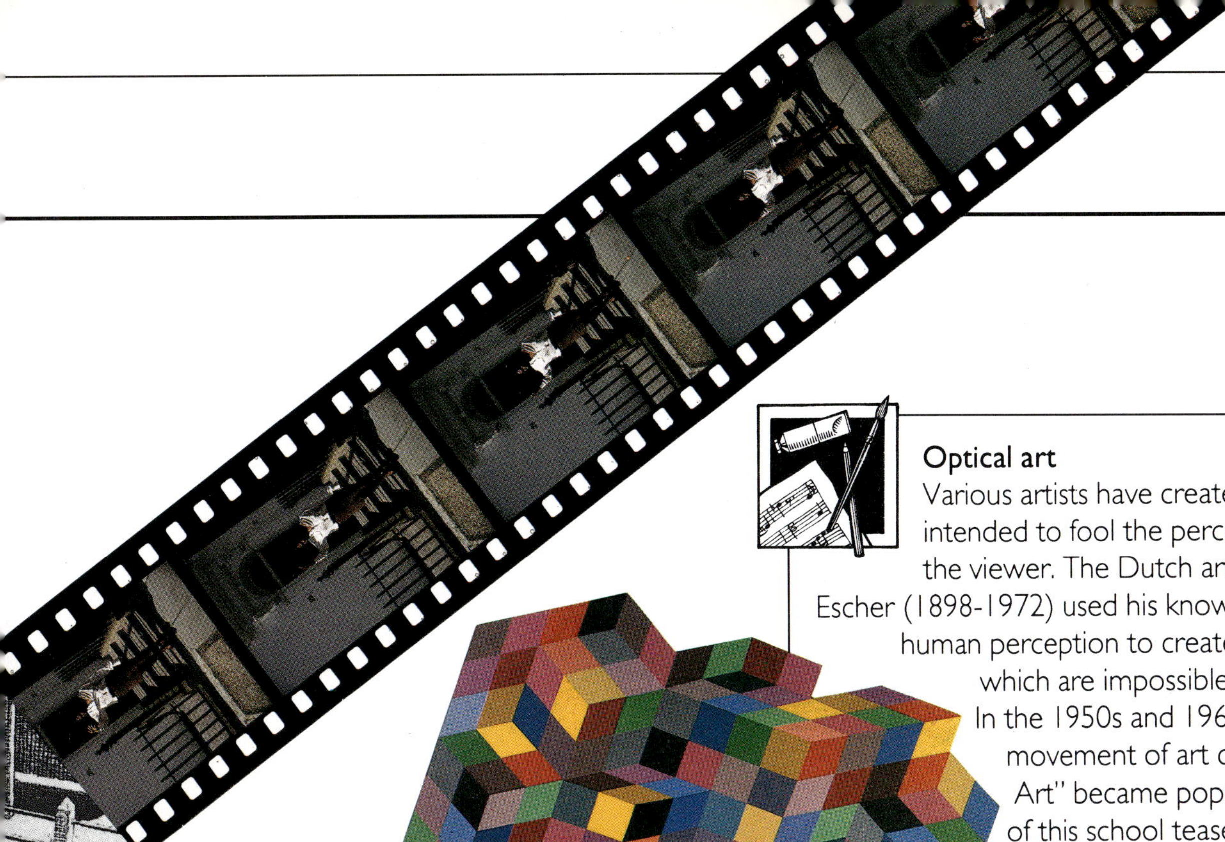

Optical art

Various artists have created works intended to fool the perception of the viewer. The Dutch artist M. C. Escher (1898-1972) used his knowledge of human perception to create images which are impossible in reality. In the 1950s and 1960s a movement of art called "Op Art" became popular. Artists of this school tease the viewer's eye with images which the brain cannot accept as reality. Op Art explored such optical effects as dazzle and vibration, and expanding and contracting space. Drawings, like the one in the top left-hand corner of the opposite page, purposely offer two perceptions. Do you see a young woman wearing a hat, or an old woman in a bonnet?

The Dutch artist M. C. Escher mixed realistic detail with strange perspectives.

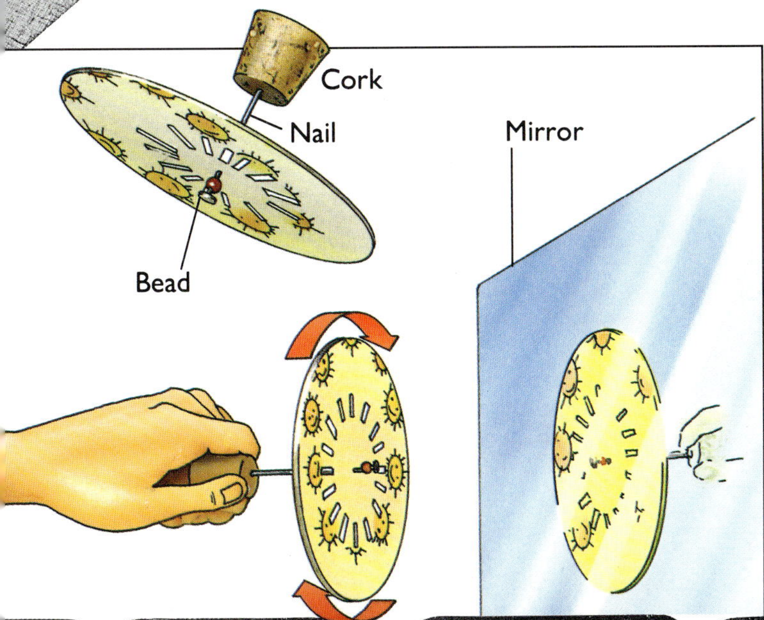

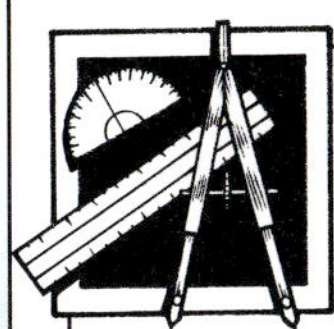

Seeing is believing?

Some images confuse the brain. Look at figure A. Are the two bars parallel? Do you think the two central circles in figure B are the same size? What about the lines in figure C? Are they the same length? Measure them and see.

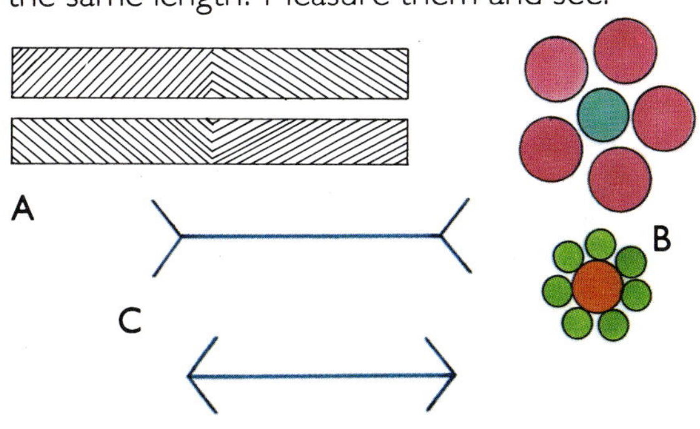

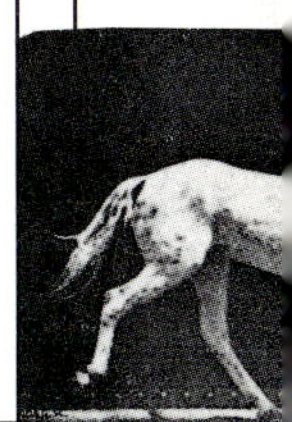

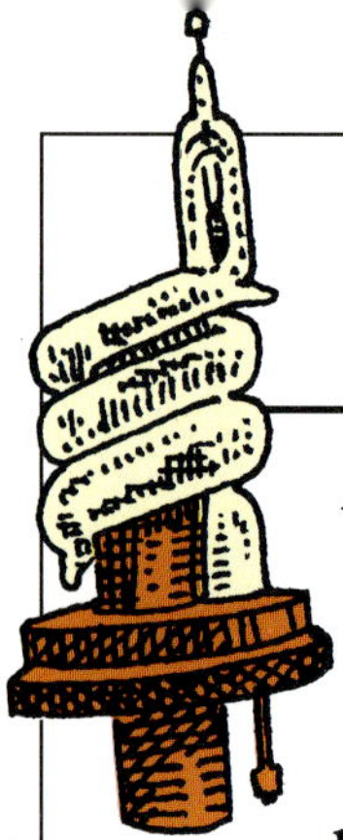

LASERS

A laser is a machine which turns an ordinary beam of light into a straight, narrow beam of very bright light. Laser light does not spread out like ordinary light, so it is concentrated and very powerful. It can cut through steel and human tissue, and can be used to measure distances accurately, make holograms and compact discs, or guide missiles. Lasers may produce visible light of one colour only or invisible infra-red rays. All the waves are in step, and reinforce each other, which is why they are so powerful, and can travel long distances without fading.

Inside a laser is a tube filled with a gas, a solid or a liquid, called the active medium. Usually, this is a man-made crystal, like ruby. Energy, such as light or an electric current, is passed through the active medium, making it give off light. Some of this bounces to and fro between two mirrors, making the active medium give off even more light. This is called lasing.

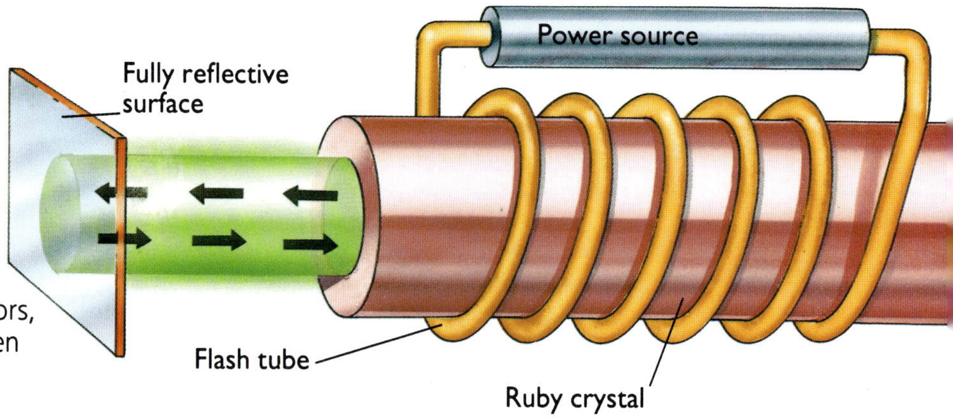

Investigating the Earth

Lasers have been very useful in increasing knowledge about our planet. The distance from the Moon to the Earth was measured by bouncing a laser beam off a reflector on the Moon. Lasers reflected off satellites orbiting the Earth can also detect tiny land movements on our planet. Scientists can use this data to measure the movements of continents or to detect earthquakes and volcanic eruptions.

Futuristic weapons

Although laser weapons are relatively new on the scene in real life, imaginative science fiction writers and filmmakers have incorporated lasers into their works for a long time. Laser weapons appear in the James Bond movie *Goldfinger* (1964), which was based on a book by Ian Fleming (1908-1964). Lasers also feature in the *Star Wars* films, where they are fired from guns and used as swords.

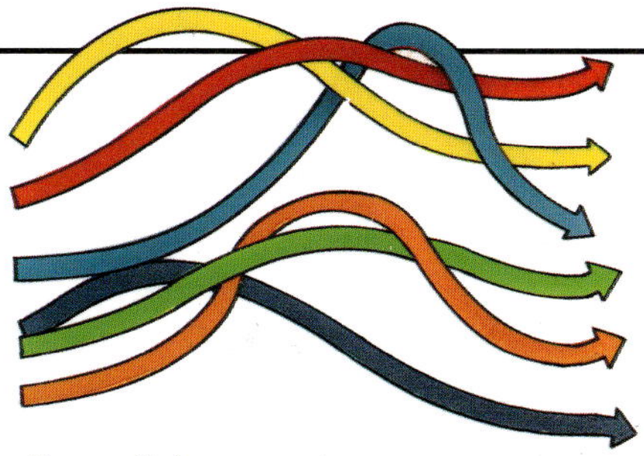

Ordinary light waves

Laser light waves

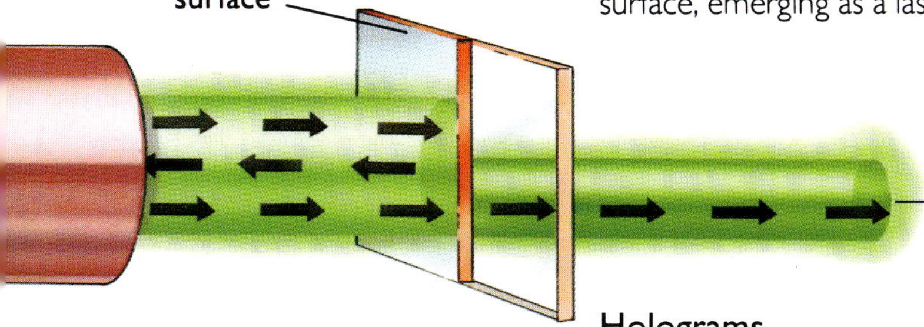

The beam of concentrated light then escapes through the partially mirrored surface, emerging as a laser beam.

History of the laser

The first laser was developed in 1960 by a scientist called T.H. Maiman.

1961 First commercially-built laser sold.
1961 First laser holograms developed.
1963 Lasers first used in surgery.
1966 Optical fibres using lasers developed.
1976 Lasers used to measure Earth's movements.
1982 Compact discs launched.
1988 First transatlantic optical fibre sends telephone messages.
1991 Laser-guided missiles used by USA in the Gulf War.
1998 Experimental high-power microlasers are developed. They are so small that hundreds could fit on the head of a pin.

Holograms

A laser beam can be used to record a ghost-like three-dimensional image called a hologram. The laser beam(1) is split into two parts. One part is aimed at the object(2), and the reflected light, called the object beam, illuminates the film(3). The reference beam (4) is aimed directly at the film, forming a complex pattern. In figure B, a beam of light identical to the reference beam(1) is directed at the developed film. A viewer(2) sees the image(3) in three dimensions.

Hologram

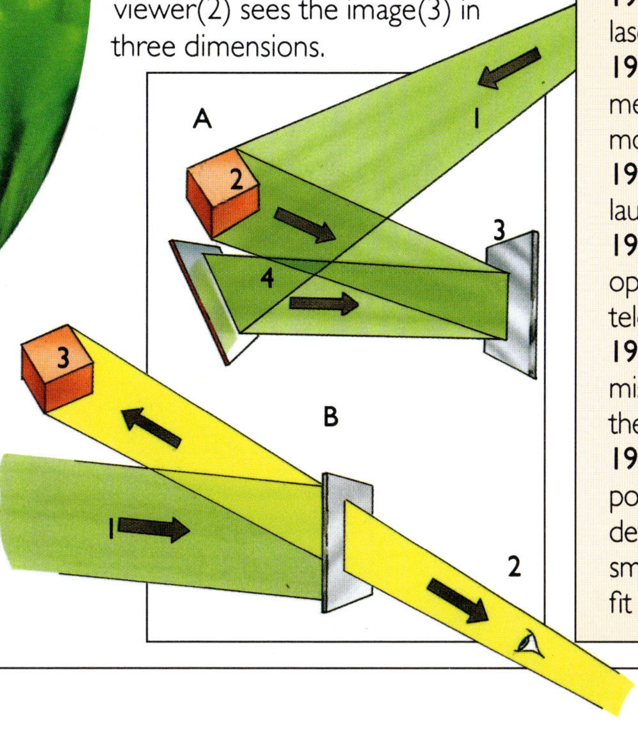

A = Recorded image

B = Viewing image

CHAPTER 3

AIR & WATER

Air and water are two natural phenomena essential for life. Air is all around us. It is the rich mixture of many gases, including oxygen that we breathe, which forms our atmosphere. This acts as a warm blanket for the Earth, producing the right conditions for life.

Water is the most abundant substance on the planet – the seas cover over 70% of the Earth's surface. Without rain, which comes from the air in the Earth's atmosphere, life would be impossible.

This chapter looks at the properties of air and water, how they are made up and the many ways in which we use them, and their importance to life on Earth.

CONTENTS

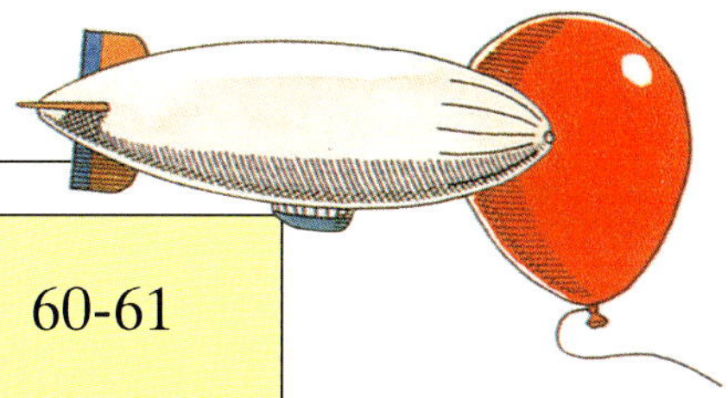

WHAT IS AIR?

Air is everywhere on Earth, even inside our own bodies. We cannot see, smell or hear air but our lives would be very different without it. Air causes changes in the weather, keeps things warm or cool, lets fires burn and allows sound to travel. Air consists of a mixture of gases, mainly nitrogen and oxygen, and can be squashed or compressed into small spaces. The air is constantly recycled by nature – so the air we breathe today is the same air that helped plants to grow millions of years ago (above left).

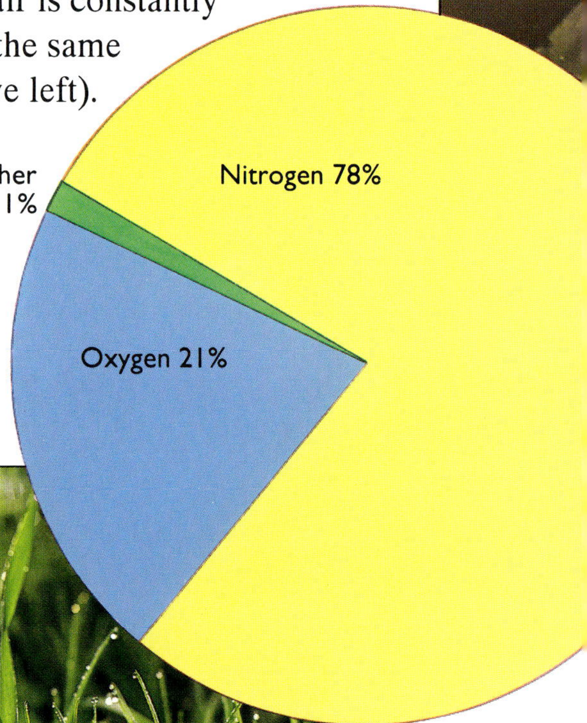

Gases in the air

Most of the air, about 78 per cent, is nitrogen gas. About 21 per cent is oxygen gas. All living things need oxygen to release energy from their food. The remaining 1 per cent of the air consists of gases such as carbon dioxide, argon, neon, helium, krypton, hydrogen, xenon and ozone. The carbon dioxide in the air helps to keep the Earth warm. The air also contains dust, and moisture in the form of water vapour.

Humidity

The amount of water vapour in the air is called its humidity. As air cools down, some of the water vapour turns into liquid water, called condensation. This happens because cool air holds less water vapour than warm air. Condensation may cause clouds, fog or dew to form.

Early morning dew

Pressure

Barometers (see above) measure air pressure, which is caused by the force of gravity pulling the air down towards the Earth's surface. Changes in air pressure signal changes in the weather. High pressure usually indicates fine, settled weather, while low pressure usually means cloudy, rainy weather.

Air studies

Before the 1700s, air was thought to be a pure substance. However, in 1754, Joseph Black discovered carbon dioxide in air. Oxygen was found by Carl Scheele in the early 1770s and by Joseph Priestly (shown right) in 1774. Nitrogen was discovered in 1772 by Daniel Rutherford, but inert gases such as argon were not detected until the 1890s.

Air particles
In a shaft of sunlight, you can often see dust floating in the air. Air always contains many tiny solid particles, from car exhausts, factory smoke and forest fires. Other sources include pollen from plants and salt from the sea. Polluted air over a large city may contain billions of particles.

Feeding a fire
Fires need the oxygen in the air to burn. People sometimes blow on a fire to give it more oxygen. To put out a fire, they cut off the supply of oxygen by spraying it with water, foam or carbon dioxide.

Rusty pipes
If iron or steel are exposed to air and moisture, they usually rust and the metal is eaten away. Rust happens when iron joins up with oxygen in the air to form iron oxide. Protective paint can stop oxygen from reaching iron or steel and therefore stops rusting taking place.

Air sayings
The word air is often used in sayings to convey different meanings. For instance, "to walk on air" is to feel elated, and for something "to be up in the air" means it is uncertain.

Can you find out the meanings of these sayings: to go on the air; to take the air; to give yourself airs; an airy-fairy idea; to be an airhead?

See if you can compose a poem or a song using some common air sayings.

Useful gases
The gases in the air can be collected separately by a process called fractional distillation. Air is made into a liquid when cooled to very low temperatures. When heated, the gases boil off the liquid at different temperatures because they have different boiling points.

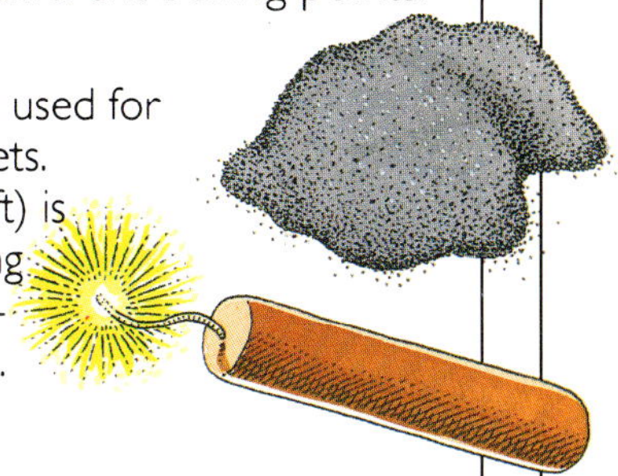

Liquid oxygen is used for powering rockets. Oxygen gas (left) is used in breathing apparatus for fire-fighters and the sick.

Nitrogen gas is used to make fertilisers (above right), while nitric acid (a compound of nitrogen and oxygen dissolved in water) is a key ingredient in explosives.

Argon is used to fill the space in most light bulbs as it is an extremely unreactive (or inert) gas.

Green plants use carbon dioxide to make their own food. Carbon dioxide fire extinguishers are used to put out fires in burning liquids and electrical fires. Carbon dioxide also provides the "fizz" in many fizzy drinks.

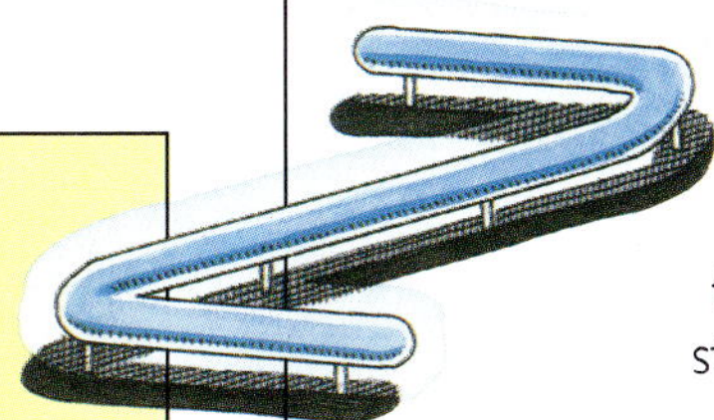

Neon, another colourless, odourless inert gas, is used in fluorescent signs and strip lighting.

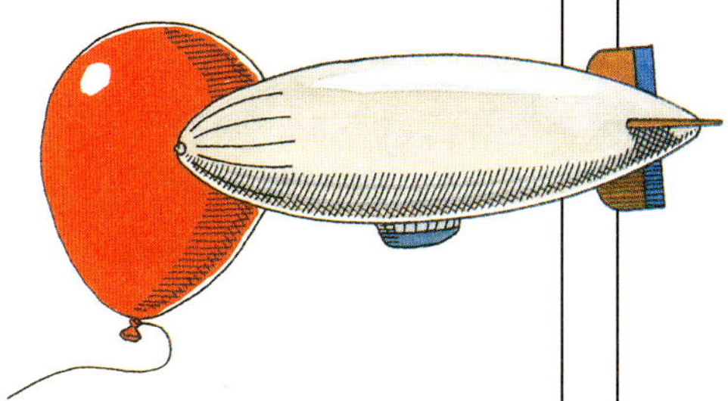

Helium is a very light, inert gas used to fill modern airships. It is also used for some types of party balloon.

AIR AND THE EARTH

The Earth is surrounded by the atmosphere, a big layer of air which formed about 4,500 million years ago. It is held in place by the pull of the Earth's gravity. The atmosphere works like a shield, keeping out harmful rays from the Sun and reducing the impact of rocks from space as they fly towards the Earth's surface. Life is only possible on Earth because the atmosphere prevents it getting too hot or too cold.

Measuring air pressure

Atmospheric pressure is endlessly changing – it pushes on us from all directions because of the gas molecules constantly jostling with each other.

To feel the effect of atmospheric pressure try this simple test. Place a piece of paper flat on a table, by the edge. Then slip a ruler between the paper and the table and lever the paper upwards with the ruler. The force you feel working against you is atmospheric pressure.

Colours of the sky

Sunlight is composed of all the colours of the rainbow. Molecules of gas in the atmosphere scatter the blue light more than the other colours. So extra blue light reaches our eyes and we see the sky as blue on clear days.

At sunrise or sunset, the Sun is low in the sky and has to shine through a thicker layer of atmosphere. More light is scattered aside by dust and gas molecules in the air and only the orange and red light gets through.

On the Moon, the sky looks black because there is no atmosphere with dust and gases to scatter the light.

Layers in the atmosphere

The atmosphere can be divided into five main layers, although there are no physical barriers and the gases in the air move freely about. More than 75 per cent of the atmosphere is in the troposphere, and all life and weather is in this layer. Above this, the stratosphere contains the ozone layer, which absorbs ultraviolet rays from the Sun. In the upper atmosphere, where the air is very thin, are the mesosphere, thermosphere and exosphere. In the thermosphere the air can reach temperatures as high as 2,000°C.

Space suits

Out in space, there is no air at all, so to travel to and from space or work outside their spacecraft, astronauts wear special space suits. These act as a kind of miniature atmosphere, providing air pressure (blood pressure would cause astronauts' bodies to explode otherwise), temperature control and pure oxygen. The early space suits used for walking on the Moon have been developed into sophisticated Manned Manoeuvring Units. First used in 1984, these have an autopilot that keeps the astronaut in position using nitrogen gas-jets.

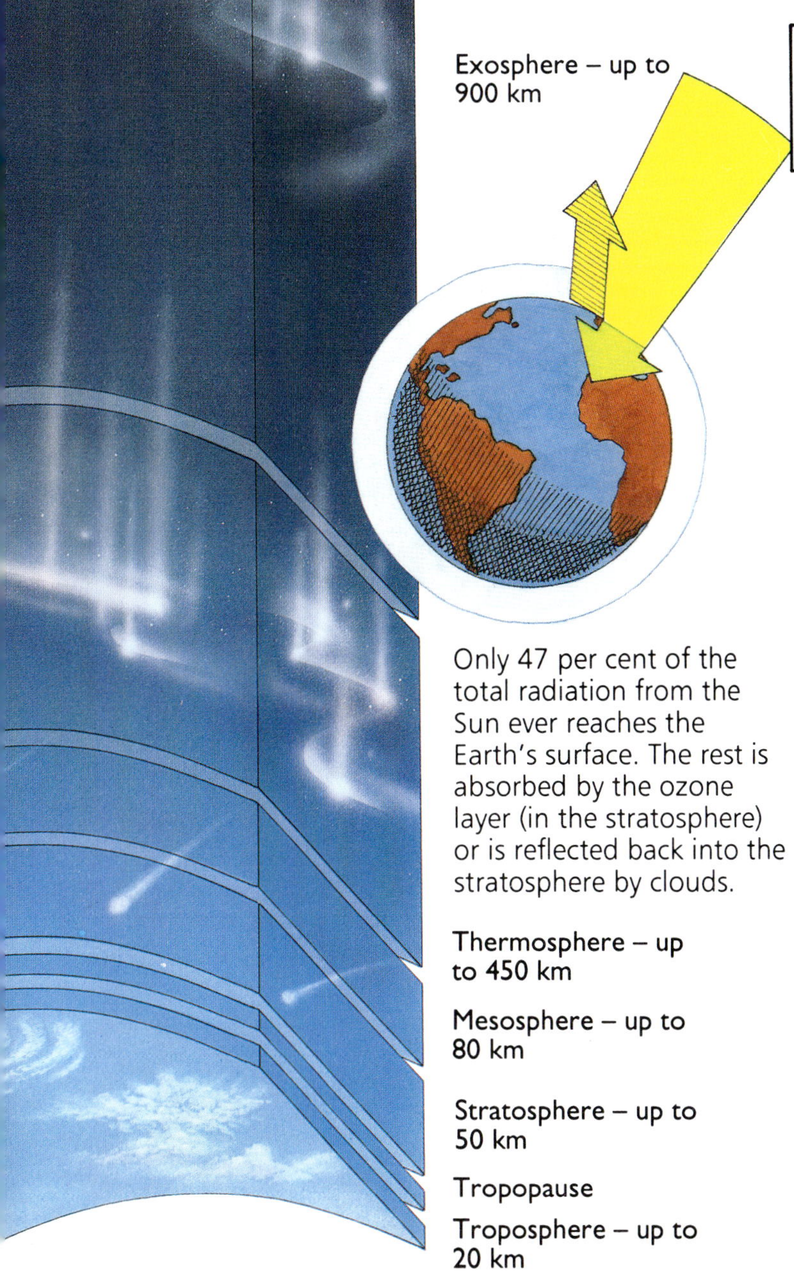

Only 47 per cent of the total radiation from the Sun ever reaches the Earth's surface. The rest is absorbed by the ozone layer (in the stratosphere) or is reflected back into the stratosphere by clouds.

Altitude

As you go higher and higher above the Earth, there is less and less air and the atmosphere becomes thinner. On high mountains, there is not enough oxygen in the air for climbers to breathe properly so they may take oxygen tanks with them. Mountain animals, and people living at high altitudes, develop large hearts and lungs to enable them to take more oxygen from the air.

Altitude sickness happens when people do not get enough oxygen. They may experience symptoms such as headaches, nausea, coughing and sleeplessness.

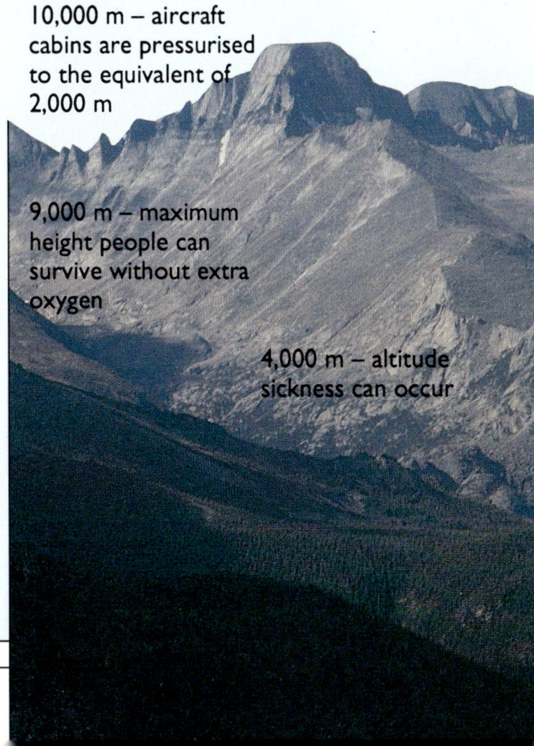

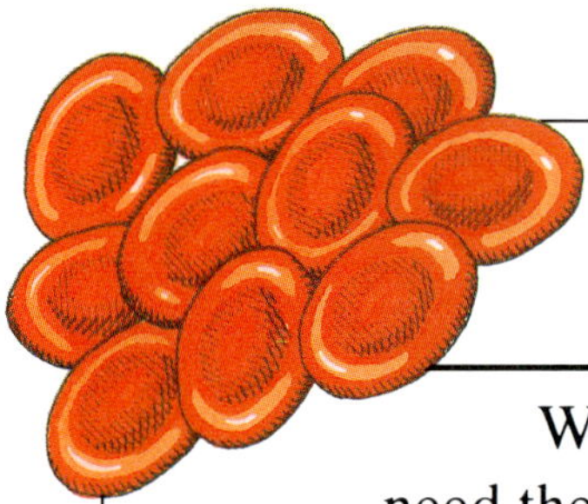

AIR AND ANIMALS

Without air, animals could not live for more than a few minutes. They need the oxygen from the air in their bloodstream to break down their food and release energy so they can live and grow. Food is combined with oxygen, then carbon dioxide and water are released as waste products. The process of releasing energy in this way is called respiration and it happens inside the cells (such as the red blood cells above left) that make up an animal's body. Animals have various special structures to take oxygen from air and water – we have lungs and fish have gills.

Greek beliefs
Ancient Greek scientists believed that air was one of the four basic elements (air, water, fire and earth) from which all things were made, and that the universe was controlled by the relationship of these four elements.

With humans, air enters the body through the nose and mouth. Here the air is warmed and cleaned before it passes down the throat to the lungs. The nostrils on a whale (below left) are called blowholes after the spout of water vapour produced when they exhale. Their wide nasal passages allow quick breathing at the surface.

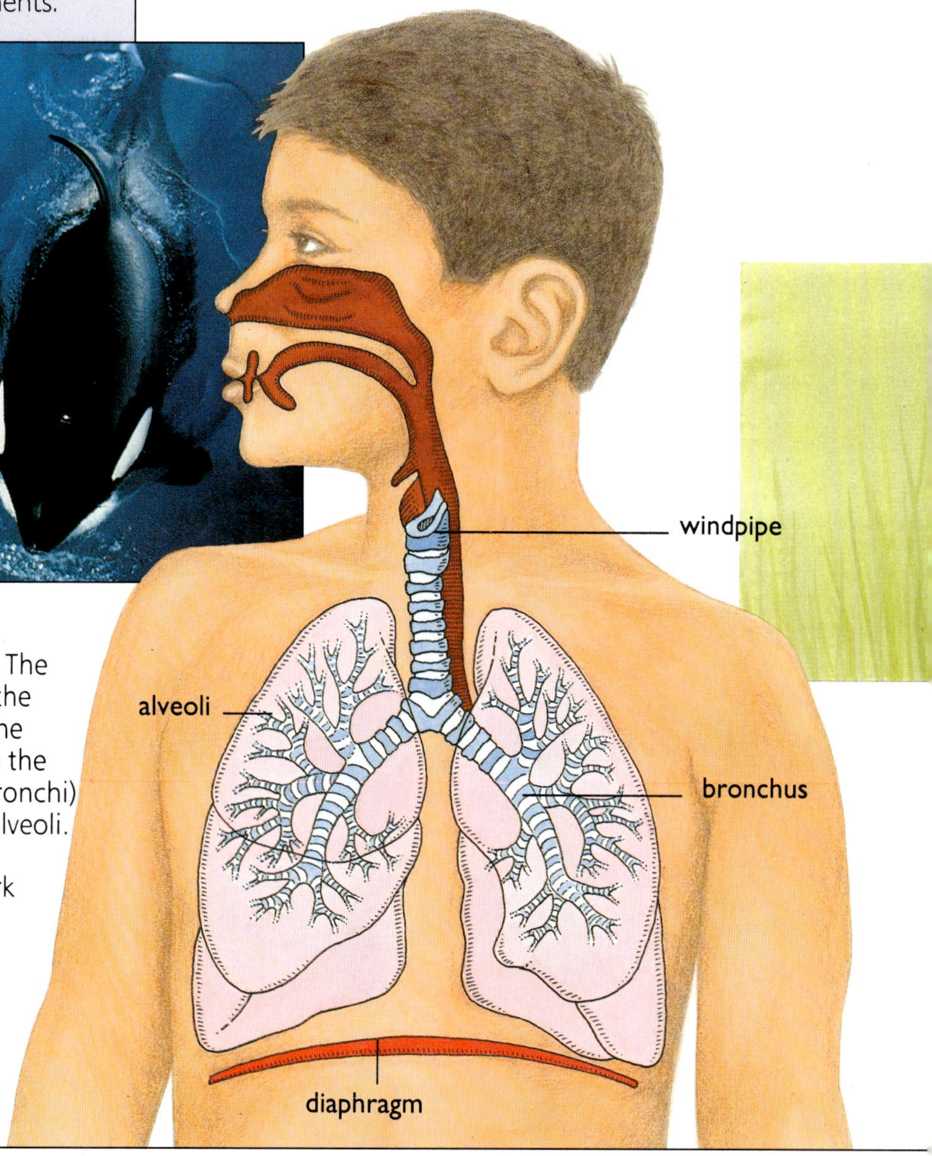

The lungs fill most of the chest cavity. The diaphragm (a sheet of muscle below the lungs) moves down to draw air into the lungs and up to squeeze it out. Inside the lungs are two branching tubes (the bronchi) leading to millions of air sacs, called alveoli. The alveoli in the lungs have very thin walls and are surrounded by a network of blood vessels, tiny tubes called capillaries. The oxygen breathed in passes easily from the alveoli into the blood. Carbon dioxide passes back in the other direction and is breathed out.

Breathing problems

People may have difficulty breathing if their lungs or breathing tubes are infected by bacteria or viruses. Smoking and air pollution also contribute to breathing problems, such as bronchitis and asthma. In an asthma attack, the muscles wrapped around the airways contract, restricting the flow of air and making it difficult to breathe.

Patients with breathing problems or people who are very ill are sometimes given extra oxygen. Their lungs do not have to work as hard and this helps a quicker recovery.

Insects

Air enters an insect's body through holes called spiracles, which lead to a network of tubes called tracheae and in turn to even thinner tubes that branch out to all parts of the body.

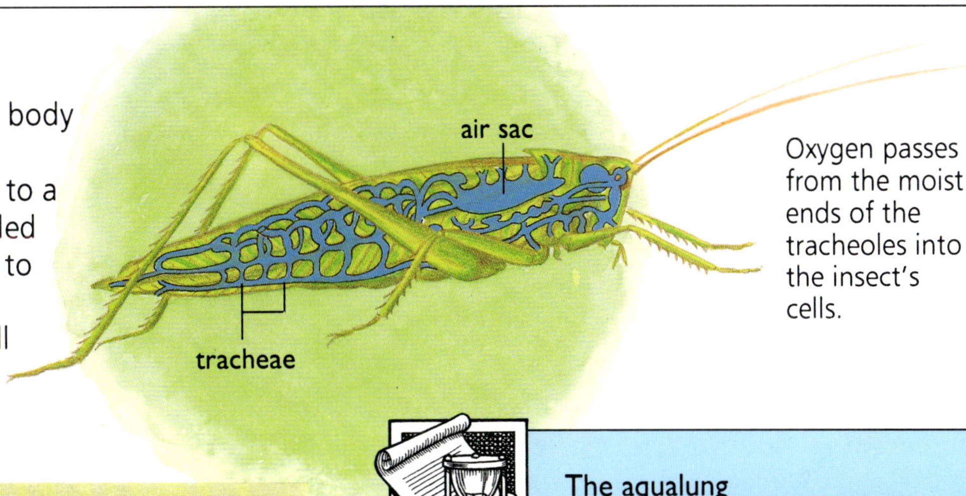

Oxygen passes from the moist ends of the tracheoles into the insect's cells.

Fish

Most fish have gills to take in oxygen from the water around them. Some fish pump water over their gills, others swim with their mouths open so that the water is forced over the gills. Fish gills are a series of tiny flaps with a large surface area and a lot of blood vessels to help the fish absorb as much oxygen as possible into the bloodstream.

The aqualung

Invented by Jacques Cousteau and Emile Gagnan in 1943, the aqualung revolutionised underwater exploration. Divers were able to move easily, without cumbersome diving suits, and could dive to depths of up to 60m. Through an aqualung, divers breathe air at the same pressure as the surrounding water. The aqualung is also known as scuba – Self Contained Underwater Breathing Apparatus.

Aqualungs consist of cylinders of air at high pressure, a valve to control air pressure and a tube to the mouthpiece.

PLANTS AND AIR

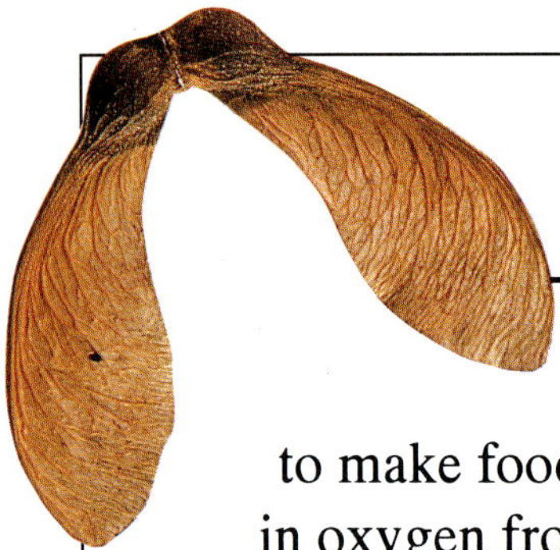

Air is just as vital to the survival of plants as it is to animals. Plants need carbon dioxide from the air to make food during the process of photosynthesis. But they also take in oxygen from the air and give out carbon dioxide, just as animals do. The waste product of photosynthesis is oxygen, which plants release into the air. During the history of the Earth, plants gradually built up the oxygen in the atmosphere. Only after there was enough oxygen in the air could animals develop.

Dispersal record

You could make your own nature diary to keep a record of seeds which are spread by the wind, such as sycamore or dandelion seeds. Stick the seeds into your scrapbook and write down the date and where you found them. In spring and summer, look out for plants that use the wind to spread their pollen, such as tree catkins.

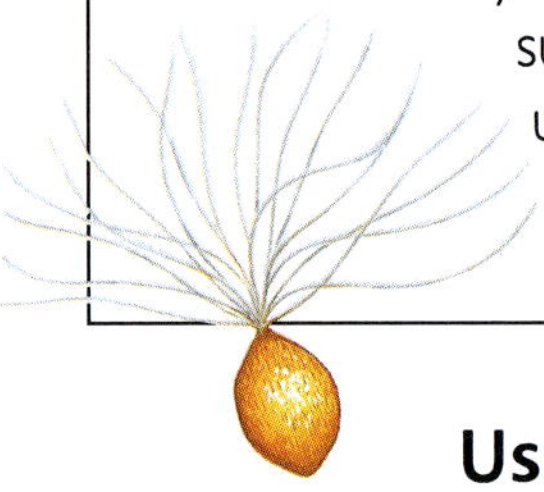

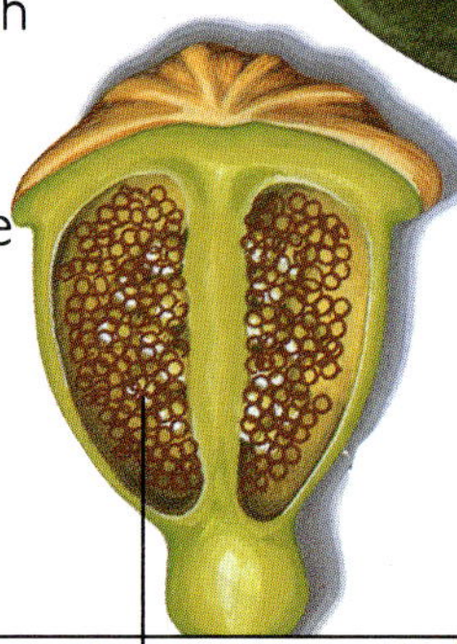

poppy seeds

Using the wind

Pollen and seeds that float on the wind are usually very light, but some use other floating devices such as little "wings", parachutes or air sacs. Seeds move away from the parent plant to reduce the competition for light, water and food nutrients.

dandelion spores

A giant puffball can produce 7,000 billion spores in a lifetime. The spores (simple seeds) puff out in clouds every time the wind blows against them. Even an ordinary field mushroom can release 100 million spores in an hour.

Land plant roots obtain the oxygen they need from water in the soil.

The epidermis is covered in a waxy layer called the cuticle. Though this prevents the leaf losing water, it also prevents carbon dioxide entering. So there are stomata (usually on the shady side) to let carbon dioxide in.

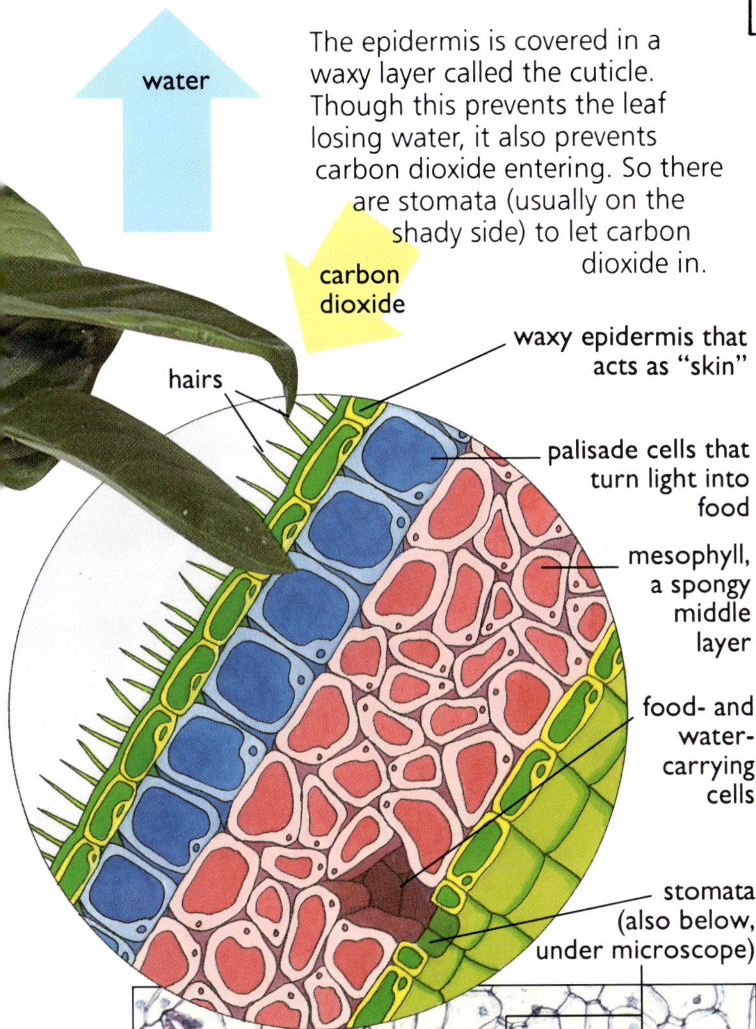

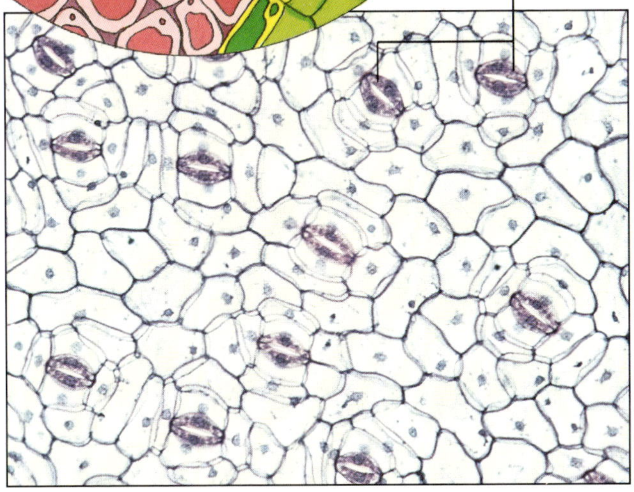

Food from air

Plants make their own food from carbon dioxide and water, using the energy in sunlight. This process is called photosynthesis. The food that plants make is a sort of sugar called a carbohydrate. Some food is broken down during respiration to release energy.

Hay fever

Many people suffer from an allergic reaction to plant pollen called hay fever. Symptoms include a runny nose, sneezing and watery eyes, but they are seasonal since plants only release pollen in spring and summer. Pollen counts are often given as part of weather forecasts to warn sufferers when to expect problems.

Plant "breathing"

Water plants take in gases from the water all over their surface. Land plants breathe through little holes called stomata in the leaves or stem. Woody stems have small raised pores called lenticels instead of stomata. The stomata or lenticels open and close to control the flow of gases and water vapour in and out of the leaf or stem. On a leaf, the stomata are mostly on the underside. There may be from 20 to over 1,000 stomata per square millimetre, depending on the species. The stomata usually open during daylight hours when the plant is busy taking in and giving out gases during photosynthesis.

Plants on mountains

At high altitudes, there is less oxygen for plants to breathe and less carbon dioxide for them to make their food. So mountain plants tend to grow slowly and function at a slower rate. The thin mountain air also fails to protect the mountain slopes from strong sunlight during the day and cold at night. Mountain plants tend to be short to hug the ground for warmth and to trap moisture, often growing in closely packed cushions for mutual protection.

WIND AND WEATHER

From carving rocks and building sand dunes to blowing over trees and buildings, the wind has the power to change the landscape. Wind is air on the move, going from areas of high pressure to areas of low pressure. The pressure differences are created by the Sun heating up some parts of the Earth more than others. Warm air is "lighter" or less dense than cold air, so it rises up and spreads out, creating low pressure. Dense, cold air sinks down, pressing heavily on the Earth to create high pressure.

Lows

Areas of low air pressure are called "lows" or depressions. They happen when warm air rises, causing the pressure to drop at the Earth's surface. The rising warm air cools as it reaches higher altitudes. Cool air holds less moisture than warm air, so some of the moisture in the air condenses into droplets of water which gather to form rain clouds.

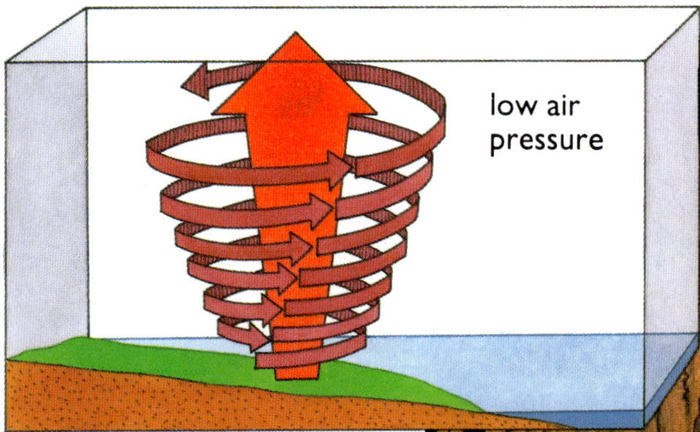

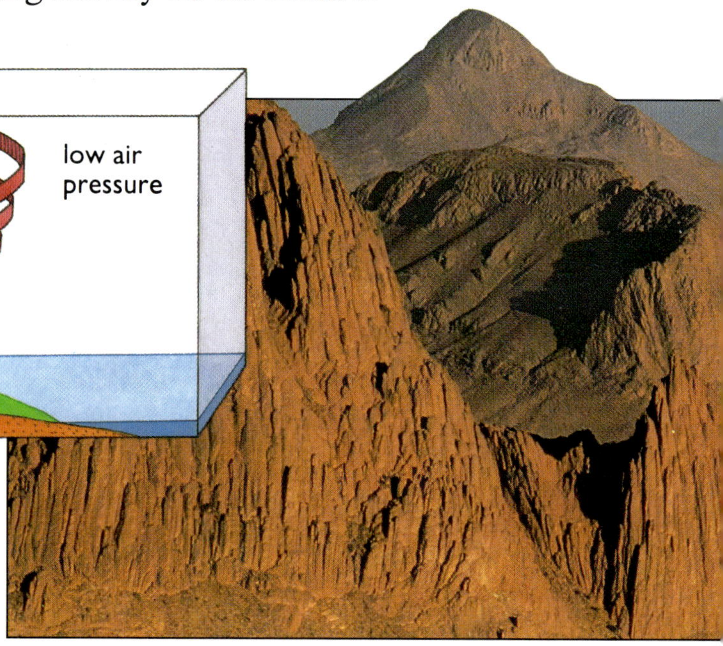

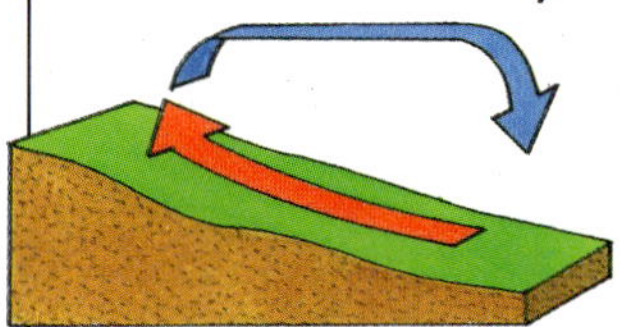

warm air rises up slopes causing daytime breezes

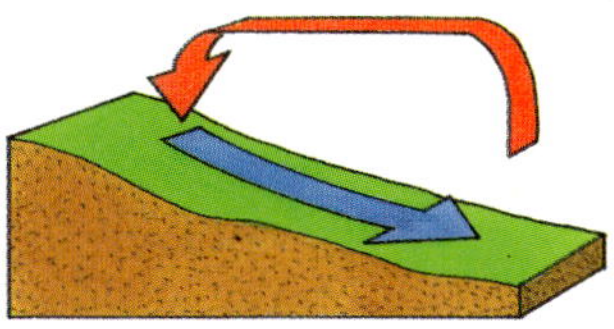

cool air falls down slopes causing night-time breezes

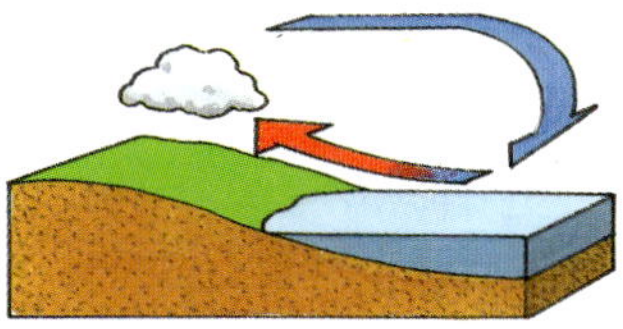
day sea breeze

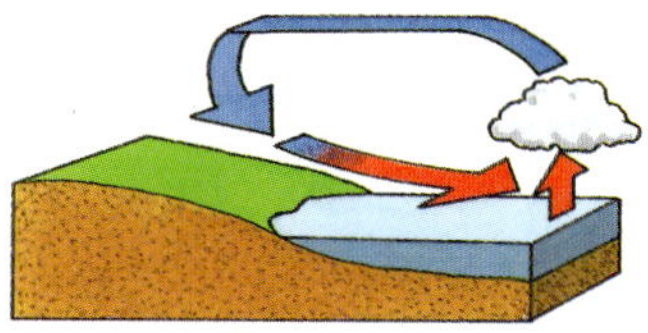
night sea breeze

Land and sea breezes

In mountainous regions, air on the valley floor heats up quickly during the day and rises up the slopes. At night, the air above the slopes cools more rapidly and is pulled down into the valley by gravity.

A similar reversal takes place in coastal regions. During the day, hot air rises off the land and cooler air over the sea is drawn in to take its place, creating a sea breeze. At night, the sea stays warmer for longer than the land, so warm air rises over the sea and cooler air from the land is sucked in, creating a land breeze.

World winds

Winds are movements of air from areas of high pressure to low pressure. The Equator is warmer than the poles, so the air rises and moves towards the poles, creating low pressure. At the cold poles, the air sinks and moves towards the Equator, causing high pressure. Around the Earth, movements of air between areas of high and low pressure result in convection cells (see right). World winds do not move from the Equator to the poles in straight lines because the planet is spinning in space, dragging the air with it. Winds bend to the east both north and south of the Equator.

The Tempest

In *The Tempest*, written by William Shakespeare, the action takes place on a remote island, where Prospero, once Duke of Milan, uses his magic to conjure up a violent storm. During the tempest, Prospero's brother Antonio is shipwrecked on the island. With the help of the spirit Ariel, Prospero confronts Antonio (who took his dukedom) and regains his rightful position in Milan.

Forecasting the weather

Weather forecasts are vitally important for people like farmers. Short-range forecasts predict the weather for the next 24 hours, and long-range forecasts predict the weather up to 8 days ahead. Information for forecasts is collected from land stations, aircraft, ships, balloons and satellites. Computer models help to predict the most likely weather.

(Above) A desert landscape shaped by the wind

Highs

Areas of high air pressure are called "highs" or anticyclones. They occur where cool air sinks down to the ground and presses on the Earth's surface. The air on the surface moves away towards surrounding low pressure areas, spreading out in the form of circling winds. Whereas "lows" are usually associated with unsettled wet and windy weather, "highs" usually bring fine, settled weather with light winds. This is because the air becomes warmer and drier as it sinks down.

The winds around a high in the northern hemisphere swirl clockwise. South of the Equator, they circle around in the opposite direction. An elongated extension of a high is called a ridge of high pressure. An extension of a low is called a trough.

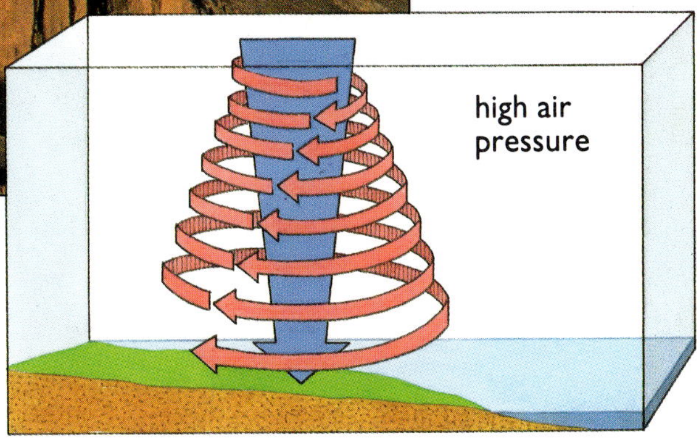

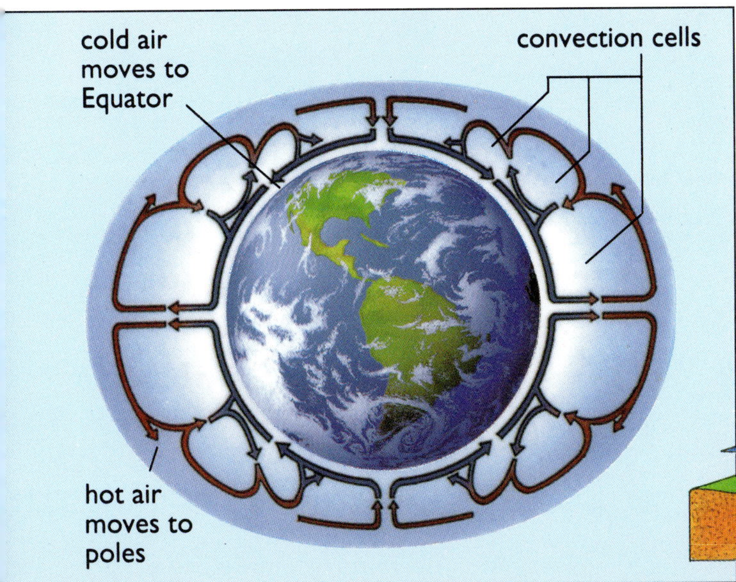

Local winds

Small-scale localised winds are often given special names. For instance, the mistral is a cold northerly wind which funnels down the Rhône valley in France. The sirocco is a very hot, dry wind that blows off the Sahara Desert in North Africa, while the chinook blows down from the Rockies of North America.

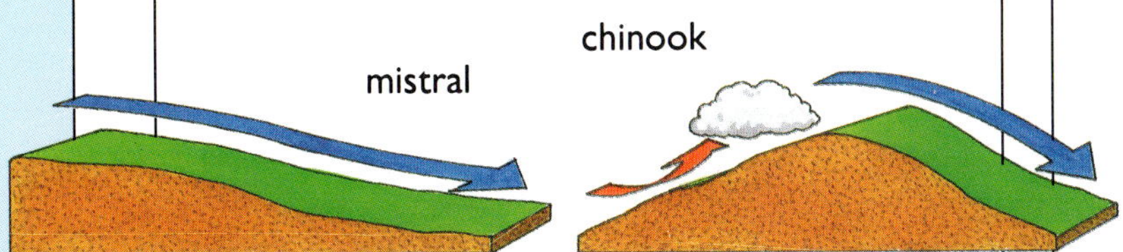

FLOATING ON AIR

Hot-air balloons, gliders and parachutes all help us to float on air without using any real power. They make use of rising currents of hot air or take advantage of air resistance or drag to slow down the rate at which they fall down through the air. Air resistance is caused by the force of air pushing against something and slowing it down. Some gliding animals are also capable of unpowered flight.

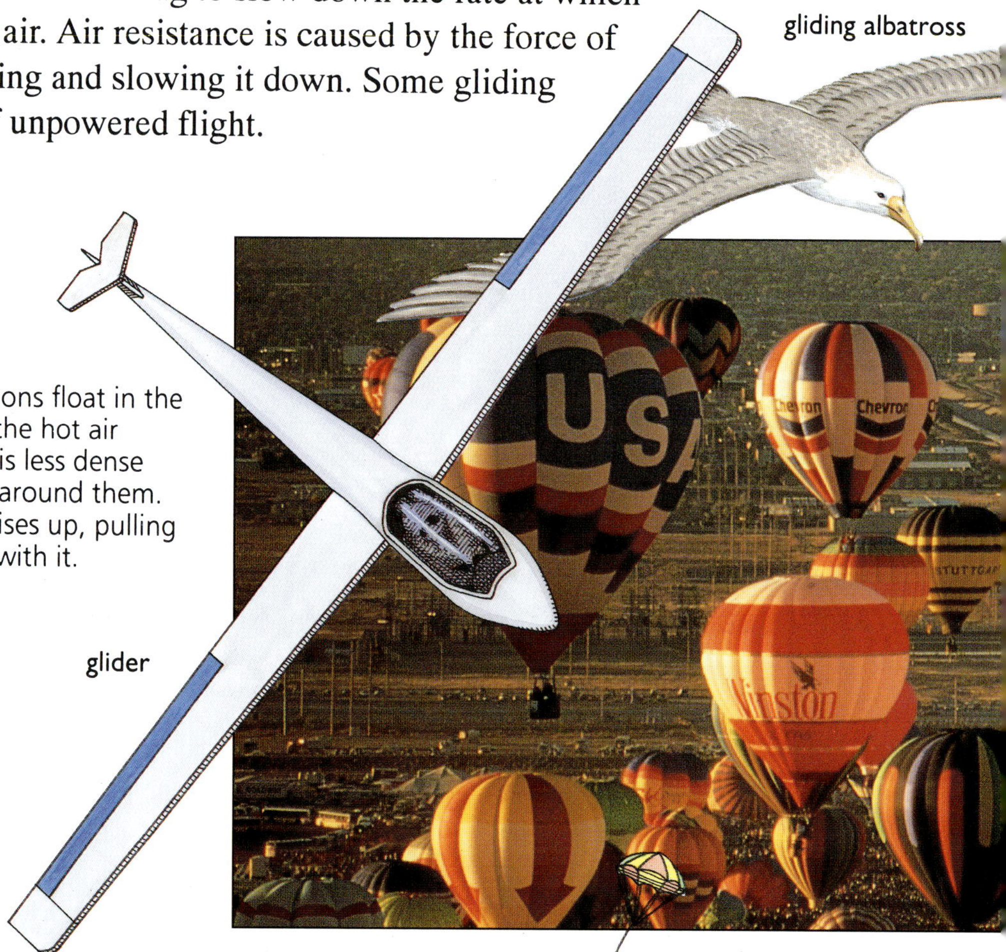

Hot-air balloons float in the air because the hot air inside them is less dense than the air around them. The hot air rises up, pulling the balloon with it.

Feathered gliders

Some birds, such as vultures or storks, soar and glide for hours on pockets of rising hot air called thermals. Gliding on thermals saves energy for birds on long migration journeys. It also helps birds of prey to stay up in the air for long periods while they search for food on the ground below. Seabirds, such as albatrosses or gulls, glide upwards on air currents rising from the waves or cliffs.

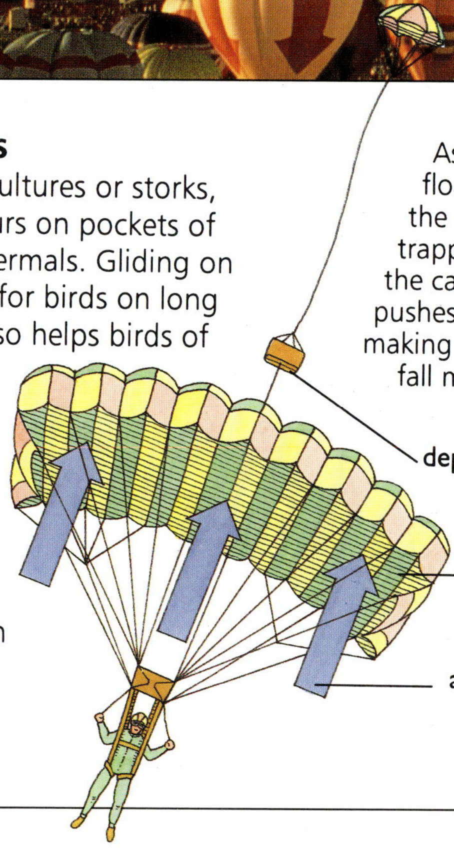

As a parachute floats down to the ground, air is trapped under the canopy. The air pushes upwards, making the 'chute fall more slowly.

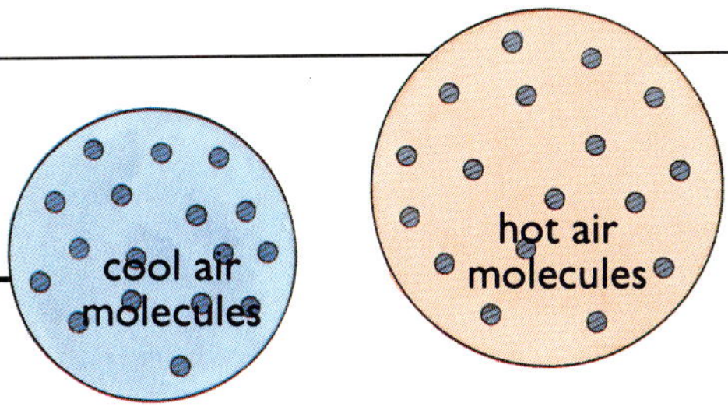

Hot air rises

When air is heated, its molecules gain energy and move further apart. This makes the hot air take up more space and become less dense, or "lighter", than cool air. So the warm air rises above the cool air.

Design a glider

See if you can build a model glider of your own following these instructions. You will need card, scissors, tape, a knitting needle and straws.

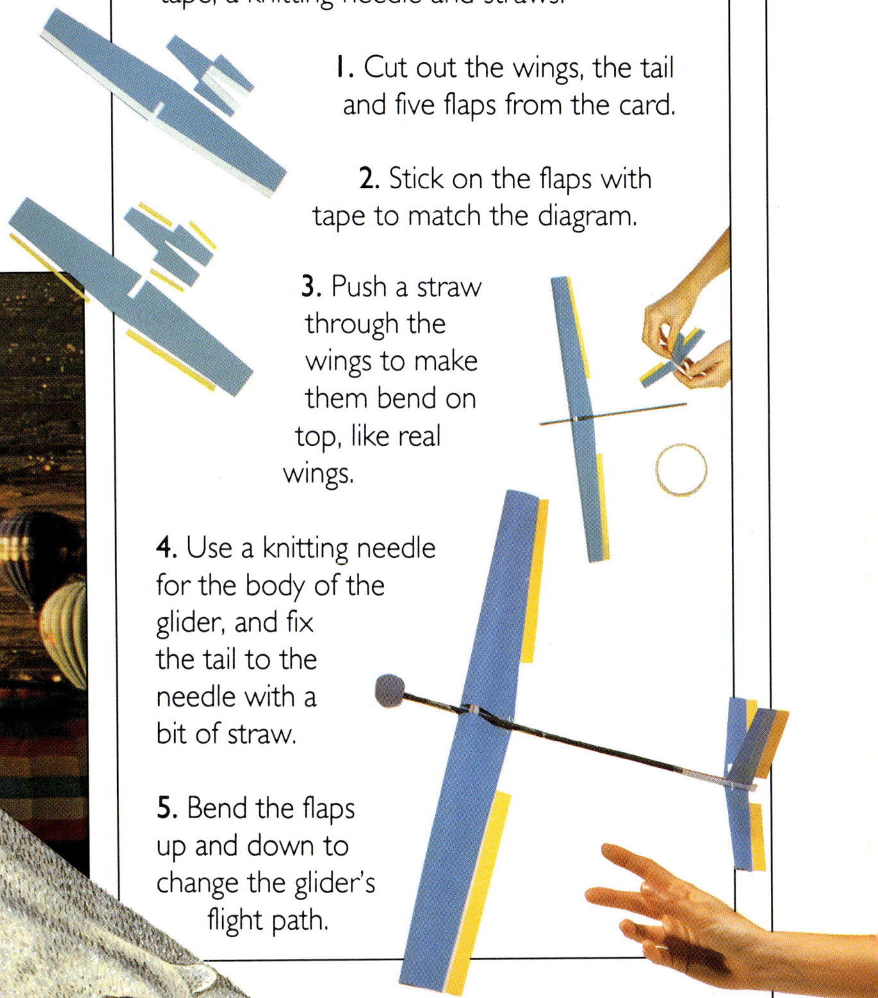

1. Cut out the wings, the tail and five flaps from the card.

2. Stick on the flaps with tape to match the diagram.

3. Push a straw through the wings to make them bend on top, like real wings.

4. Use a knitting needle for the body of the glider, and fix the tail to the needle with a bit of straw.

5. Bend the flaps up and down to change the glider's flight path.

Gliding animals

Gliding animals such as flying squirrels (above) or tree frogs use air resistance to help them fall slowly through the air. They have developed webs or flaps of skin which they spread out like living parachutes. The air pushes up against the skin flaps and slows down their falling speed. Flying fish glide over the waves for about 500 metres to escape from predators. A gliding mammal called the flying lemur glides up to 135 metres between rainforest trees in southeast Asia. On the ground, its folded "wings" get in the way and it cannot even stand up.

Flying frogs have enormous webbed feet to glide up to 12 metres when jumping from tree to tree.

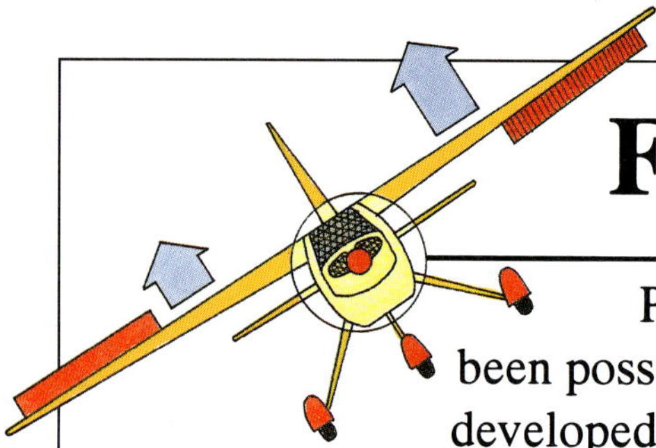

FLYING MACHINES

People dreamed of flying for centuries, but flight has only been possible in the last hundred years. In that time, aircraft have developed from small wood and fabric planes to the gigantic jumbo jets and supersonic aircraft of today. Great leaps in speed and design were made during wartime as people tried to build better fighting planes. But modern planes still work on the same idea of aerofoil-shaped wings creating enough lift to support the weight of the aircraft and keep it up in the air.

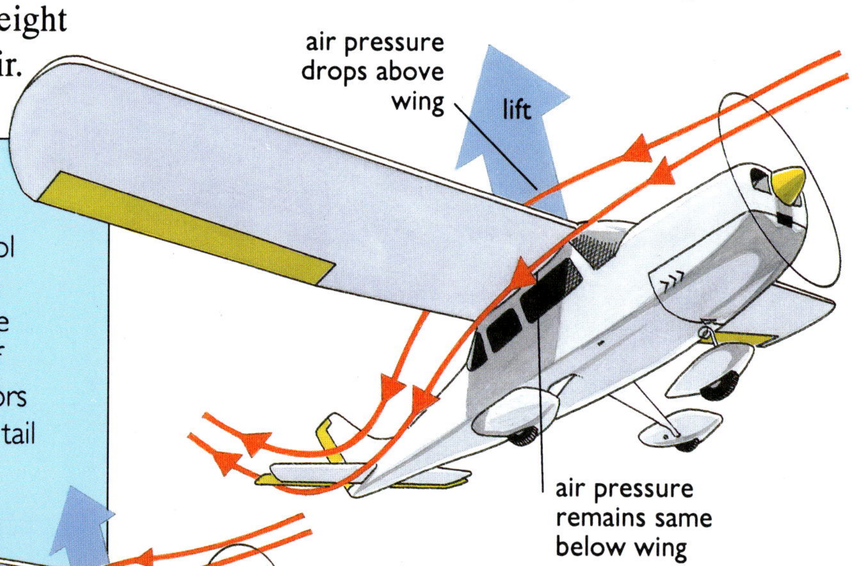

Controlling an aircraft

A typical aircraft is controlled by movable flaps, called control surfaces, which allow the pilot to make the aircraft turn, climb and dive. On the wings are ailerons, on the back edge of the tail wings (the tailplane) are elevators and on the upright part of the tail (the tail fin) is a rudder.

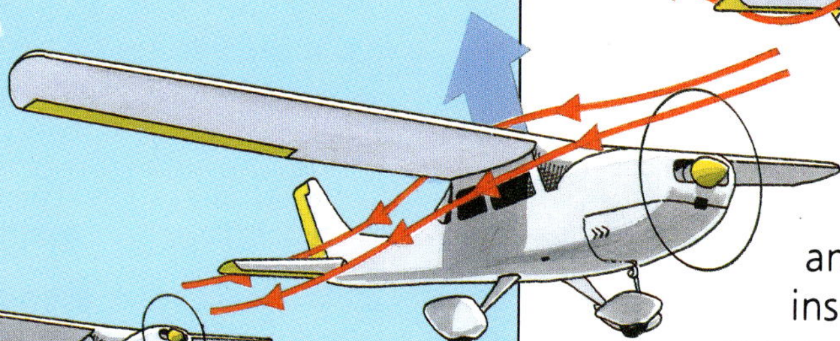

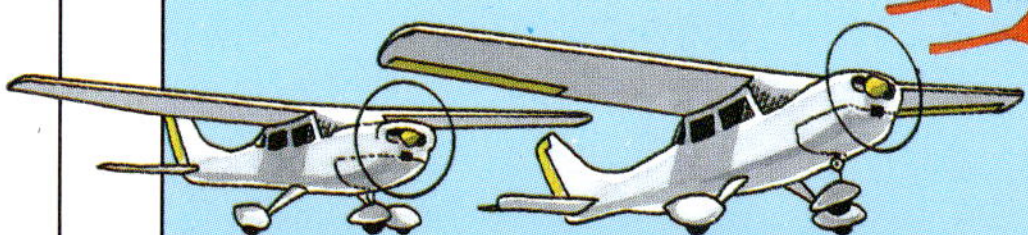

The ailerons on the wings are used together with the rudder to make the aircraft turn in the air. By moving the elevators, the pilot can make the aircraft climb or dive.

Jet engines

Most modern, high-speed aircraft are pushed along by jet engines. Fans at the front of the engine suck in air like a vacuum cleaner but at very great speed. Inside, the air is compressed in a series of turbines, sprayed with fuel and set on fire. The hot gases rush out of the back of the engine, pushing the aircraft forwards. It's rather like letting the air out of a balloon to make it zoom through the air.

Helicopters

Helicopters can twist and turn in the air rather like insects. They are much more manoeuvrable than an aeroplane, but they use up a lot of energy when they fly. Their aerofoil-shaped rotors produce lift as they spin around, so a helicopter does not have to go fast through the air to create lift like an aeroplane. To move up or down, forwards or backwards, the angle of the rotor blades is adjusted.

The tail rotor stops helicopters spinning around by balancing the turning movement of their main rotors.

F-14 Tomcat

BAe 146

Concorde

Wing types

Concorde has a streamlined delta-shape wing to allow it to cruise at speeds of 2,300 kph, but it requires a long runway for take off. In contrast, the BAe 146 is designed for the short runways of city airports, its stubby wings giving maximum lift at take off. The F-14 Tomcat has the best of both worlds with its swing-wing technology. This allows it to swivel its main wings forward for extra lift on take off from aircraft carriers. In fast flight, the wings are swung backwards to form the aerodynamic delta wing shape.

Wind tunnel tests

In wind tunnels, smoky air is sucked over scale models (such as the one of Concorde below) to show the pattern of airflow over the surfaces of the aircraft. Designs can then be altered to reduce the amount of drag caused by tiny whirlwinds or eddies of air, formed as the air flows over and around the body surfaces.

Flying into history

Since the first record-breaking aeroplane flight by the Wright brothers in 1903, many people have flown their way into the history books. Some have crossed oceans or mountains, others have broken speed or distance records.

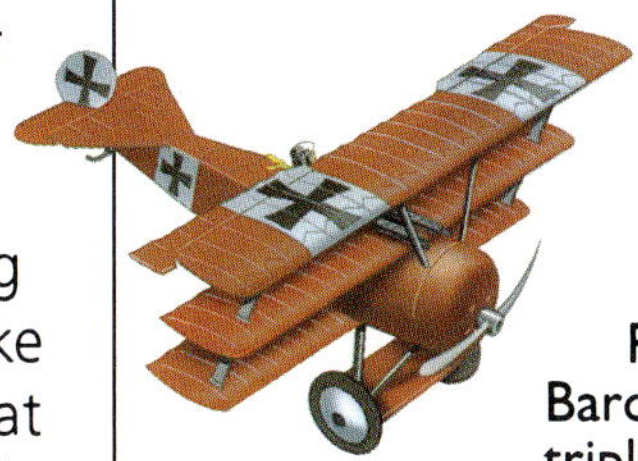

Red Baron's triplane

1909 Louis Blériot flew across the English Channel in 36 minutes.
1919 First non-stop flight across the Atlantic by Alcock and Brown in a Vickers Vimy in 16 hours 27 minutes.
1927 Charles Lindbergh made the first solo flight across the Atlantic.
1930 Amy Johnson became the first woman to fly solo from England to Australia.
1932 Amelia Earhart was the first woman to fly the Atlantic alone.
1936 Amy Johnson completed a return flight from England to South Africa in 8 days.
1937 The first fully pressurised aircraft, the Lockheed XC-35, came into service.
1939 Igor Sikorsky designed and built the first helicopter.
1949 The De Havilland Comet, the first jet airliner, entered service. James Gallagher made the first non-stop flight around the world.
1969 Concorde was the first passenger plane to fly faster than the speed of sound.
1970 The Boeing 747 Jumbo jet entered service.
1976 The world air-speed record of 3,529 kph was set in California.
1979 First crossing of the English channel by a human-powered aircraft.
1986 First non-stop flight around the world without refuelling.

McDonnell Douglas MD-12

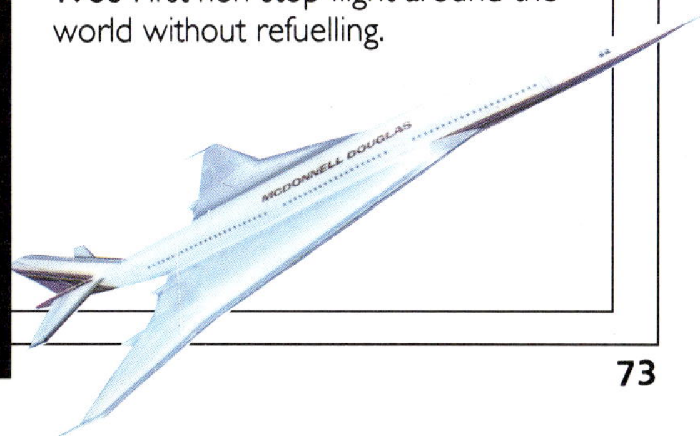

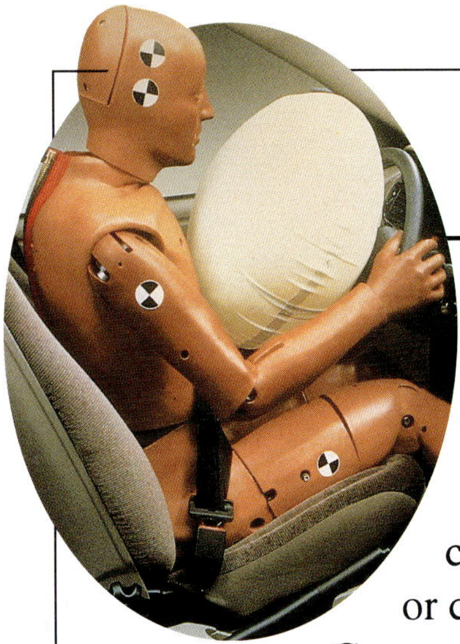

AIR AT WORK

We use air to improve our quality of life, both at home and at work. Many recipes mix air or gases with the ingredients, and fizzy drinks contain bubbles of carbon dioxide gas. Home appliances such as vacuum cleaners and tumble driers all make use of the properties of air. Air bags improve safety on cars and coaches (above left). In industry, air is used to keep things warm or cool, to extract harmful fumes or dust and to burn things. Compressed air is a powerful source of safe energy for pneumatic tools.

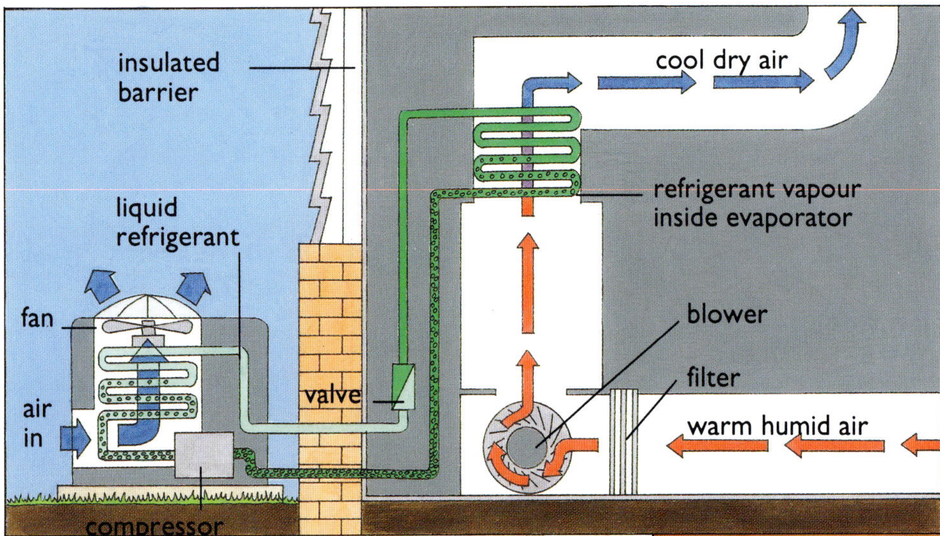

Air conditioning
Inside an air conditioner a fan extracts air from the room. A liquid called a refrigerant turns into a gas (evaporates), taking heat from the air as it does so. The heat is released outside and the cool air returns to the room. The refrigerant gas is compressed to turn it back into a liquid so it can be used again.

Air in cooking
A lot of the food we cook is full of air. The bubbles in bread and cakes are carbon dioxide gas. This comes from yeast in bread-making or from baking powder or bicarbonate of soda in cakes. The bubbles expand on cooking to make the bread and cakes rise and give them a light, spongy texture. If bread is baked without yeast, it won't rise, producing unleavened bread. Mousses, meringues and soufflés are light and fluffy because of all the air whisked into them.

Expanded polystyrene

Expanded polystyrene is a kind of plastic with lots of air bubbles in it. The air does not carry heat well, so polystyrene makes a good insulating material. It is also often used for packaging because it is light yet rigid.

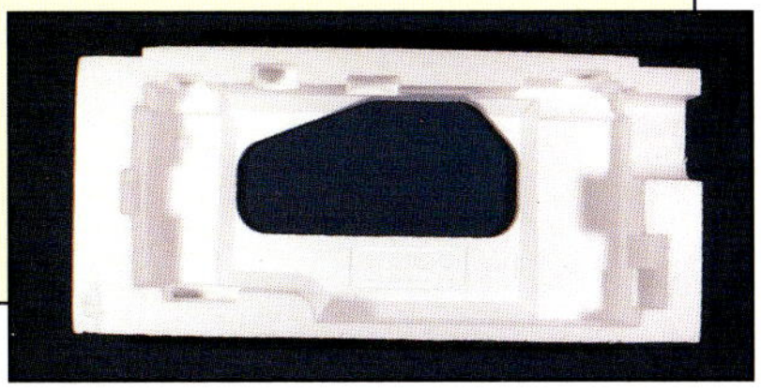

Making iron and steel

Blast furnaces (below) extract iron from a rocky material called iron ore. They are named after the blast of hot air that heats up the raw materials – iron ore, limestone and coke – inside the furnace. As the coke burns, it produces chemicals which take oxygen from the iron ore, leaving iron metal behind. The iron metal melts and sinks to the bottom of the furnace. Most iron is converted into steel.

Airbrush art

An airbrush sprays air and ink to produce a flat, even colour. The air comes from a compressed air supply called a propellant, which may be an aerosol can or an electric air compressor plugged into the mains. As compressed air blows across the nozzle, it creates a vacuum. This sucks ink up a tube to fill the vacuum, creating a spray of air and ink.

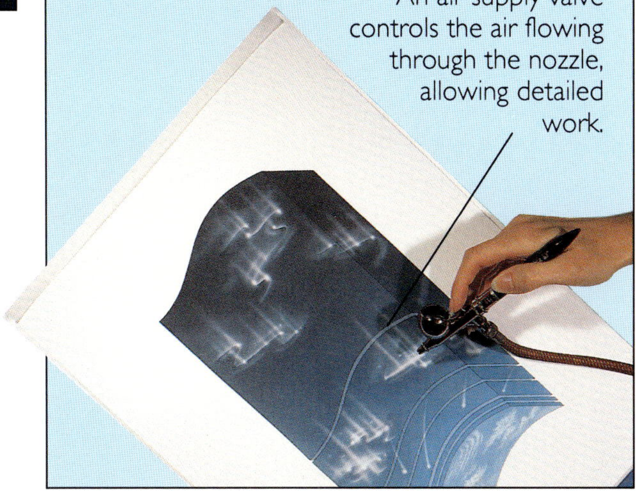

An air supply valve controls the air flowing through the nozzle, allowing detailed work.

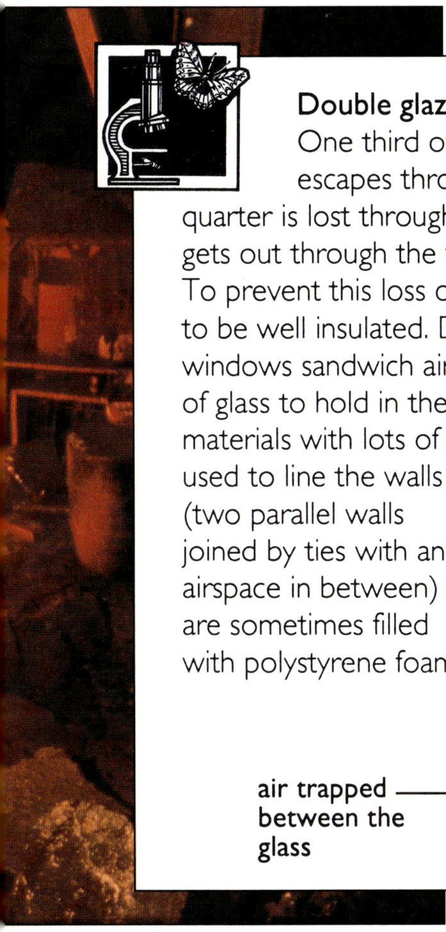

Double glazing

One third of the heat in a building escapes through the walls, a quarter is lost through the roof and the rest gets out through the floors and windows. To prevent this loss of heat, buildings need to be well insulated. Double-glazed windows sandwich air between two layers of glass to hold in the heat. Insulating materials with lots of air pockets can be used to line the walls and roof. Cavity walls (two parallel walls joined by ties with an airspace in between) are sometimes filled with polystyrene foam.

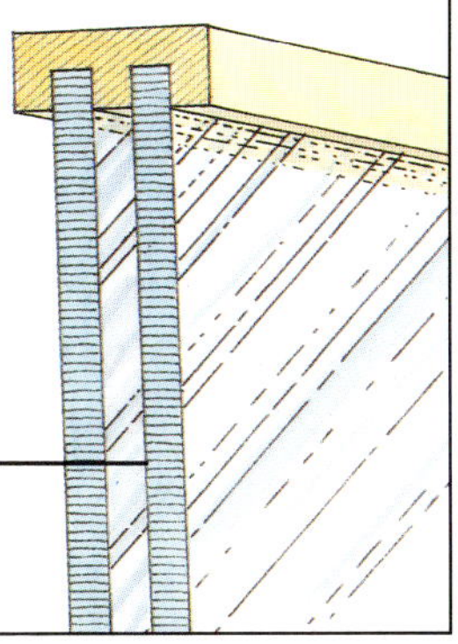

Squashing air

When air is squashed or compressed into a small space, it can be used to provide a safe source of energy for power tools, called pneumatic tools. There is no danger of sparks to start fires and no chance of getting an electric shock. It works well for rotary tools such as dentists' drills where the compressed air is forced against a rotor with several blades. Compressed air is also used to inflate tyres and work air brakes.

The pressurised air under a hovercraft lifts it off the ground.

WHAT IS WATER?

Water is not only one of the most common substances on Earth, it is also one of the most unusual. Unlike any other substance, water exists as a solid, liquid and gas in everyday life. Each drop of water is made up of millions of molecules (tiny particles). Water molecules consist of even smaller particles called atoms. Two atoms of hydrogen combine with one atom of oxygen to form the chemical compound H_2O (water). Over 70 per cent of the Earth's surface is covered by water. Water is everywhere – it fills oceans, rivers, lakes, soaks into the ground and is even present in the air that we breathe.

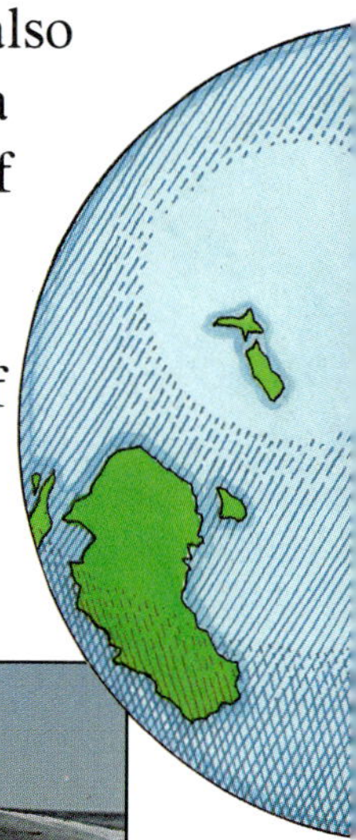

Forms of water

Water can exist in three different forms – as a solid, a liquid and a gas. The form water takes depends on how fast the molecules of H_2O are moving. In ice (right), the molecules are tightly bound and move slowly. However, in its liquid form, water molecules can move more quickly. The molecules in water vapour (a gas) move faster still and travel freely in the air.

When you breathe out on a cold day, the water vapour in your breath cools down and turns into droplets of liquid water, which form a mist in the air.

Salt water

About 97 per cent of the world's water is the salty water in the seas and oceans. Seawater is "salty" because it contains minerals and salts washed off the land and carried to the sea by rivers. Objects float more easily in salt water than in fresh water. The salt makes the water "thicker" or more dense. The Dead Sea (below), in the Middle East, is about eight times more salty than seawater, allowing bathers to float with ease.

Beliefs and ceremonies

Water is a powerful symbol of purity and cleanliness, and is used in many religious ceremonies around the world. Hindus believe that the sacred River Ganges, in northern India, cleanses their souls as well as their bodies, and transports the dead to heaven. The bathing ghats at Varanasi, on the banks of the Ganges, have been used by Hindu pilgrims (right) for thousands of years. In the Christian ceremony of baptism, holy water is sprinkled onto a person's head, to mark the start of their new life as a Christian.

Life in water

The first life on Earth probably evolved from simple chemicals on the surface of early oceans about 3,500 million years ago. Today, the oceans contain about 20 per cent of all the animal species on Earth and watery environments on land, such as marshes and swamps – wetlands – are especially rich in wildlife. One of the largest wetlands in Europe are the salty marshes and shallow lakes of the Carmargue Nature Reserve in southern France. The grazing of the famous white horses helps to maintain the marshes by stopping trees and scrub taking over. Tens of thousands of wildfowl migrate here for the winter months. Colonies of pink flamingos (shown left) breed in the summer months, despite the industry, housing and airports which surround the park borders.

Water words

There are many sayings which include the word water. To "be in deep water" implies being in great difficulties; to "spend money like water" is to spend money recklessly as if you had an endless supply. Do you know the meanings of these sayings: "water under the bridge"; and "to be like a fish out of water"?

Water energy

Over the centuries, people have harnessed the energy of moving water using water-wheels, and more recently, with hydro-electric power plants or wave and tidal power stations. Water power is a form of renewable energy – it does not use up limited resources, such as coal, gas or oil. Water is often seen as a clean energy resource as it does not pollute the air or produce dangerous toxic waste. However, water power can cause serious environmental problems. Dams alter the landscape and tidal barrages destroy estuaries which are often very rich in wildlife.

LIVING ON WATER

People and animals often build their homes near the coast or on rivers and lakes. Living near water is useful for transport, trade and food supplies. Some people even live on houseboats or sampans floating permanently on the water. In the future, as space begins to run out on land, more cities may be built floating on water or on artificial islands reclaimed from the sea.

In some parts of the world, houses are built on a platform fixed to poles above shallow water. These houses are called pile dwellings; they provide protection against flooding.

Venice

Venice, in Italy, was built on over 100 islands in a lagoon near the Adriatic sea. The foundations of the buildings were built on pine-wood piles, driven into the bedrock, and its "streets" are canals (shown right) which criss-cross the city. In the 14th century, the city became a wealthy world centre for shipping and trade. Today, Venice is a major tourist attraction, but its waters are badly polluted and it is slowly sinking into the Adriatic.

Animal builders

Safety from enemies and a good food supply are reasons why animals build homes on or in the water. Beavers build lodges in the middle of rivers. Reed warblers tie their woven nests to reed stems, while caddis fly larvae carry their home of sticks and stones under water. China mark caterpillars live in air spaces inside floating leaves until they turn into adults.

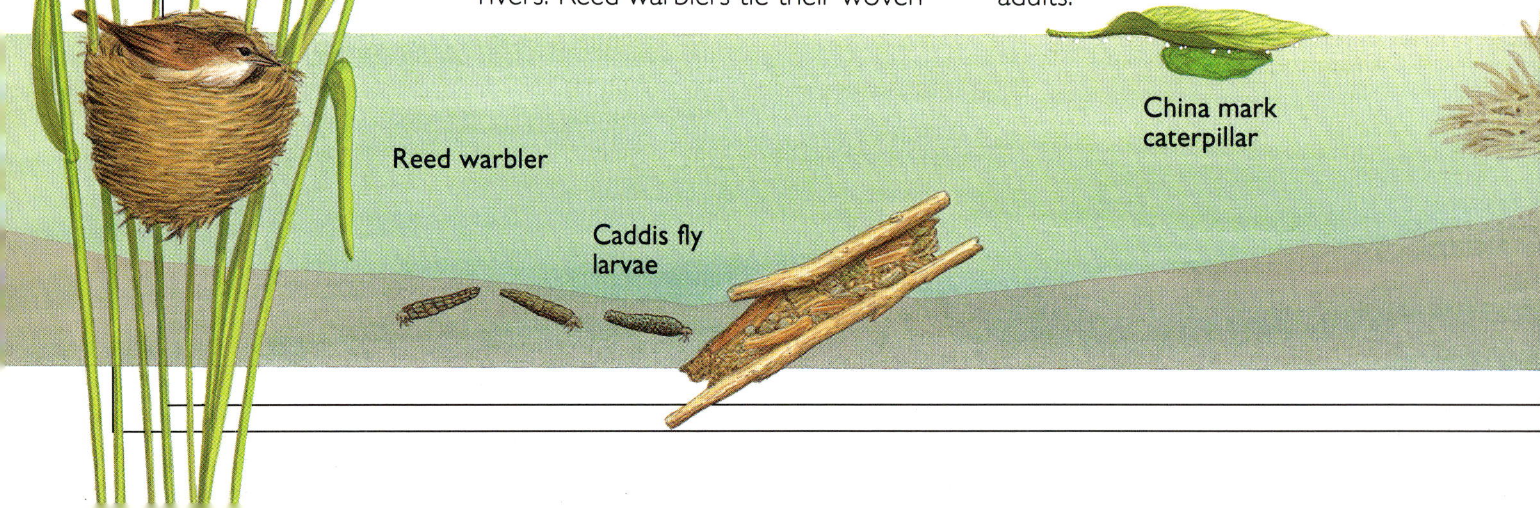

Land from the sea

More than one third of the Netherlands is below sea level. To reclaim land from the sea, engineers built dikes (barriers of earth) around areas of shallow water. Pumps were used to drain out the water, leaving behind fertile areas of land, called polders, which are used for farming. Prins Alexander Polder, the lowest point in the Netherlands, is about six metres below sea-level.

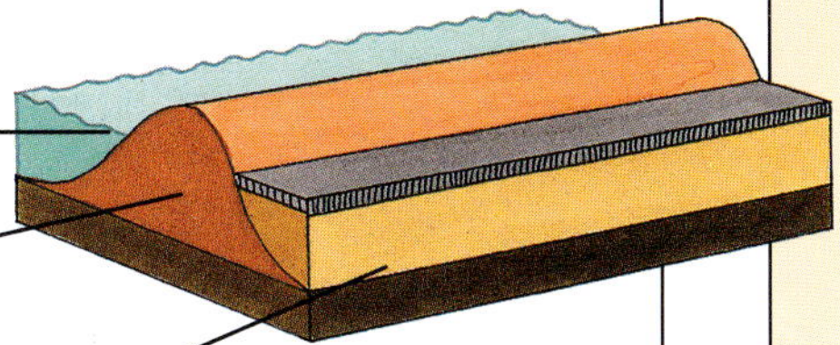

Bridges

The first bridges were probably made by laying tree trunks across rivers or placing flat stones in shallow streams. Later, people made bridges from rope or built stone bridges with arches. The first bridge known to historians was built in the ancient city of Babylon (in modern day Iraq) about four thousand years ago. Modern bridges are made from concrete, steel or other modern materials. Suspension bridges have thick steel cables that carry the weight of the bridge. They can span long distances because they are lightweight. The Akashi-Kaikyo bridge, in Japan, is the world's longest suspension bridge which was completed in 1998. It spans 3,560 metres (11,680 ft).

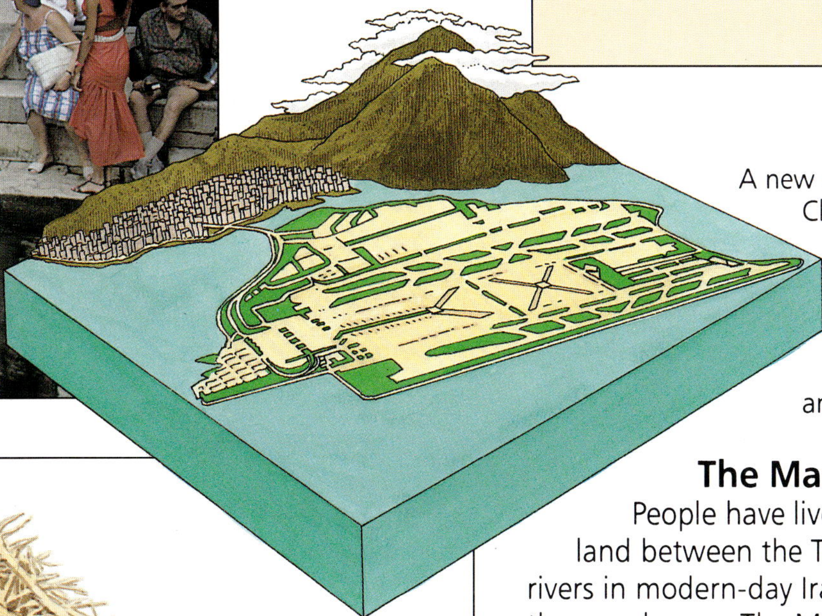

A new airport was built on Chep Lap Kok island (left) in Hong Kong. The island has been levelled and then enlarged using tonnes of rock and sand.

The Marsh Arabs

People have lived on the marshy land between the Tigris and Euphrates rivers in modern-day Iraq for five or six thousand years. The Marsh Arabs of today make reed houses on small, natural islands in the marshes, or make their own artificial islands from mud and reeds.

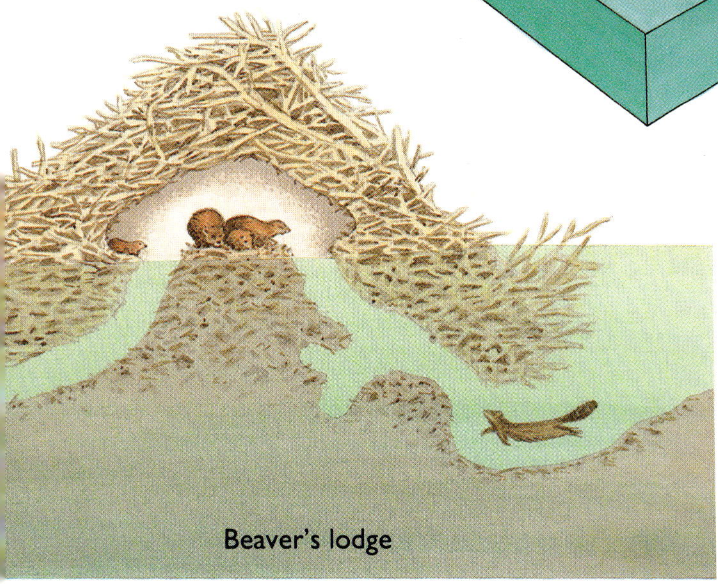

Beaver's lodge

ANIMALS IN WATER

From seas and oceans, to rivers, lakes and ponds, the waters of the Earth teem with all sorts of animal life. Fish live in water all the time, while animals, such as frogs, are amphibious (specially adapted to living on land and in water), and only spend part of their life-cycle in water. Some of the largest animals in the world, such as the whale, can only live in water, because it supports its massive body. Ocean currents carry sea mammals, fish and microscopic animals, called zooplankton, around the world. Most animals are adapted to either fresh or salt water, but a few, such as eels and salmon, can survive in both.

Water birds
Ducks, geese and swans have webbed feet which help them swim. Rails and coots have long toes to walk over soft mud without sinking in. Long legs allow herons and storks to wade in deep water.

Animals in shells
Shellfish, such as crabs, limpets and mussels, have strong, hard shells to protect their soft bodies. Crabs are scavengers, eating almost anything edible from the seabed or seashore.

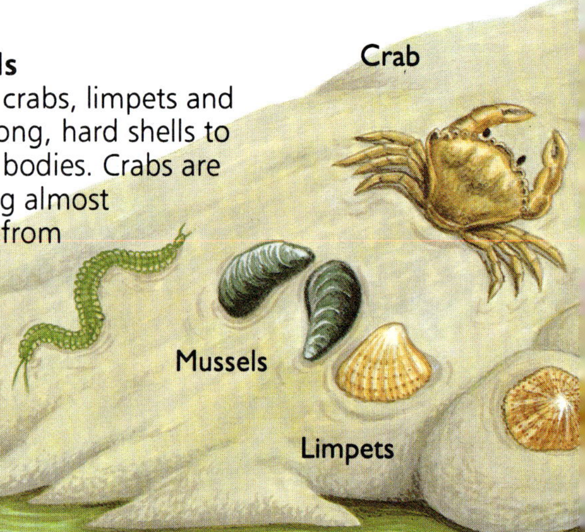

Insects
Water bugs, such as water boatmen and water beetles, inhabit freshwater ponds, slow-moving streams and still pools.

Fish
Roach and bream are freshwater fish which live in lakes and rivers all over Europe. Eels can survive in both salt and fresh water.

Sea mammals
Dolphins, sea cows and whales, like this humpback whale (left), spend their whole lives in the water. Thick layers of fat, called blubber, help to keep them warm. They come to the surface to breathe air through a blowhole on the top of the head. Other sea mammals include seals, sea lions and walruses.

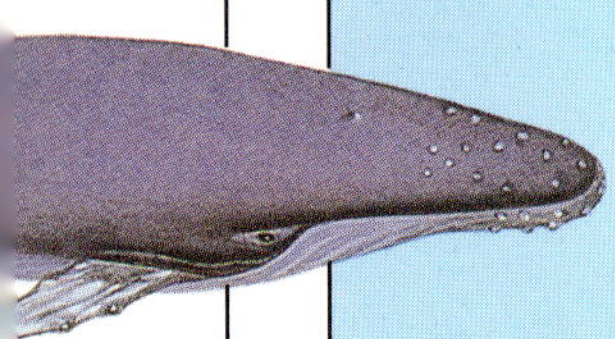

Dolphins and porpoises have a smooth, sleek, streamlined shape. Water flows past them easily, allowing them to swim faster.

Mermaids

Mermaids have appeared in stories about the sea for hundreds of years. The top half of a mermaid is like a woman, and the bottom half is like a fish. People used to believe that mermaids lured sailors to their deaths with their beauty and enchanted singing.

Breathing in water

All animals need to take in oxygen, which allows them to release energy from their food. There is oxygen dissolved in water which fish absorb by gulping in water and forcing it over tiny, featherlike structures called gills (shown right). Gills are rich in blood vessels, and oxygen is absorbed directly into the blood and carried around the body. Like other animals which breathe oxygen, fish produce carbon dioxide as a waste product. It passes from the blood through the gills and into the water. Gills, or gill-like structures, are also found in molluscs (animals in shells), crabs and water insects, such as mayfly nymphs.

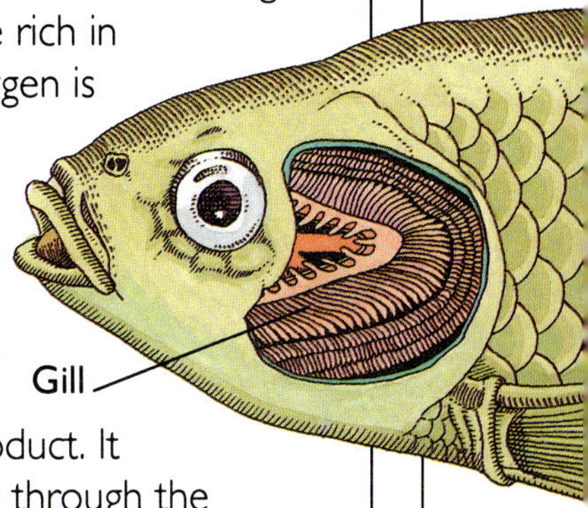

Otter

Mammals

Otters are specially adapted to living both in and out of water. They have soft underfur which traps air, keeping water out and body heat in, and webbed feet for swimming.

Leeches and medicine

Doctors once believed that too much blood in the body was the cause of some diseases. They put water animals, called leeches, on a patient's body to suck out some of the blood. When a leech feeds, it produces a chemical that stops blood from clotting (thickening). A single leech can rapidly take in three or four times its own weight in blood.

Reptiles

Most reptiles live on land but some, such as sea-turtles, crocodiles and alligators, spend much of their lives in the water, coming to land mainly to lay eggs. Turtles swim with their paddlelike flippers, while crocodiles and alligators use their powerful, flattened tails for swimming.

Crocodiles and turtles are ancient reptiles which have lived in the world's seas and rivers for thousands of years.

PLANTS AND WATER

Like animals, plants are full of water. Water helps to support land plants so they stay upright and keep their shape. Water is essential for all the chemical processes that keep a plant alive, especially photosynthesis – the process by which plants make food. Water also acts as a transport system, carrying important minerals and nutrients from one part of a plant to another. Plants that live in dry places have special adaptations to store water and prevent water loss. Water plants have the opposite problem – they need to stop themselves becoming waterlogged.

Rising water

You can see how plants take up water by doing this experiment with carnations. Take a white carnation with a short stem and stand it in a container of coloured water. Use food colouring to colour the water. After several hours, you should be able to see how the flower has taken up the water. The petals will have tints from the food colouring.

Transpiration & photosynthesis

Land plants take in water through their roots and release it into the air through their leaves. Water is drawn upwards, through the roots and stem, to the leaves. This is called the transpiration stream, and the evaporation of water from the leaves is called transpiration. Water escapes from the leaves through tiny holes called stomata.

Transpiration helps the plant to cool down, as well as draw up more water from the soil. Unlike animals, plants make their own food by a process called photosynthesis. They contain a green pigment, called chlorophyll, which enables plants to use the energy from sunlight to turn carbon dioxide gas from the atmosphere, and minerals and water from the soil, into sugars – the plant's food.

Waxy surfaces
A waxy surface on some leaves seals in water or stops plants absorbing too much water and becoming waterlogged.

Hairy leaves
Hairs on leaves help to trap valuable moisture and stop it escaping into the air.

Spines and needles
Long thin leaves and needles have a smaller surface area and lose less water to the atmosphere than a wide, flat leaf.

Roots
Roots draw up moisture and certain minerals from the soil. Water is absorbed by tiny hairs which cover the roots.

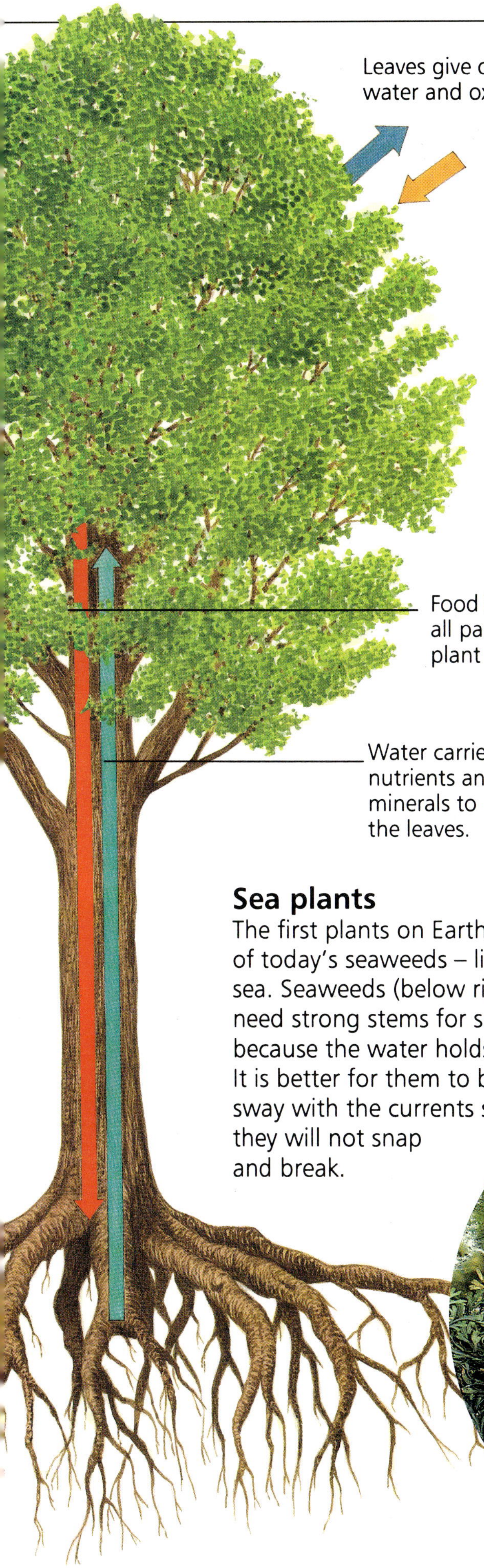

Succulents

Plants with large, fleshy stems and leaves which store water are called succulents. They include cacti and stonecrops. Many succulents live in deserts or on areas of bare, rocky ground where water is hard to find. Most cacti live in the hot, dry deserts of Mexico and the south-western parts of the USA. Money plants are also succulents. They have thick, fleshy leaves which are covered in a waxy skin to store as much water as possible.

Money plant leaf

Pond plants

Some pond plants, like duckweed, float freely on the surface of the water. Others, such as flowering water crowfoot (shown below) and water lilies, have leaves floating on the surface, and strong roots which firmly anchor the plant to the bottom of the pond.

Sea plants

The first plants on Earth – relatives of today's seaweeds – lived in the sea. Seaweeds (below right) do not need strong stems for support because the water holds them up. It is better for them to bend and sway with the currents so they will not snap and break.

SHAPING THE LAND

Water is a powerful force which is constantly changing the shape of the land both above and below ground. It wears away, or erodes, stones, rocks and mountains. Rivers carve valleys, canyons and caves but also build estuaries, deltas and beaches where they meet the sea. Frozen rivers of ice, called glaciers, grind and tear away at rocks, shaping valleys and mountains. Where the sea meets the land, the effect of waves, tides and currents constantly alters the shape of the coastline.

Glacial landscapes

During the history of the Earth, there have been a series of ice ages at regular intervals. Ice sheets spread out from the Poles to cover much more of the Earth than they do today. Clues to the presence of the ice remain long after the ice has melted away. Valleys become U-shaped instead of V-shaped and rocks have scratched or polished surfaces where ice has moved over them. The Briksdal glacier (shown right), in Norway, is one of Europe's largest glaciers.

Rivers

Near the source of a river, the water flows quickly. As the river gathers more water, it flows more slowly, bending from side to side and depositing mud and sand along the riverbanks. Eventually, rivers flow into the sea, dropping the rest of their load of sand and mud to form an estuary or delta.

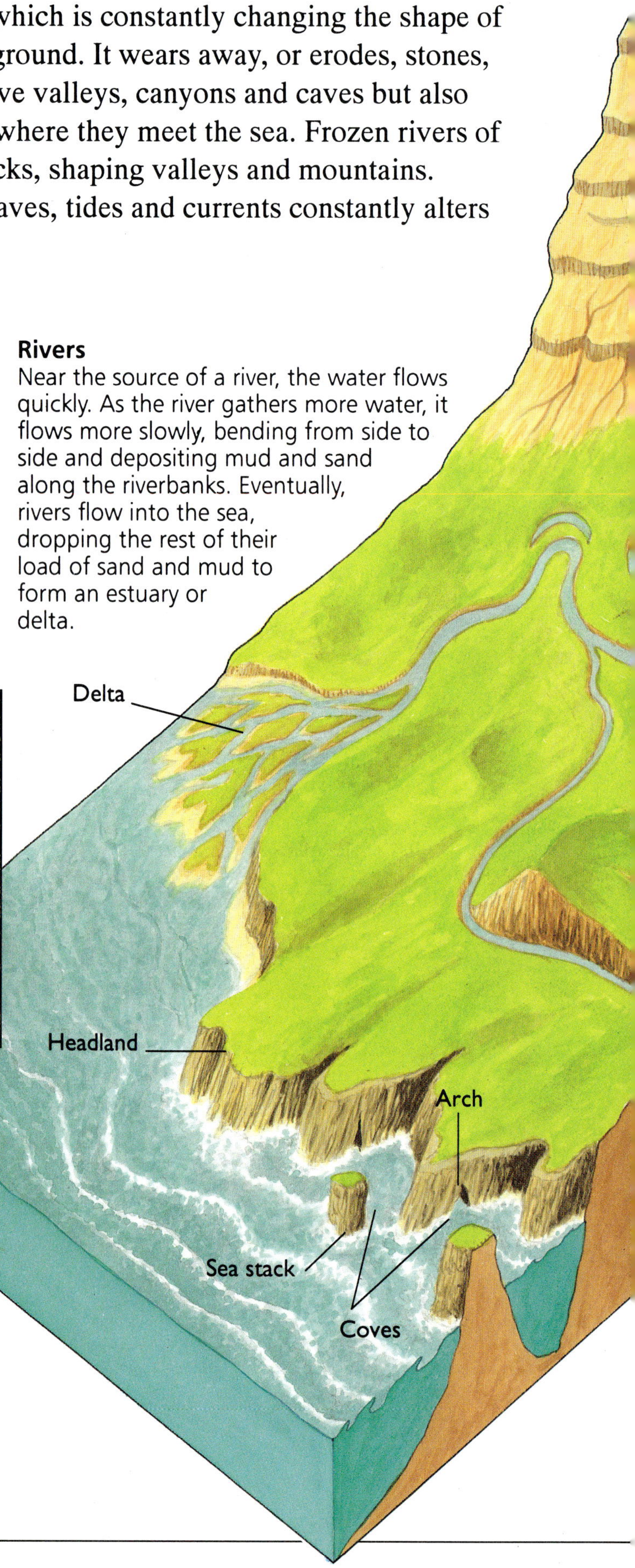

Waves at work

Waves wear away land by the sea, using rocks and pebbles as cutting tools. Chemicals in seawater make it slightly acidic, so it eats into rocks, especially soft rocks, such as chalk or limestone. Soft rocks are worn away to form bays, while hard rocks jut out as headlands. Coves on opposite sides of a headland may meet in the middle to form an arch. If the roof of an arch falls in, a column of rock, called a stack, is left standing at the foot of the cliff.

Canyons

In dry areas, where rivers carry water from mountains or rains outside the region, they carve out deep valleys called canyons. One of the most spectacular canyons is the Grand Canyon in Arizona, USA. It is 354 km long and about 1.6 km (1 mile) deep.

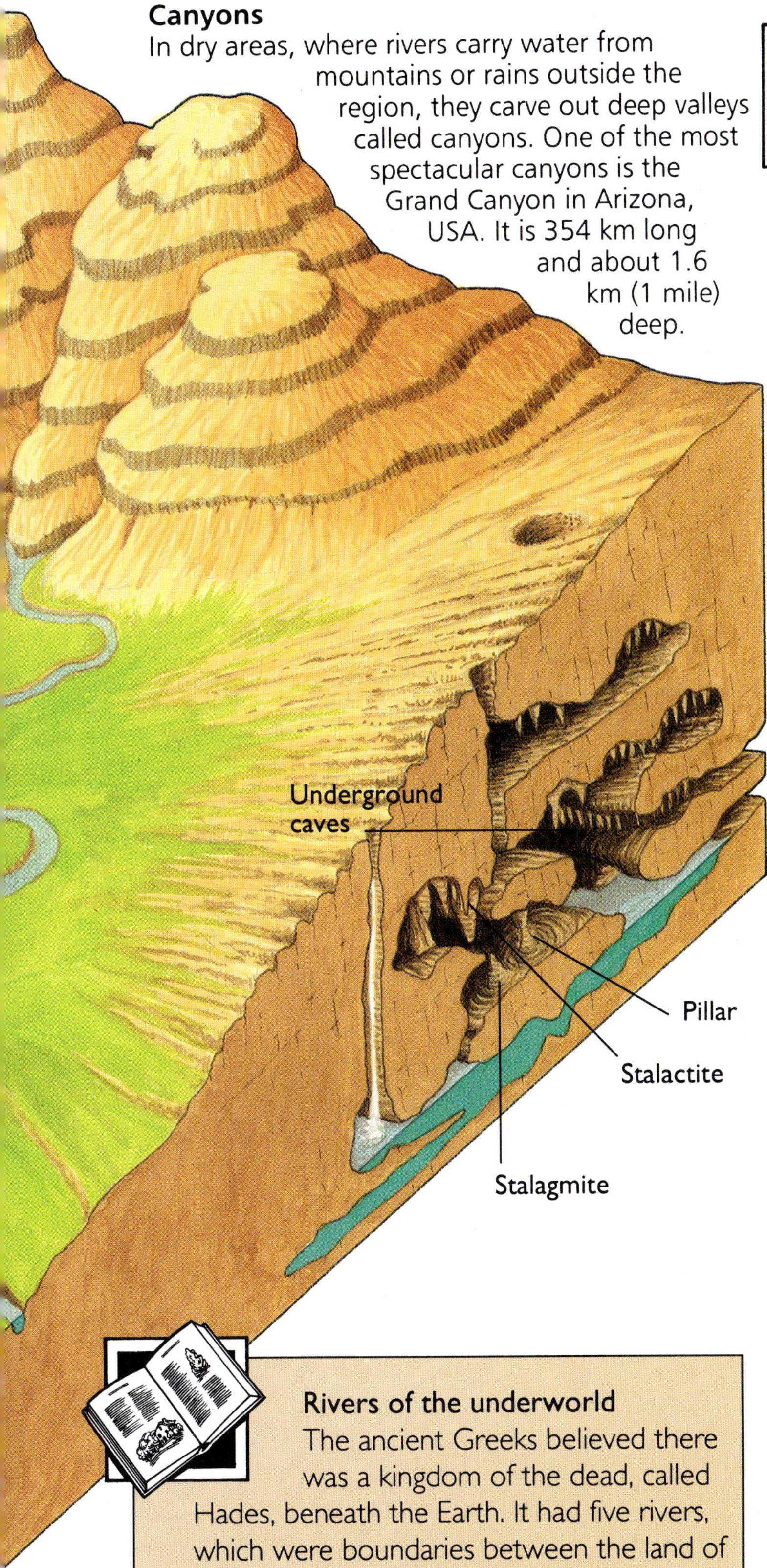

The frozen continent

Antarctica contains 90 per cent of the world's ice, and most of the Earth's fresh water is locked up in this ice. In the centre of the continent, temperatures range from -50°C to -60°C and winds can gust at up to 160 kilometres per hour (100 mph). In the summer, as the ice around the coast melts, penguins, like these Chinstrap penguins, come ashore to breed on the exposed shoreline.

Underground water

Underground water is slightly acidic and eats into soft rocks, such as limestone, forming tunnels and caves. Eventually, the water may collect into large underground rivers, which erode the rocks still further. As water drips through the cave roof, it evaporates, leaving behind columns of minerals which were dissolved in the rocks. These are called stalagmites (which grow up from the floor) and stalactites (which hang down from the roof). Over hundreds of years, stalagmites and stalactites may meet, forming pillars.

Rivers of the underworld

The ancient Greeks believed there was a kingdom of the dead, called Hades, beneath the Earth. It had five rivers, which were boundaries between the land of the living and the land of the dead. The Styx was the best known river in Hades. To cross the Styx, a soul had to be ferried by a boatman called Charon, who demanded payment for his work. This is why the ancient Greeks placed coins in the mouths of their dead before burying them.

Waterfalls

Waterfalls, like this one in South Wales, often form where rivers flow over layers of hard and soft rock. The soft rock is worn away, leaving behind a step of hard rock, which becomes a steep cliff over thousands of years. The water tumbles over the cliff as a waterfall. Waterfalls may also occur where river valleys have been widened by glaciers.

THE WEATHER

The blanket of air around the Earth – the atmosphere – is full of water. Most of the moisture is in the form of an invisible gas, called water vapour. When the air is cool enough, some of the water vapour turns into the tiny water droplets that form clouds, rain, mist and fog. If the temperature near the ground is below freezing, frost and snow may occur. The amount of rain and snow that falls to the ground varies at different times of the year, as the movement of the Earth around the Sun causes seasonal changes in the weather.

The water cycle

The amount of water on the Earth never changes because the water moves round and round in a continuous cycle, called the water cycle. Water is recycled and used over and over again. The warmth of the Sun makes the liquid water in rivers, lakes and especially oceans evaporate and rise up into the atmosphere as water vapour. During evaporation from seawater, salt is left behind and the water that rises is freshwater. When this cools down, it changes back into droplets of liquid water, forming clouds. These droplets of water eventually fall back to the Earth as rain, sleet or snow. The cycle is completed as the water collects on the ground and in lakes, rivers and oceans.

Monsoon myths

In South-East Asia, there are monsoon rains at certain times of the year. These winds are full of moisture from the ocean and bring torrential rainfall. The rains are vital for agriculture. The dragon became a symbol of the monsoon rains to the Chinese. Like the dragon, the rains could be violent and powerful, but were also very important since they brought the precious gift of water.

Weather forecasting

Weather forecasting is a complex process involving satellites, radar and weather stations all over the world. Weather satellites carry television cameras that photograph weather systems around the world. The photograph shown here was taken by a NASA weather satellite and shows the centre, or eye, of a tropical storm.

Clouds

Millions of droplets of water or ice floating in the sky make up the clouds we see. There are three main types of cloud – cumulus (meaning heaped), cirrus (feathery), and stratus (layered). Fluffy cumulus clouds are usually a sign of fair weather, while flat blankets of stratus cloud bring rain or drizzle. Large, dark cumulonimbus clouds bring storms while altocumulus (like cotton wool balls) are a clue to unsettled weather to come.

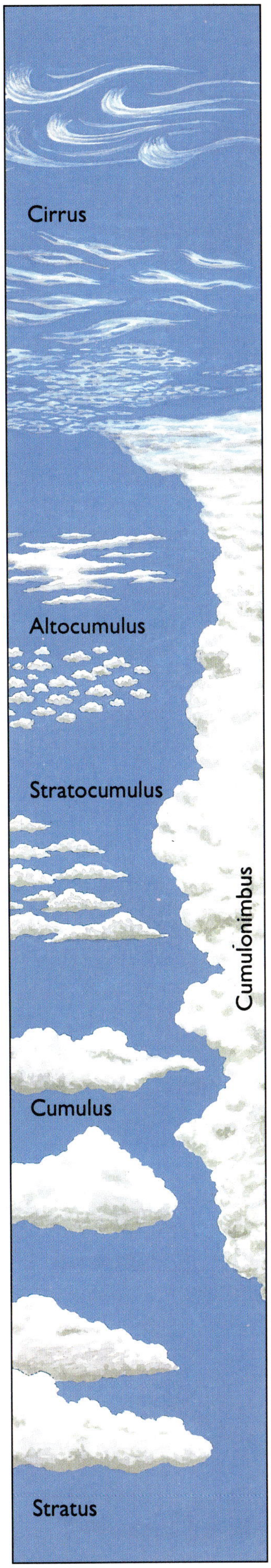

Weather damage

The weather can cause a lot of damage to people's homes. Rain and damp air make wood rot. If bricks and stones soak up water they crack and crumble. A thick layer of felt or plastic can be placed between bricks a little way above the ground. This damp-proof layer stops water from getting to the bricks above it. In very cold weather, the water in pipes sometimes freezes into ice. As water freezes, it expands and presses against the pipes, causing cracks. When the ice melts, the water pours out of the cracks, and damages the building.

Icicles form when snow or ice melts and freezes again.

WATER AT WORK

From industry to agriculture, to generating power for factories and homes, we make water work for us. To make the paper for this book, about 16 litres of water were used, and other industrial processes, such as making cars, use vast amounts of water. Some power stations use water to generate electricity, while others need large quantities of water to cool machinery – you can often see water vapour escaping into the atmosphere through huge cooling towers (shown above).

The Itaipú Dam (shown above), on the Paraná River in Brazil, is one of the world's largest hydro-electric dams. Its 18 turbines can produce 13 million kilowatts of electricity.

Water power

Water generates power when it flows from a higher to a lower place. Water-wheels were originally used to capture the energy of flowing water and use it to turn millstones that ground corn or wheat into flour. Today, turbines use moving water to generate electricity. Modern turbines are huge machines weighing thousands of tonnes. They are usually placed at the bottom of a dam to make the best use of the energy made by falling water.

Water-wheel

Industry

In the USA, industry uses around 1,360 million litres of water each day. Water is used for washing, cleaning, cooling, dissolving substances and even for transporting materials, such as logs for the timber industry (above). About 30,000 litres of water are needed to make a car, and eight litres of water are used to produce just one litre of lemonade. The largest industrial users of water are paper, petroleum, chemicals and the iron and steel-making industries.

Dam problems

Dams can cause problems for people and for the environment. Before a dam is built, people and animals have to be cleared from the area. If trees or plants are left to rot under the water, they make the water acidic and the acid may corrode (eat away) the machinery inside the dam. Reservoirs may become clogged by mud and silt which cannot be washed away downstream.

Flood irrigation is used to grow rice. The fields of young rice plants are flooded, covering them in water. These fields are called paddy fields (above). It takes about 4,500 kilogrammes of water to grow just one kilogramme of rice.

An Archimedes screw lifts water up a spiral screw to a higher level. The device was invented by the Greek scientist Archimedes over 2,000 years ago. It is still used in some parts of the world today.

Solar salt

For centuries, salt has been a vital part in people's diets and has even been used instead of money. In countries such as China, India and France, salt is harvested from seawater and used for food flavouring or to make industrial chemicals. Seawater is left in shallow pools in the hot Sun so the water evaporates, or disappears, into the air. Salt crystals are left behind and can be raked by hand or collected by machines. The salt is then taken to a refinery where it is crushed, ground and sorted before being packaged and sold. Evaporating seawater is the oldest method of obtaining salt. This kind of salt is called solar salt.

Irrigation

Crop plants, such as wheat or rice, need large quantities of water to grow properly. In places where there is not enough water, or the supply varies with the seasons, farmers irrigate the land. Most irrigation systems involve a network of canals and ditches to carry water to the crops. The sprinkler irrigation system (below) has an engine and wheels and moves across a field spraying crops with a fine mist of water.

Hydroponics

Plants can be grown without soil using a watering technique called hydroponics. A carefully controlled mixture of nutrients are dissolved in water and passed over the roots of plants which are suspended in a tank of water. Hydroponics does not produce better or larger crops, but it is important in the study of plants and can be used in areas where soil is not readily available, such as on board a ship or in Arctic areas.

CHAPTER 4

HEAT & ENERGY

The universe began in an incredibly hot ball of energy and from that time to the present day, the effects and uses of heat and energy are everywhere. Everything we do uses energy – running, cycling, walking and reading a book all need energy.

Since humankind began, we have found new ways to store and use the power of heat and energy. In this chapter we explore the scientific principles and everyday applications of heat and energy and their vital roles in today's world.

CONTENTS

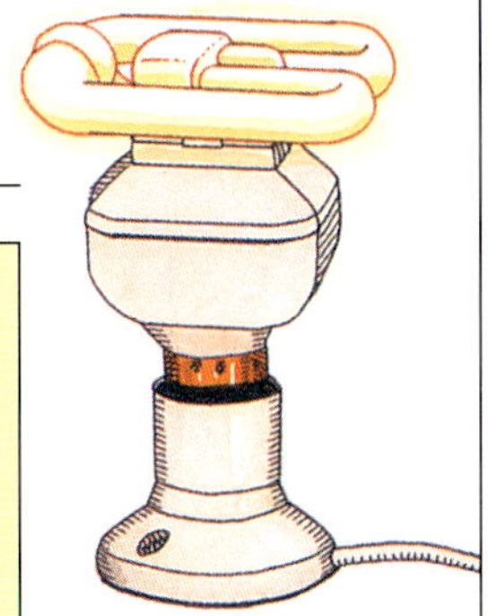

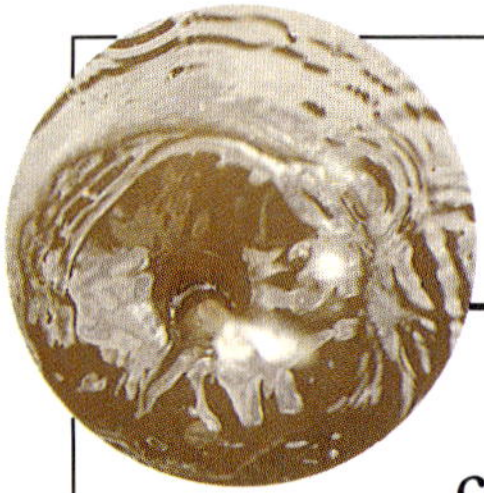

WHAT IS ENERGY?

Energy is the ability to do things. Without it we couldn't get up in the morning, or turn on the lights or drive the car. Plants wouldn't grow, the rain wouldn't fall, the Sun wouldn't shine. Everything we do needs a supply of energy, which is used to make things work: the word energy is Greek, and means "the work within". Energy comes in many forms, which can be stored and used in different ways.

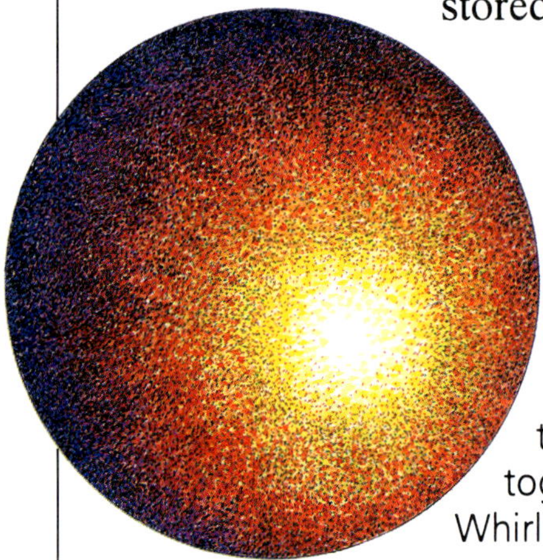

The universe was born 15 billion years ago in an incredibly hot ball of energy (left). It began to expand at an astonishing rate, creating matter and cooling rapidly as it grew. After 10,000 years, atoms appeared and in two billion years began to group together to form stars and galaxies. Whirling gases around the stars condensed into the planets, like Earth and Mars, about five billion years ago.

Matter and energy

Energy and matter seem very different, but they're not: in fact, matter can be turned into energy. This is how the Sun produces its enormous energy, and how nuclear power stations and nuclear bombs work. The physicist Albert Einstein showed that the amount of energy produced is given by the equation $E = mc^2$, where E is energy, m is mass, and c is a very large number – the speed of light.

The energy we need comes from food. Some foods, like sugar or fat, contain more energy than others. In the body, food is digested to release its energy, which then flows through the bloodstream to the muscles. An active person needs more food than somebody who sits down all day.

Aristotle and Galileo

The Greek philosopher Aristotle (384-322 BC) was among the first to try to explain energy. He believed that a heavier stone would fall faster than a lighter one – but he never tested it. If he had, he would have found that both fell at the same rate. They did not fall simply because they were heavy, but because they had energy from being lifted. It was the Italian physicist Galileo Galilei (AD 1564-1642) who first began to understand this and to challenge many of Aristotle's incorrect theories.

All machines need a source of energy. Viking longboats were driven by muscle power, which is limited. But the petrol or diesel engines in a modern mechanical digger are far more powerful. Until the invention in the 19th century of engines that could turn heat from coal or oil into work, the methods by which people altered their environment were very different.

Energy expressions

There are many sayings which use ideas about heat and energy. To "get into hot water" means to get into some kind of difficult situation. To "go full steam ahead" means to do something with all your energy. To "blow hot and cold" is to change your attitude towards something many times. Do you know these sayings: "too hot to handle"; and "firing on all cylinders"?

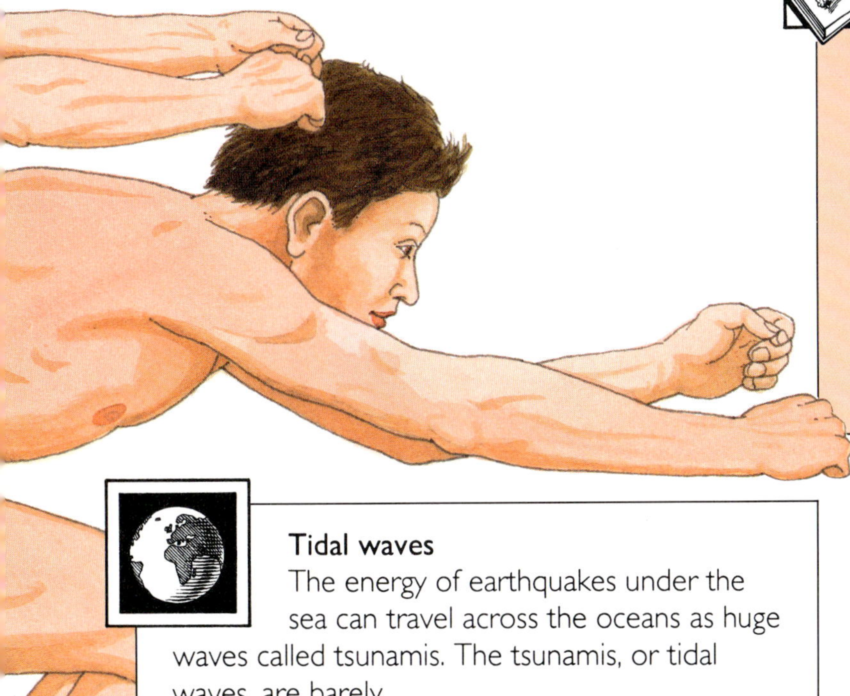

Tidal waves

The energy of earthquakes under the sea can travel across the oceans as huge waves called tsunamis. The tsunamis, or tidal waves, are barely visible out at sea, but when they reach land they sweep ashore, causing destruction. Systems around the Pacific Ocean warn people to move if a tsunami approaches.

Sound is a form of energy, created by vibrations, such as the sound of a tuning fork. It is transmitted through the air in waves, which travel at about 1,126 kph (700 mph). The vibrations of the air are picked up by our ear drums, which vibrate in time, sending signals to our brains.

ENERGY CYCLE

Nearly all the energy we use comes originally from the Sun. It radiates through space and reaches Earth, causing plants to grow. These plants provide us with food energy in the form of crops, and feed the animals which we eat as meat. They also provide fuel because plants and microscopic creatures that lived millions of years ago formed the fossil fuels – coal and oil. Rainwater, evaporated by the Sun's heat from the oceans, fills the rivers and provides hydro-electric power, while the wind is also produced by the Sun.

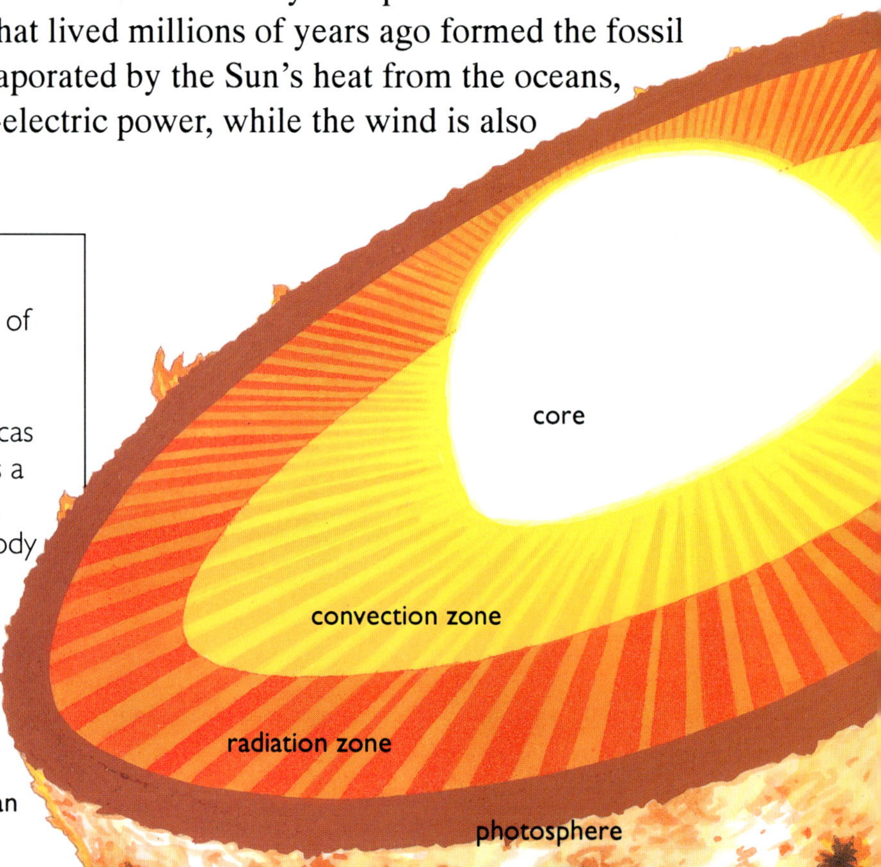

Sun worship

The Incas, Mayas and Aztecs, of South and Central America, worshipped the Sun with sacrificial offerings on Sun temples (left). The Incas thought the emperor was a descendant of the Sun. When he died, his body was preserved and kept in his palace, where servants continued to wait on him.

an Egyptian Sun-god

In ancient Egypt, the Sun was one of many gods until King Akhenaten decreed that the Sun-god, Aten, should be the only god.

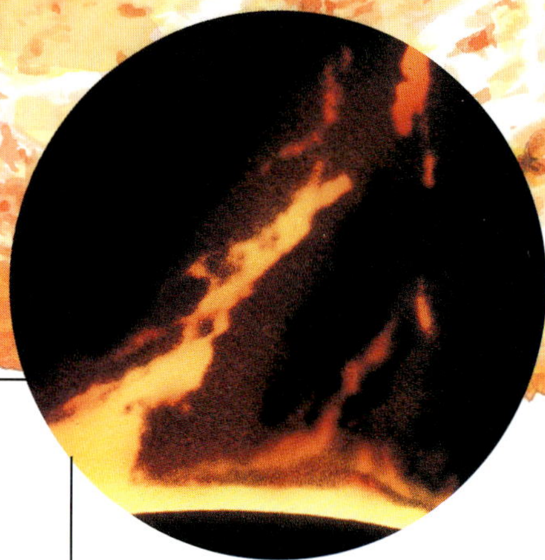

From the rim of the Sun, flares (above), called solar prominences, leap out. They are huge eruptions of hot gases linked to sunspots – slightly cooler areas on the Sun's surface.

Myths and legends

In Greek mythology there were many gods. Phaeton, the son of the Sun-god Helios, was granted his wish that he should control the chariot of the Sun for a whole day. But Phaeton lost control of the horses and the Sun came too close to the Earth. He was about to burn the Earth up when Zeus, the chief god, struck him down with a thunderbolt.

The light of the Sun comes from the outer shell, or photosphere. Heated by nuclear reactions in the core, the photosphere glows brightly. The light from the Sun looks white, but it is a mixture of colours in the visible spectrum (above), or the range of colours visible to people.

Food energy

Different foods provide different amounts of energy, measured in kilocalories (or kcals). Each day we need 2,200 - 2,900 kcals from food. A gramme of fat contains nine calories; a gramme of flour or sugar just under four; a gramme of fish between one and two. Just sitting still uses 1.1 kcals a minute, while walking uses 3-4 kcals a minute and running fast about 15 kcals a minute. Sportspeople have a special diet to give them enough energy to compete.

Plants capture the Sun's energy by a chemical process – photosynthesis (left). A green pigment, chlorophyll, creates sugars from water, in the plant's roots, and carbon dioxide gas from the air. Other chemicals – nitrogen, calcium, phosphorus and potassium – come from the soil.

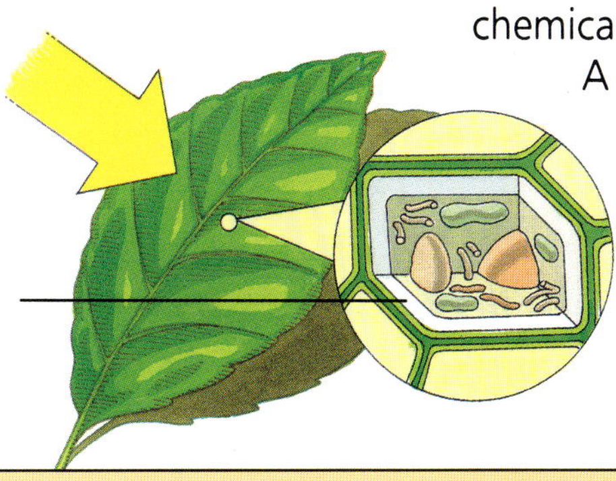

a single plant cell

Wheat worldwide

Six crops – wheat, rice, maize, barley, oats and rye – provide about half of all human food energy. Wheat is used for making bread and is very efficient at converting sunlight into food energy, while for thousands of years rice has formed the basic diet of half the world's population. Wheat grows easily in cold, northern climates with low temperatures as opposed to rice, which needs warmer, wetter conditions in order to thrive and is grown on graduated terraces.

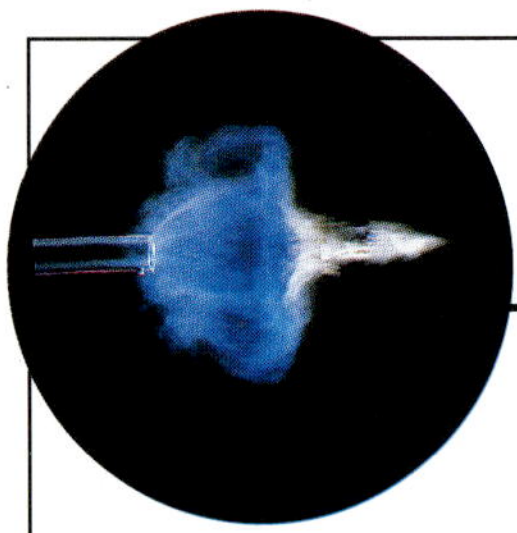

ENERGY CHANGES

Energy cannot be created, nor can it be destroyed. It can only be converted from one form into another. A fire converts chemical energy from its fuel into heat, while a steam engine goes further and converts the heat into work by generating steam in a boiler. A torch converts electrical energy stored in its battery into light. There are dozens of ways in which energy can be stored and used, all governed by scientific rules known as the laws of thermodynamics.

Making fire
When two surfaces rub together, the work of rubbing is turned into heat. This is the simplest way to create a fire and was used by our ancestors in a device called a fire drill (below). A rod is inserted into a hole in a piece of wood. The rod, attached to a bone and a leather bow, is turned rapidly and held in place by a mouthpiece. The base hole heats up, begins to smoulder and eventually catches fire.

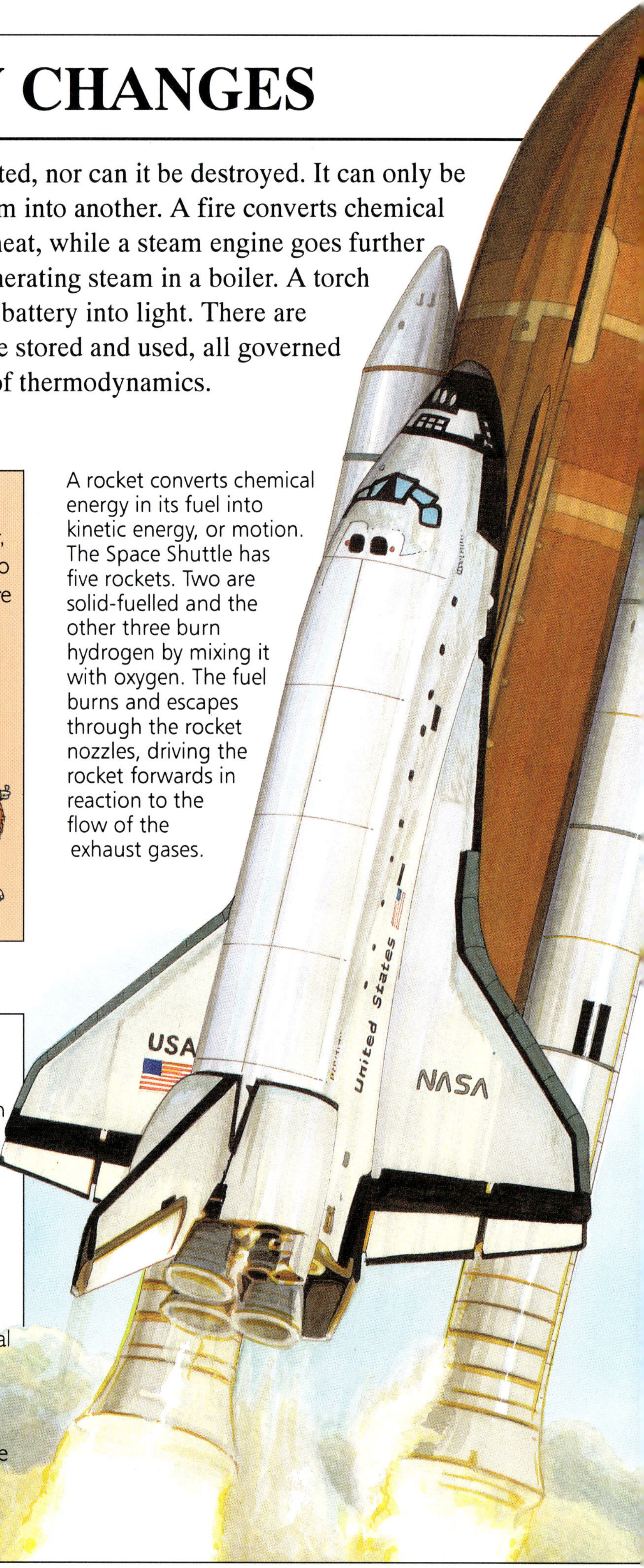

A rocket converts chemical energy in its fuel into kinetic energy, or motion. The Space Shuttle has five rockets. Two are solid-fuelled and the other three burn hydrogen by mixing it with oxygen. The fuel burns and escapes through the rocket nozzles, driving the rocket forwards in reaction to the flow of the exhaust gases.

James Joule
The English scientist James Joule (1818-1889) was so interested in the study of heat energy that he took a thermometer on his honeymoon. He spent much of the time studying the temperatures of the water at different points of a waterfall. His work played a vital role in showing that heat was in fact a form of energy. The unit of measurement for energy, the joule, was named after him.

Art and energy

The English artist J.M.W. Turner (1775-1851) lived at a time when new machines were transforming life. His paintings use vivid colours and an impressionistic style to create a sense of the forces of energy and the power of nature, whether painting a storm at sea, an Alpine scene, or a steam train.

An archer preparing to shoot works on the bow to make it bend. The bow then has energy called potential energy. As soon as the archer lets go of the bowstring, this potential energy is released and converted into the kinetic energy of the arrow, sending it speeding away.

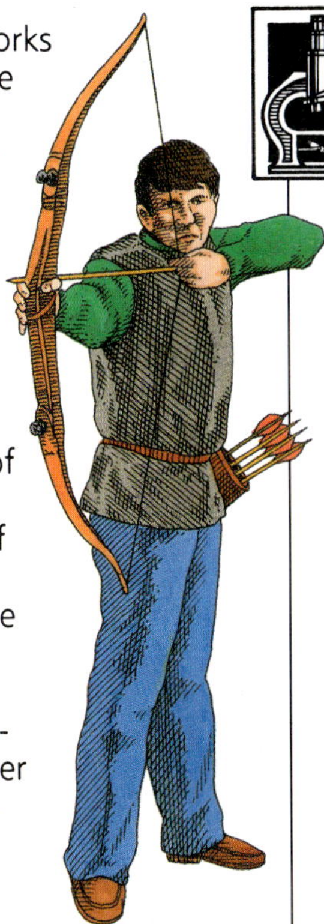

A drum is a way of converting the kinetic energy of the drumsticks into sound. The harder the drummer hits the taut drum-skins, the bigger their vibrations and the louder the sound.

Lifting and dropping

Lifting an object gives it potential energy. This turns into kinetic energy as the object falls. Galileo showed that heavier objects do not fall faster. Test this by rolling two marbles of different sizes down a slope at the same time. With no air resistance, they will arrive at the bottom together. In a vacuum, where there is no air, a feather will fall as fast as a marble.

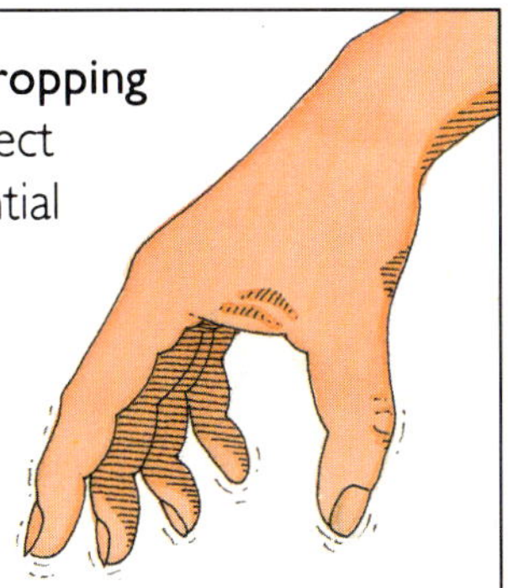

Old Faithful

This geyser in California is famous for its regular eruptions. Every day, jets of hot water shoot high into the air. The water, from below ground, is heated by the Earth's heat, building up pressure until it erupts. Geysers convert the Earth's energy, or geothermal energy, into kinetic energy – the moving jet of water – and then into potential energy.

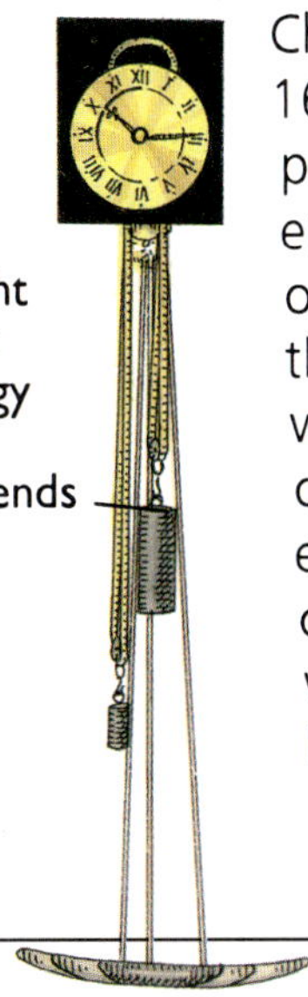

Christian Huygens (1629-1695) invented the pendulum clock. The energy to drive the hands of the clock comes from the falling lead weight, which releases a fraction of the weight's potential energy with each tick. The clock stops when the weight reaches its lowest position.

HEAT AND TEMPERATURE

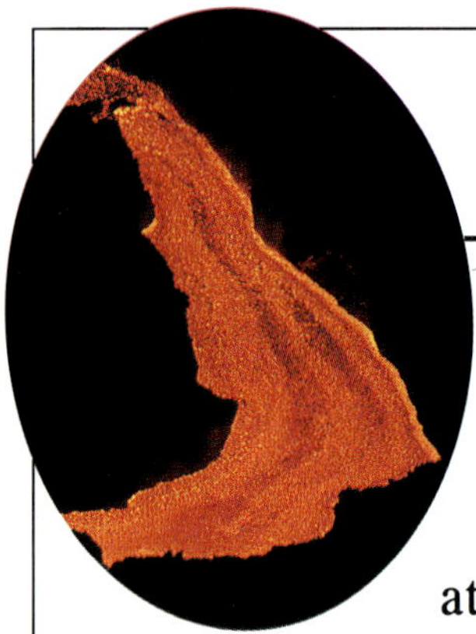

Once it was thought that heat was a kind of fluid that could flow from hot to cold, but this is not so. Heat is actually a form of kinetic energy, caused by the atoms and molecules of matter vibrating to and fro. The hotter a thing is, the more violently its atoms vibrate, and the greater its heat content. Heat always transfers energy from a hotter place to a cooler one – for example, the energy in a hot drink moves from the drink to the cooler air around it. The intensity of the heat in any object can be measured by its temperature.

Heat from the Sun reaches us directly by radiation through space. Radiant heat travels in straight lines and can be blocked by clouds.

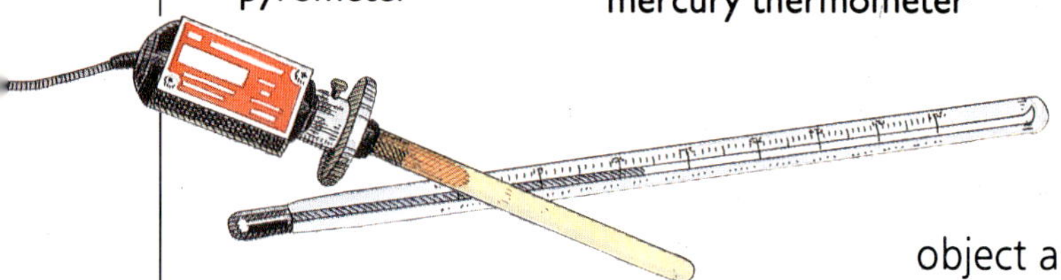

pyrometer

mercury thermometer

Thermometers and pyrometers are used to measure temperature. A radiation pyrometer works by converting heat into electricity; an optical pyrometer observes the colour of the object and matches it with a known temperature.

Infra-red radiation

Warm objects radiate heat, mostly in the form of infra-red radiation. This lies just beyond the red end of the visible spectrum – hence its name – and can be detected by film sensitive to those wavelengths. Infra-red images show small variations in temperature and are useful for assessing the growth of crops or the extent of forests.

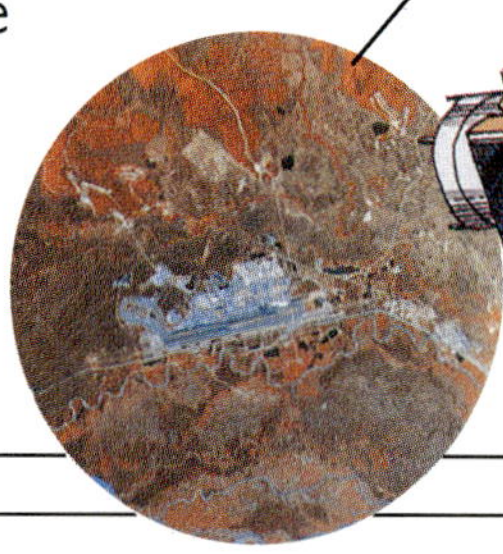

infra-red satellite picture of the Earth

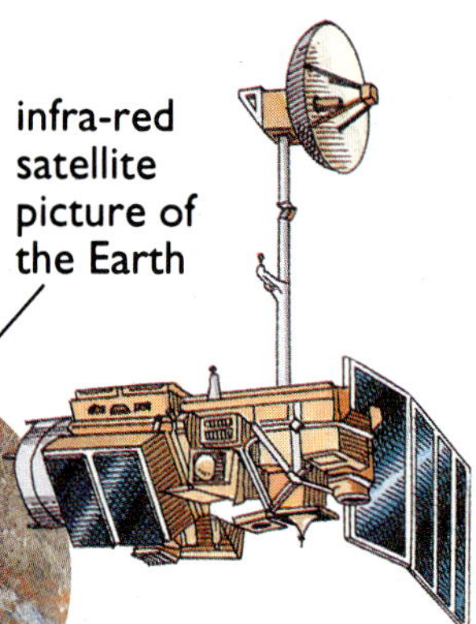

The Landsat 5 satellite system (left) was designed to acquire data (below left) about the Earth's resources. The strongest readings are of healthy vegetation.

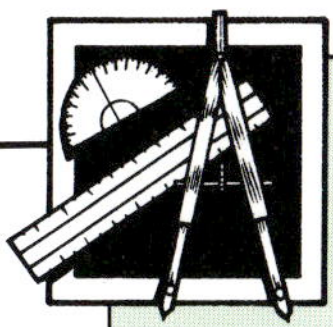

Body heat

You can measure temperature with a thermometer (right). A column of mercury inside a glass tube expands along a graduated scale as the temperature rises. A healthy human body is always at the same temperature, but what is it? Take your own temperature to find out.

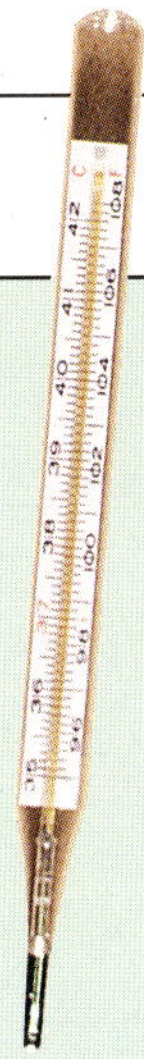

Substances expand as they get hotter because the atoms are vibrating more quickly and tend to be further apart, increasing volume. Different materials expand differently. The Eiffel Tower grows 18 cm on a hot day.

Heat is spread in fluids by convection. Near the source of heat the fluid warms up, becomes less dense, and rises, to be replaced by the colder fluid.

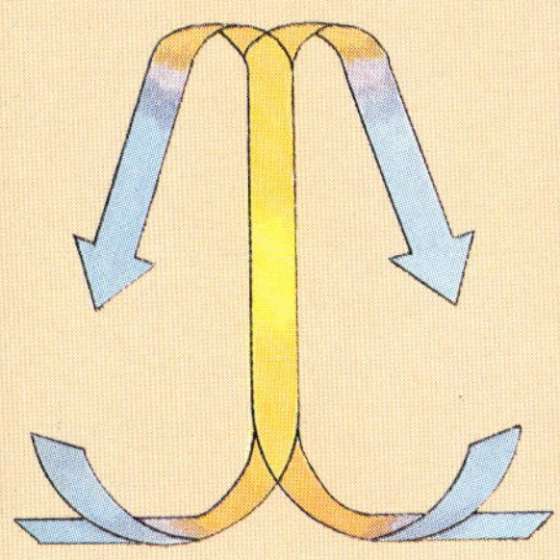

In solids, heat flows by conduction. Atoms vibrating violently at one end, because they are hot, agitate those further along and cause heat to flow.

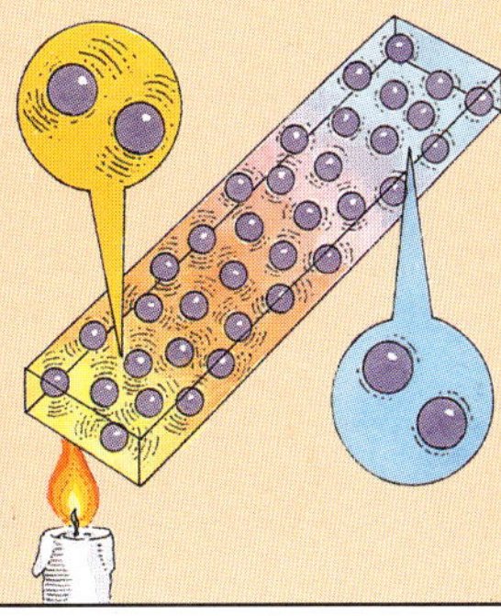

Animal heat

Some creatures have warm blood, others have cold. Birds and mammals have warm blood. This means that in cold climates they have to conserve heat, with hair, feathers or blubber, and use heat generated by their muscles to keep them warm. Reptiles, amphibians, fish and invertebrates are cold-blooded. Their blood is the same temperature as the outside world, which makes them slower in cold weather.

Cool colours

Different colours express different temperatures and also different emotions, something that painters have always understood. Red is a hot, dangerous colour, because when things are very hot, they glow red. We also get red in the face when we are angry. Blue is a cool colour, borrowed from the sky and the sea. African Americans invented the Blues as a vivid expression of their despair.

FIRE AND BURNING

A fire is a chemical reaction, in which a burning object combines with oxygen, producing an energy change. Most of the energy from fire is heat energy, but fire also releases energy in the form of light and sound. This is why fire can be seen, felt and heard. Fires need high temperatures and a supply of oxygen to keep them burning, so removing either of these can put out a fire. Substances such as water, sand or foam can also be used to smother a fire and dampen the flames.

Prometheus

In Greek myths, Prometheus (right) was a god who created people and gave them reason. He stole fire from heaven and gave it to humans. Zeus chained him to a rock and sent an eagle each day to eat his liver, which grew back at night. After many years, Prometheus was rescued.

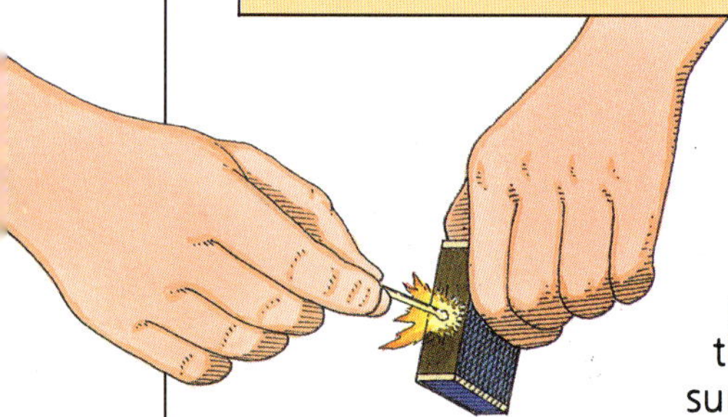

Matches have heads made of a substance that is easily ignited by rubbing. The heat generated by rubbing them on a rough surface is sufficient to ignite the match.

The Great Fire of London

The Great Fire of London, in 1666, destroyed much of the city. It spread swiftly through the narrow streets filled with wooden houses. As there was no proper fire service in England at that time, people had to wait for the fire to burn itself out, which took days. When the citizens returned, they found their homes and their city in ashes.

Modern fire fighters do not always use water to douse flames, because if fuel is burning, water may spread it and make the fire worse. Foam is used in airports, swamping the fire and cutting off the supply of oxygen that it needs to keep burning.

Some things burn very slowly. Piles of old car tyres can smoulder for years, releasing smoke and filthy liquids. Putting them out is very difficult.

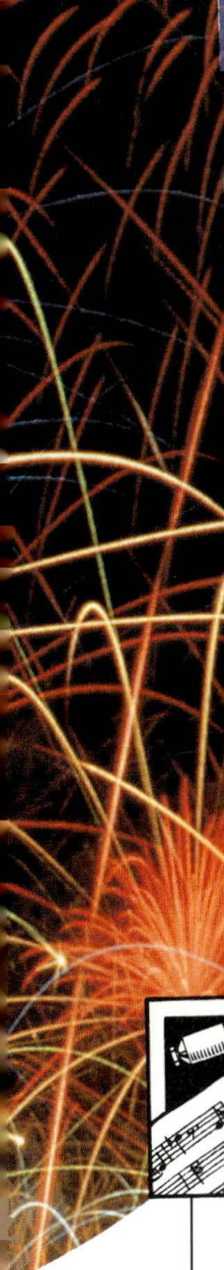

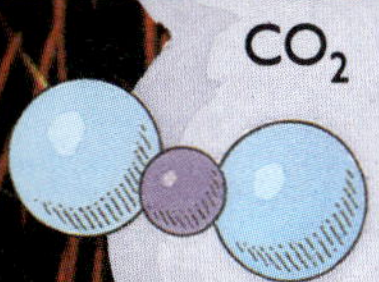

Most combustible materials contain carbon, the basic building block of life. Coal, wood, oil and gas all contain carbon as a major constituent. When they burn, the carbon combines with oxygen to produce the gas carbon dioxide, which drifts away as smoke. Some people fear that we are producing so much carbon dioxide that it will cause the Earth to warm up, by blocking the radiation of heat in a "greenhouse effect".

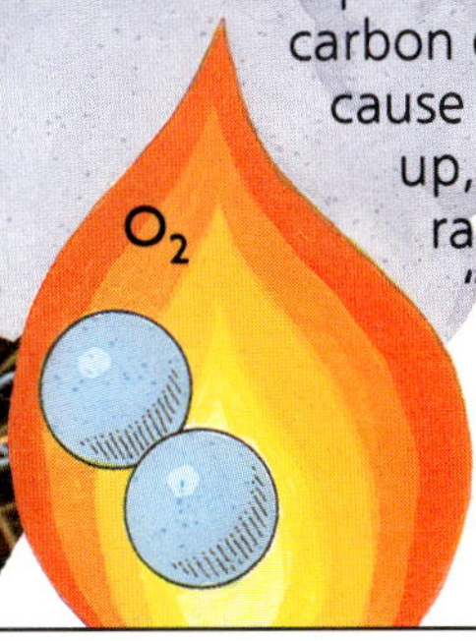

Hell fires
Hell is supposed to be a place where evil people burn forever. The theme was often used by religious artists of the Middle Ages, such as the Dutch painter Hieronymus Bosch (1450-1516). His teeming Hell is full of people regretting that they didn't lead better lives.

The internal combustion engine
The internal combustion engine emerged during the late 19th century as an alternative to steam power. The engine burns a mixture of petrol and air inside the cylinders, driving a piston with little power. Steam engines burn fuel outside the cylinders and use it to produce steam, which drives the pistons. Modern Grand Prix engines in Formula One racing cars have 8 or even 12 cylinders. For extra power, fuel can be blown into the cylinders using turbo-chargers.

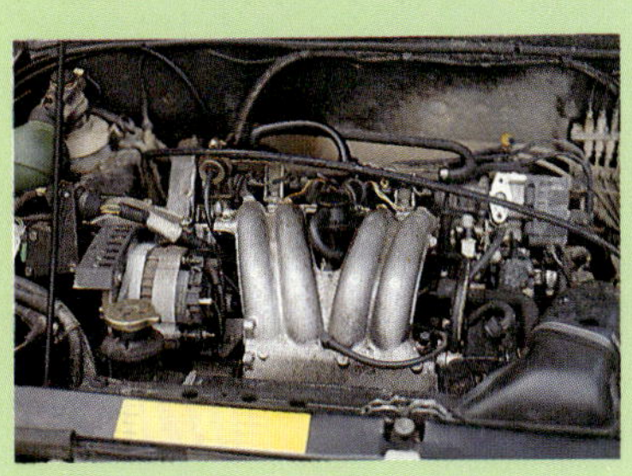

Candle combustion
Burning or combustion needs a supply of oxygen for it to continue. In order to prove that this is true, try this experiment. Light a candle in a saucer containing water, then put a Pyrex glass over it, with its rim in the water to seal it. Ask an adult to help you with this experiment, taking care with matches.

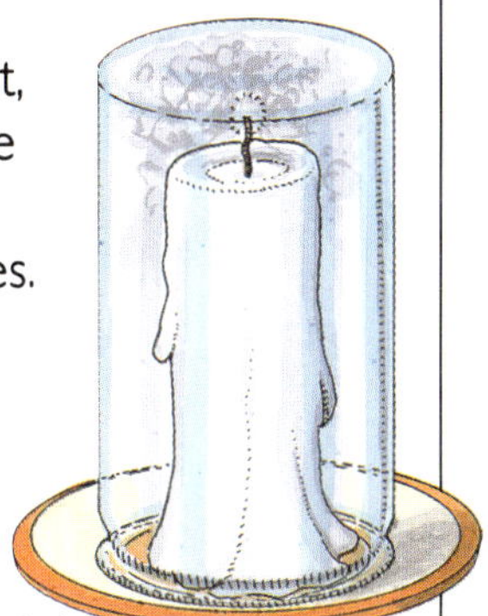

As the candle burns, it uses up the oxygen, and goes out when there is none left.

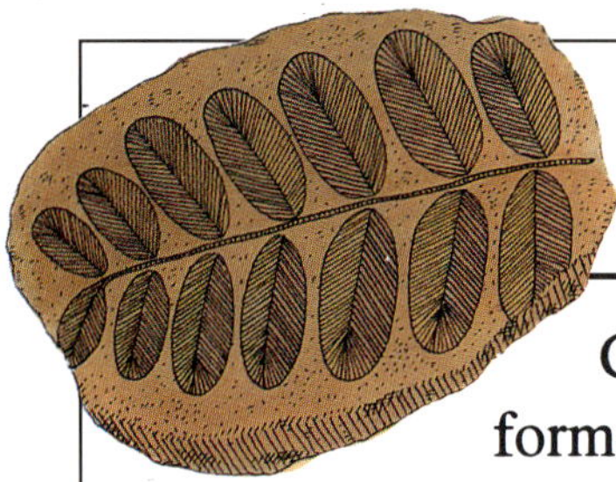

FOSSIL FUELS

Coal, oil and natural gas are known as fossil fuels. They were formed from plants and the tiny creatures that lived on them, which were buried and subjected to the heat and pressure of the Earth over many millions of years. As energy from the Sun is stored in plant leaves as potential chemical energy (by photosynthesis), fossil fuels are a form of stored solar energy. The amounts available are large, but one day they will run out. Until then, we can use them as fuel and as raw materials for plastics, fertilisers and chemicals.

Vincent Van Gogh

The painter Vincent Van Gogh (1853-1890) knew a lot about coal-mining communities, as he spent some time working as a missionary among the miners before becoming a painter in 1880. His early paintings were mainly of people in their work places, such as *The Return of the Miners* (below).

Coal deposits vary in location as well as quality. Coal can be extracted from near the surface by opencast mining. Often, however, the seam is deep underground and vertical shafts must be dug down to the seam. Tunnels or galleries are then cut into the seam as the coal is extracted.

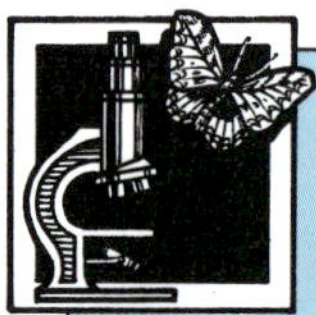

SWOPS

When oil is found under the oceans, huge production platforms can be built to extract it. But if the well is small the cost may not be justified. Then a wellhead can be placed on the seabed, and oil pumped up to a tanker above, in a system called SWOPS – the Single Well Oil Production System. A single tanker, with room for 300,000 barrels, can serve up to three small fields.

seismic truck

the SWOPS system

The study of sound, or seismic, waves in the Earth can help companies to locate oil and gas. Trucks can be fitted with equipment which sends controlled sounds into the Earth.

Coal gas has now been replaced by cleaner natural gas, found in reservoirs in the Earth's crust, often with oil. It consists mainly of methane. The cheapest fuel available, gas, is ideal for heating and cooking.

Gas lighting

In 1792 a Scottish engineer, William Murdoch, produced gas by heating coal in a closed container. By 1814, the first streets were lit by gas in London. However, really good lights were not available until 1885.

Swamp land

Plants and animals flourished on Earth 300 million years ago. At that time, large areas of the Earth were swampy forests. These waterlogged conditions preserved the vegetation as part of its slow change to coal.

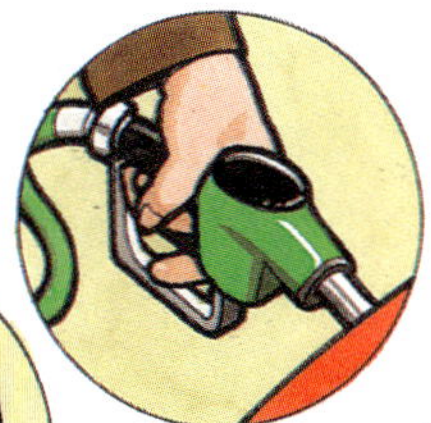

Crude oil is a heavy liquid which must be broken down, or refined, before being used. The process used to refine oil is distillation, and is based on the fact that different parts (fractions) of oil boil at different temperatures. Some of the lighter fractions make petrol, with heavier fractions being used for heavy fuel oil and tar.

Oil is less plentiful than coal, and is found where rocks prevent it escaping. Exploration rigs all over the world drill through ice and seabed in the hope of striking oil. When they do, pipelines and tankers take it away. It is so valuable that its discovery can make a country very wealthy.

D.H. Lawrence

Coal mining was a major industry in the 19th century and produced mining communities around pits. It was a dangerous job which bred a strong community spirit. The novelist D.H. Lawrence (1885-1935), the son of a miner, wrote novels centred in these communities from his own life and experiences.

ELECTRICITY

Electricity is the most convenient form of energy, available at the flick of a switch and able to provide light, power and heat. It is generated mostly by huge machines called turbo-generators, driven by steam produced by coal, oil, gas and nuclear boilers. It is also produced in smaller generators powered by wind and water. The first public supplies were installed in New York in 1882, and today, almost everybody in developed countries has access to mains electricity, transforming our lives.

Natural electricity

Electricity occurs naturally in the form of lightning and in electric shocks that some creatures can produce. The electric ray has muscles on either side of its head that can produce a shock wave sufficient to stun nearby prey. Sharks can detect tiny electrical currents from other fish, tracking them even in darkness. But until the work of Faraday (see page 105), it was not known that this natural electricity was the same as that produced by batteries.

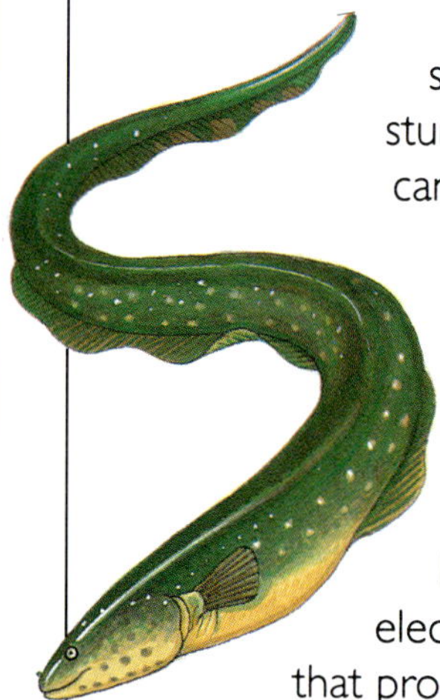

A fuel cell (above) converts chemical energy into electrical energy. It is a way of making electricity directly by reacting together hydrogen and oxygen, to create electricity and water. The principle has been known for many years but only recently have fuel cells become practicable. Now buses powered by fuel cells are being tried out.

In a coal-fired power station (right), coal is burned in a huge boiler and its heat produces steam. Water is fed through pipes that pass through the hot region of the boiler, turning it into steam. The steam is then superheated to a very high temperature before passing to the steam turbines. Even the most efficient power stations turn less than about 35 per cent of the energy in the fuel into electricity: the rest is lost as low-temperature heat through cooling towers, or in some modern plants is used to heat buildings.

A battery is a way of turning chemical energy into electricity. Inside a battery there are two metal parts which are covered by a special chemical. When the circuit is made by switching on an appliance, the chemicals inside the battery react to produce charged particles. The negative particles collect at one terminal and the positive ones at the other. In the circuit the charged particles flow from the negative to the positive terminal in a current.

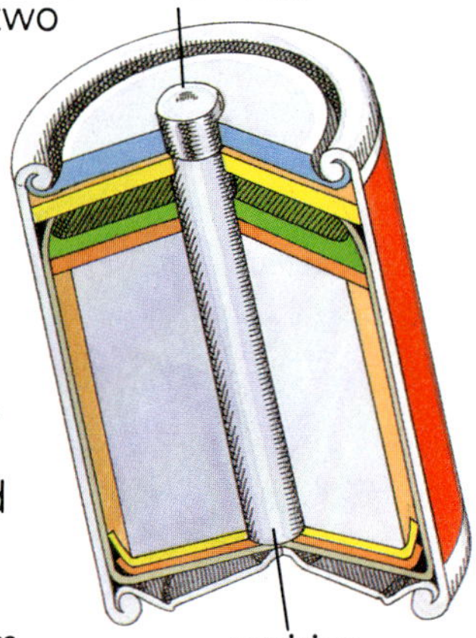

Michael Faraday

The scientist Michael Faraday (1791-1867) discovered how electricity worked whilst working at the Royal Institution in London. In his most famous experiment, he showed that if two coils of wire were wrapped around an iron core shaped like a ring (right), a current was created in the second coil every time the current in the first was switched on or off.

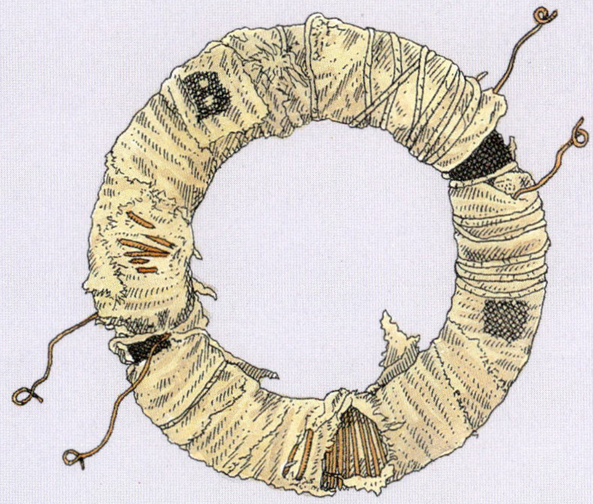

Steam turbines (left) consist of a series of fine-bladed fans running inside a tight-fitting case. High-pressure steam is fed into the turbine from a boiler, and expands past the successive rows of fans, driving them round. All the fans are connected to a single shaft, which runs directly to a generator. As the steam condenses, it is returned to the boiler again.

Frankenstein

When Mary Shelley (1797-1851) wrote the novel *Frankenstein* in 1818, electricity was all the rage. Scientists had shown that an electric current applied to the muscle of a frog made it jump. So what better way for Dr Frankenstein to bring his monster to life than by giving it a huge jolt of electricity? The story has remained one of the most popular ever written.

Make an electromagnet

You will need a coil of copper wire and a battery. Wind the coil round a steel knitting needle and use a compass to detect the magnetic field produced when the current flows. Does removing the needle make any difference?

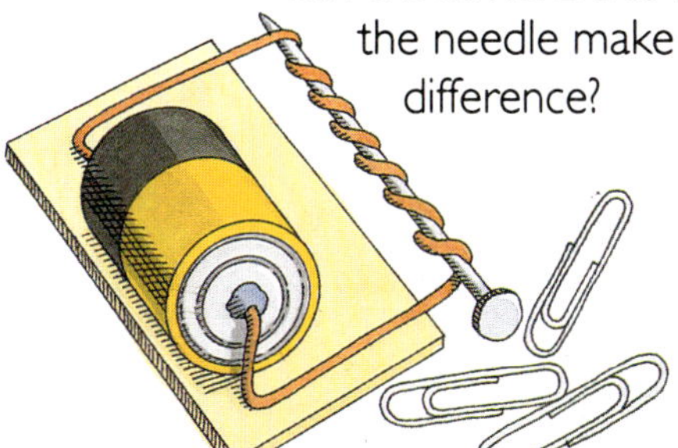

Power stations send electricity through thick cables, often carried high above the ground by pylons (right). The power in the cables is at a very high voltage and is reduced by transformers for use in offices and homes.

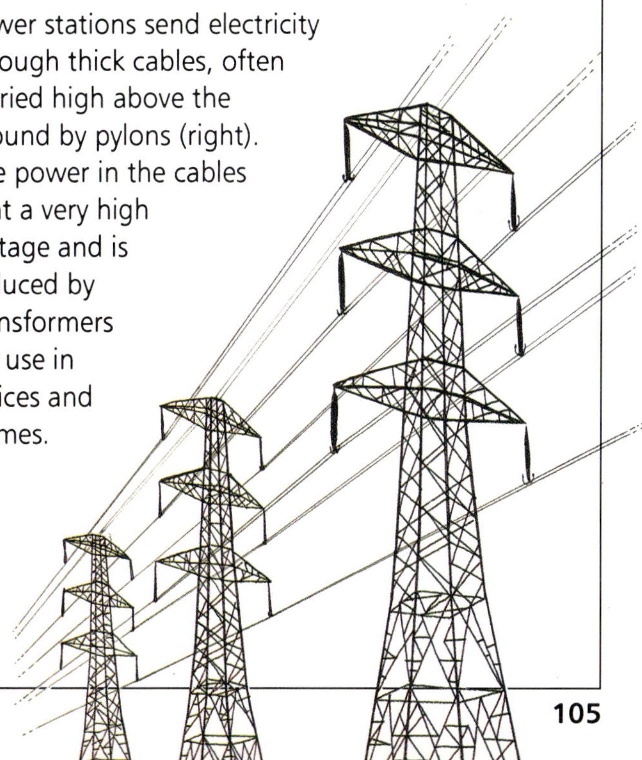

ALTERNATIVE ENERGY

Fossil fuels are plentiful, but one day they will run out. Then we will need to use alternative energy sources, such as wind, waves, geothermal, solar, nuclear and tidal power to generate electricity. Most of these are renewable sources, so called because they do not rely on a resource which can be used up. None are fully developed yet but a lot of money has been invested in the past few years in trying to find an economical and safe alternative. The best prospect at present appears to be solar energy, but wind power may also be a worthwhile source.

The Earth's energy

The heat of the Earth itself can be used to generate power in some places. Powerful jets of steam emerging from geysers can be used directly to generate electricity. Attempts have also been made to tap geothermal heat (heat from underground rocks) by drilling holes into dry rock and pumping down water.

Thorium reactor

Scientists are researching a safer, more efficient form of nuclear power plant that runs on the element thorium. The thorium is hit by particles, called neutrons, from a device called a particle accelerator. The neutrons cause the thorium to convert into a type of uranium.

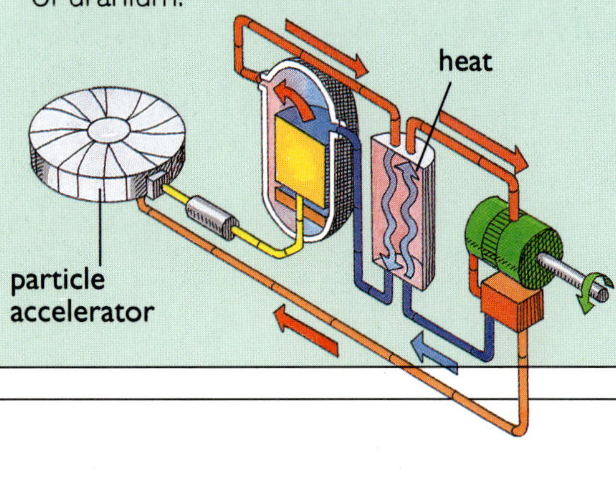

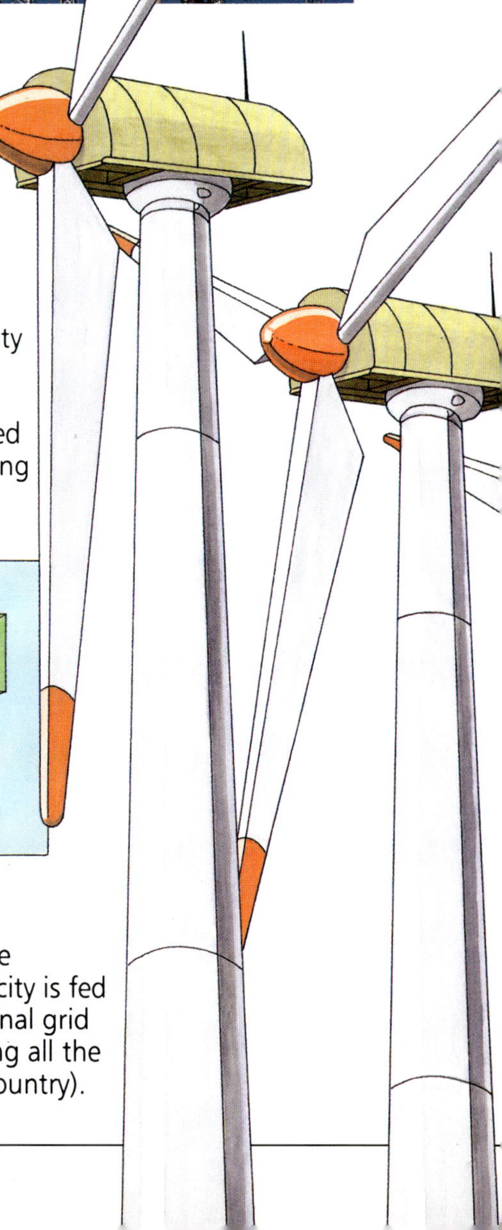

Wind power is practical, and close to being economical. In the US, 600,000 households are now supplied with electricity from wind turbines. Wind "farms", with many turbines grouped together, are now being built in windy places.

A wind turbine has a two- or three-bladed rotor, which drives the generator. The electricity is fed by cables into a national grid (the system connecting all the power stations in a country).

Nuclear power

Nuclear power works, and uranium fuel is plentiful. It also produces large amounts of power, unlike most other alternatives. But its costs are higher than fossil fuels and it faces campaigners who claim that it is unsafe, following several alarming incidents concerning safety, such as the major fire at Sellafield nuclear power station, England (right), in 1957. These difficulties have reduced the building of nuclear plants worldwide.

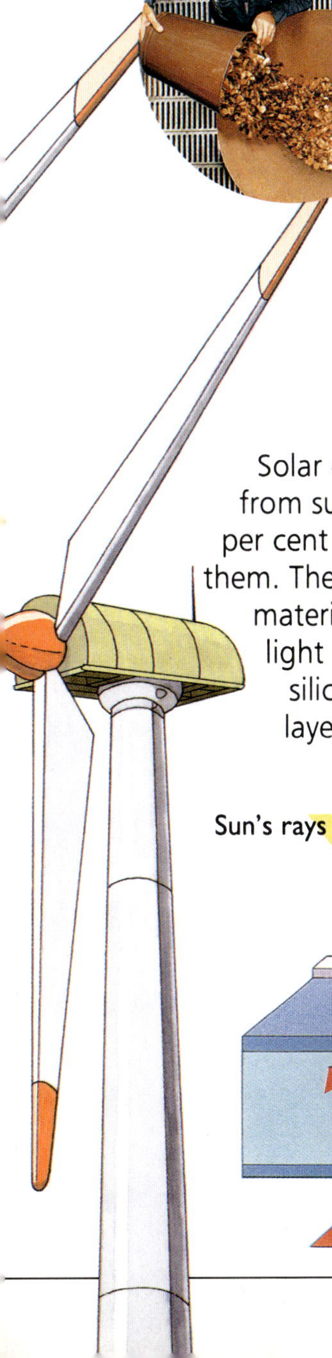

Fuel from plants is created from timber, grown specially and turned into woodchips (left) to burn in a furnace. Wood can also be turned into a gas which is useful for cooking. Fuels like this are called biomass.

Solar cells make electricity directly from sunlight, but convert about 10 per cent of the energy that reaches them. They are made of layers of a material such as silicon. The Sun's light creates electric charges in the silicon which flow between the layers, and produce a current.

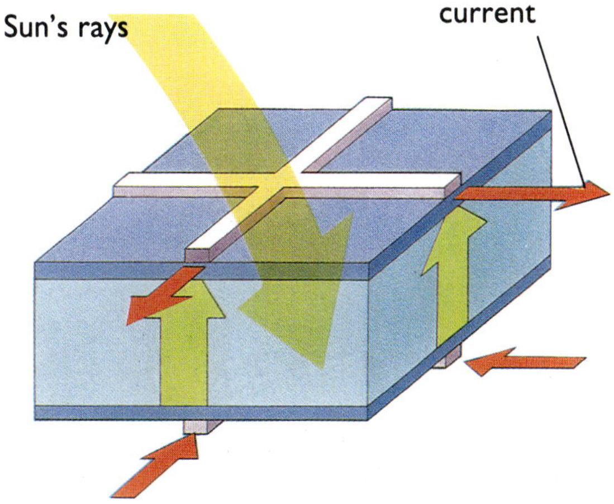

Wave power

Tidal power stations are dams across estuaries which capture water at high tide, then allow it to escape through turbines to generate electricity. The Rance plant, in France, is the only large one ever built, due to the high building costs.

Sun energy

Solar cells can generate electricity at nearly economic prices in places where there is a lot of sunshine. The Solar One power station, in the Mojave Desert in California, uses solar cells to convert the Sun's light energy into electricity. Nearly 2,000 computer-operated mirrors reflect the Sun's rays at a central tower. There the heat energy is absorbed by oil. Heat from this is then used to turn water into steam and generate electricity.

TRANSPORT

Getting around uses a lot of energy. Almost all of it comes from oil, refined to produce petrol, diesel and aviation fuel. But burning fuel produces polluting gases such as the oxides of nitrogen, so great efforts are now being made to produce cleaner vehicles. Catalytic converters can clean up exhausts, and efficient cars that use less fuel, or run on batteries, are being developed to meet the new standards.

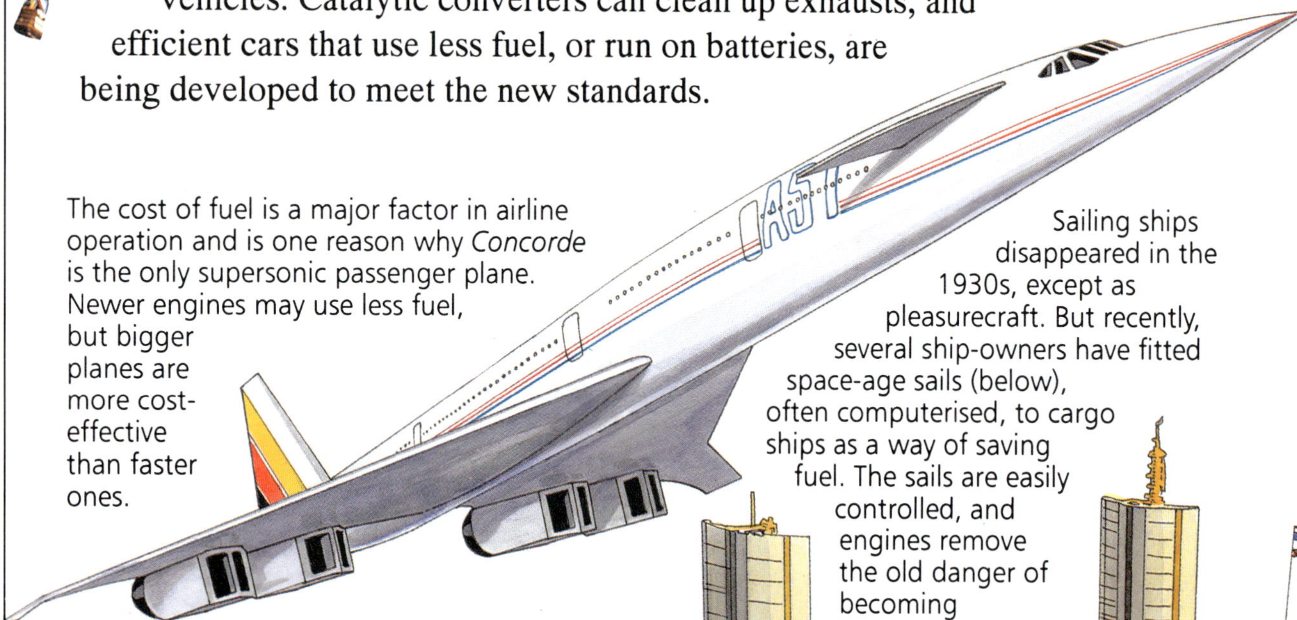

The cost of fuel is a major factor in airline operation and is one reason why *Concorde* is the only supersonic passenger plane. Newer engines may use less fuel, but bigger planes are more cost-effective than faster ones.

Sailing ships disappeared in the 1930s, except as pleasurecraft. But recently, several ship-owners have fitted space-age sails (below), often computerised, to cargo ships as a way of saving fuel. The sails are easily controlled, and engines remove the old danger of becoming becalmed.

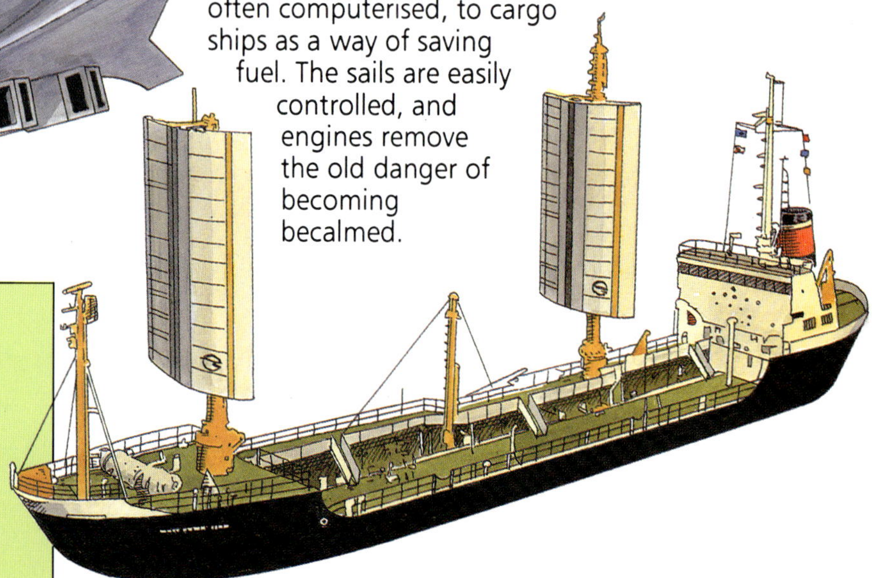

Alternative fuels

The world's oil is unequally distributed, and countries that have it try hard to keep the price high. This is a problem for countries buying oil, such as Brazil, inspiring them to create fuel from plants. Alcohol can be made by fermenting many plants and used on its own or added to petrol to make it go further. The problem is that although oil costs a lot, producing alternative fuels often costs even more. Because of this cost, countries normally depend on their own government for financial help.

Claude Monet

Claude Monet, a 19th-century impressionist painter (1840-1926), was inspired by the power of steam. His *Gare de St. Lazare* shows life in a major Paris station. It was one of a series of paintings showing the scene at different times of the day.

Future wheels

The bicycle is one of the most efficient means of transport ever invented. The Lotus racing bike (right), used by Chris Boardman to win an Olympic gold medal in Barcelona, has a frame made of reinforced carbon fibre. Wind-tunnel testing proved its speed.

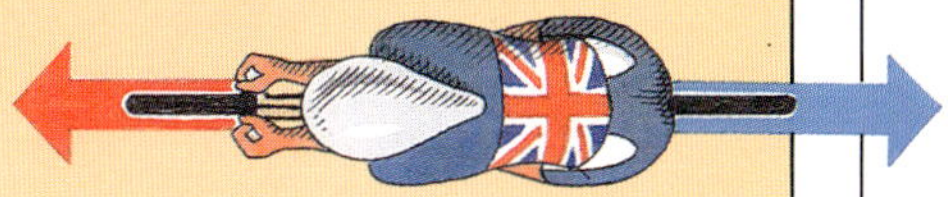

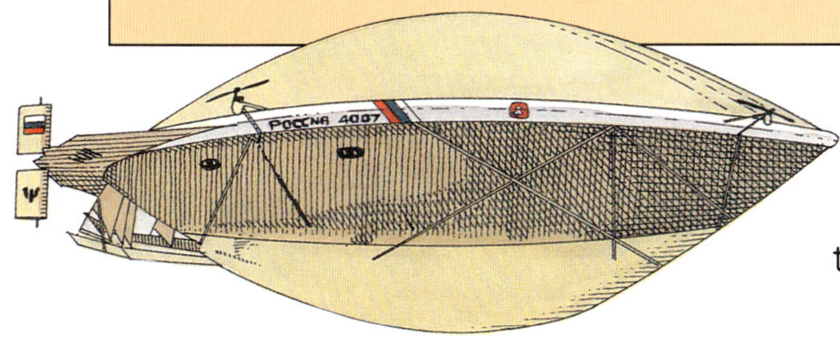

The era of the great airships ended in 1937 with the crash of the Hindenburg in New Jersey. Since then, attempts have been made to revive the airship (above) by using helium rather than inflammable hydrogen. The latest design is a Russian cargo carrier designed for use in remote areas.

In the future, more trains may run not on rails but on a magnetic cushion holding them above their tracks. The Japanese train MLU00X1 will reach 500 kph (300 mph). It rests on its wheels but as it moves, electromagnets on the side make currents in coils on the track. The magnetic fields repel each other and the train lifts.

Hybrid cars (above), combining both electrical and conventional engines, could cut pollution. They have a small engine that runs efficiently and will recharge the batteries which provide the main power. They have a much greater range than cars depending on batteries alone, but they are likely to be expensive. Traditional batteries are heavy and bulky, while smaller nickel-cadmium or sodium-sulphur batteries could cost thousands of pounds per vehicle.

Hansom cabs

Before cars, cities were crowded with horsedrawn vehicles. For 70 years, from the 1830s, the Hansom cab was London's most popular form of transport. The driver sat above the passengers and could talk to them through a trap-door in the roof.

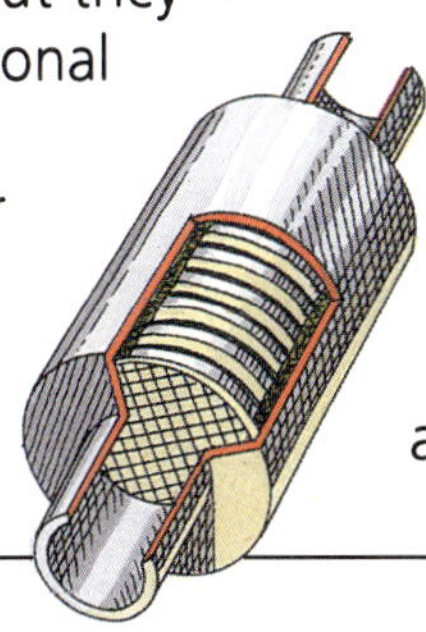

Catalytic converters (left) are part of the exhaust systems of modern cars to reduce pollution. They use catalysts – substances that make chemical reactions more quickly – to reduce the amounts of unburned petrol and carbon monoxide in the exhaust.

INDUSTRY

Industry would not exist without sources of energy. Heat is used to transform ores into metals, and machines need power to turn those metals into finished products. The first factories were built close to streams, getting their power from running water. After the invention of the steam engine, areas with plenty of coal attracted industry. Today, the availability of oil, gas and cheap electricity are all important factors in deciding where a company locates.

The Alaskan pipeline

When oil was found in Alaska, a pipeline was built to get it out. It crosses mountain ranges and rivers, over frozen ground. To keep the oil moving it is heated. For more than half its length, the pipeline is on supports with coolers. The supports contain ammonia. In warm weather, the ammonia vaporises, ensuring that the ground stays frozen around the supports.

Making steel uses huge amounts of energy. Iron ore is mixed with coke and smelted in a blast furnace (above). Hot air allows carbon in the coke to burn, at a high temperature. This reduces the ore to pig iron. To make steel (below), the carbon in pig iron is reduced by adding oxygen. The oxygen and carbon form carbon dioxide, leaving behind steel.

Modern industries, like radio, television, hi-fi, computers and electronics, use far less energy than the traditional industries such as coal and steel. Nevertheless, they all depend on electricity. This is the source of power that transformed life in the 20th century. Cable television has enabled news reports to be collected and sent all around the world.

The Industrial Revolution

During the Industrial Revolution, machines were created to do the work of people. Among the first was the spinning jenny, patented in 1770 by James Hargreaves, a carpenter and weaver. The jenny replaced the spinning wheel as a means of creating yarn from cotton. From 1790, such machines were driven by steam engines whose efficiency had been much improved by the inventions of James Watt. By 1812, the cost of making cotton yarn was one tenth of what it had been in 1780.

Water power

For nations which are short of energy, water can still provide the best option. By building dams to create reservoirs and using the water to generate electricity, they get power without pollution. One fifth of the world's electricity is generated by such hydro-electric plants. The Itaipú dam in Brazil is the world's most powerful dam.

The chemical industry (right) turns raw materials – crude oil, sulphuric acid and silica, for example – into a vast number of products ranging from explosives to fertilisers and plastics to glass.

Coalbrookdale

After the world's first iron bridge was built in Coalbrookdale, Shropshire, England (below), artists came to record the drama of the smoke rising and the steam engines at work there.

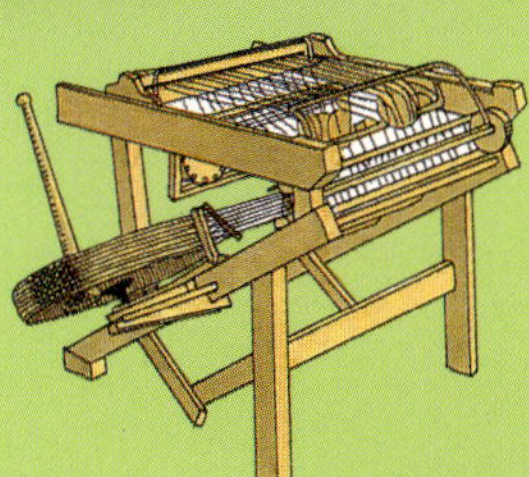

The spinning jenny was invented in the 1760s.

The Watt steam engine was invented in 1812.

Cleaning up

Both coal and oil usually contain small amounts of sulphur. When they burn, this becomes sulphur dioxide, which mixes with air and produces acid rain. This damages buildings and stunts the growth of plants. To meet new laws, power plants must burn low-sulphur fuels, or fit enormous scrubbers to remove sulphur dioxide from the gases before they leave the chimney.

a Japanese power plant

ENERGY IN THE HOME

We use energy in the home for heating, lighting, cooking, cleaning, listening to music, watching TV, shaving and making telephone calls. There is hardly a single thing we do that doesn't depend on energy being instantly available. Yet until a century ago – and even today in many parts of the world – none of these devices existed. People got up with the Sun, and went to bed when it set.

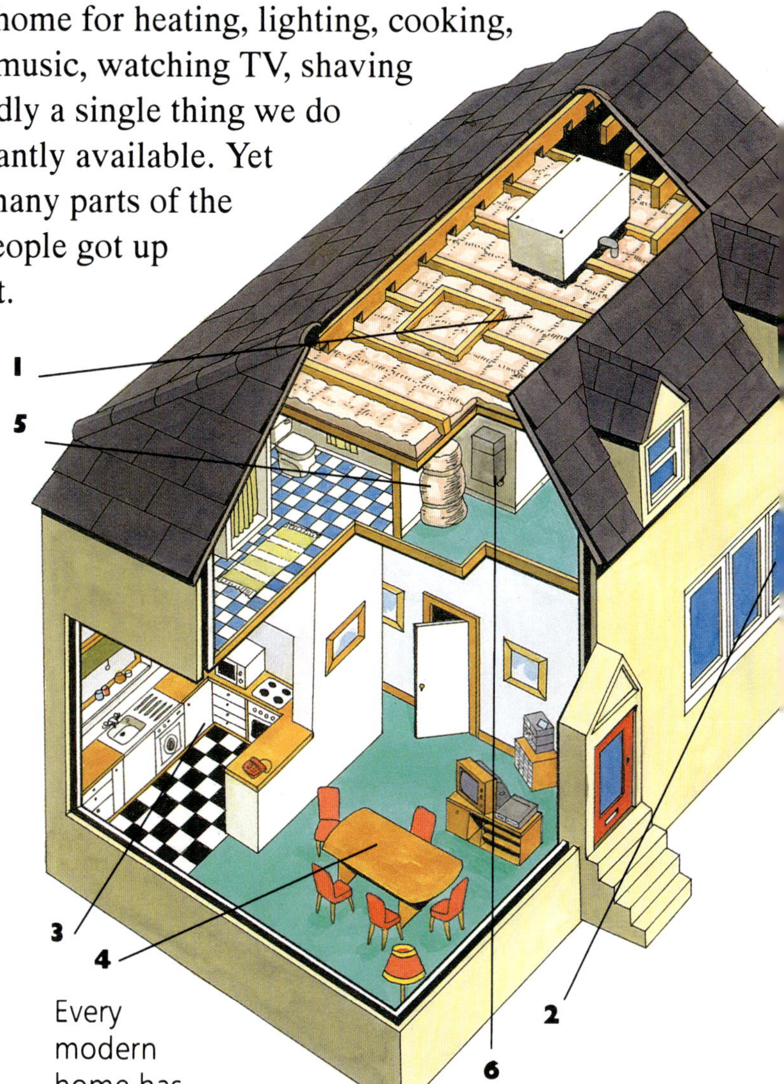

Every modern home has devices that use different energy sources. Because energy has always been available, most are not as efficient as they could be. The key (facing page) shows places in the house above that have been improved to save energy.

Early home-help

The first vacuum cleaner was the idea of engineer Hubert Booth in 1901, after watching cleaners at a railway station using air to blow dust and dirt out of a train. He thought that sucking dirt into a bag would be better than blowing it out. W.H. Hoover, a harness-maker from Canton, Ohio, sold his first vacuum cleaner in 1908, and soon cleaned up. The Hoover was designed by J. Murray Spangler, but it is Hoover's name which is now famous.

Microwave power

Microwave ovens first appeared in 1945. They were developed after research into radar at Birmingham University, England, produced powerful radio-frequency waves. It was soon clear that these waves could be used in cooking. The waves spread throughout the oven, penetrate into the centre of the food and create intense heat and the food cooks quickly.

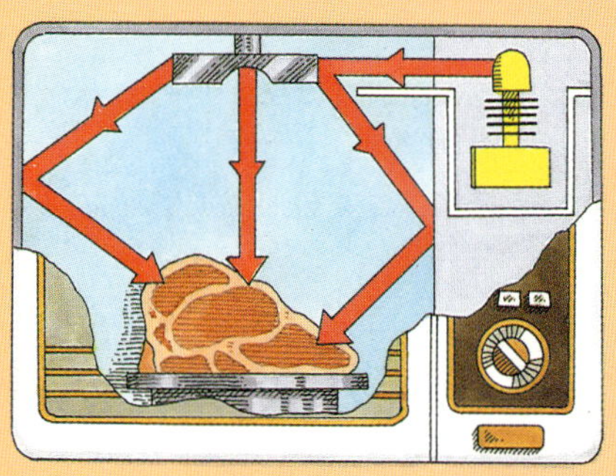

Power needs

Some devices use lots of power, while others need little. One kilowatt-hour of electricity will only cook the lunch in an electric oven for about 20 minutes, but it will power a 100 watt bulb for ten hours, run a TV for three hours and keep time for three months using an electric clock.

Key
1. Lagged loft
2. Double glazing
3. Microwave and other efficient power uses
4. Food management
5. Lagged hot water tank
6. System saving water

A century ago, some families would have used gas to light their home, though most were still using candles and oil lamps. To cook, they used a cast-iron range, though gas cookers were beginning to appear. Electricity was still a great novelty. For amusement people read or played card games or musical instruments – activities that need no outside source of power. Today, many families in developing countries have electricity for lighting and television.

In hot climates, homes may be more comfortable if they are cooled. In the Western world, some homes have air conditioning, but in developing countries shade is used to keep cool. In other hot climates, houses are built in light colours to reflect the Sun's rays.

Office blocks depend entirely on technology to make them habitable. Large areas of glass would make them too hot without air conditioning. Better-designed blocks can be more efficient in energy.

Deforestation

In the world's poorest countries, people are forced to move into the forests and use the land to plant their crops. However, this has become increasingly difficult as the forests are fast disappearing. Over the last twenty years, people have realised the great damage that has been done by industries that clear forests for timber and burn the ground in order to develop it. This is called "slash and burn".

SAVING ENERGY

In the 1970s, the oil-producing nations twice put up the price of oil. Though it has since declined, the shock made many nations think carefully about saving energy. More efficiency, less waste and greater efforts to recycle materials are the results. Homes, offices and factories now use less energy, while the fuel consumption of cars has improved. More could be done, but the high cost of saving energy is often seen as a disadvantage.

Industry has always recycled valuable materials; a quarter of every new car is made of metal from old cars. Paper can also be used again, once it has been bleached to remove ink. Recycled paper is never as clean and crisp as new paper, so it can't be used for high-value products. Often, it may simply be cheaper to plant more trees and use them as raw material.

BMW have produced a totally recyclable car, in which every item can be dismantled and re-used.

Insulation

A simple experiment shows the value of insulation in saving energy. Use two identical mugs and wrap an old scarf around one. Fill both with hot water at the same temperature. Take the temperature of each at regular intervals and plot them on graph paper. Also try a thermos flask. Why is that so much better?

Pedal power

Bicycles are the most energy-efficient form of transport in towns. They don't burn fuel and are quicker in heavy traffic. The police in Seattle, USA, use bicycles instead of cars. The biggest drawback is the danger from other vehicles.

Scientific research has shown that the lead in car exhaust fumes is dangerous to the body, even in small quantities. Lead-free petrol was introduced to reduce pollution but it doesn't save energy because it burns less smoothly than leaded petrol.

a bottle recycling plant

Brighter bulbs

Compact fluorescent light bulbs use about a fifth as much energy to produce the same light output as normal light bulbs. They also last longer but cost more. This means they are most effective in lights that stay on for many hours. However, they do not produce heat, so more energy may be used in heating your home.

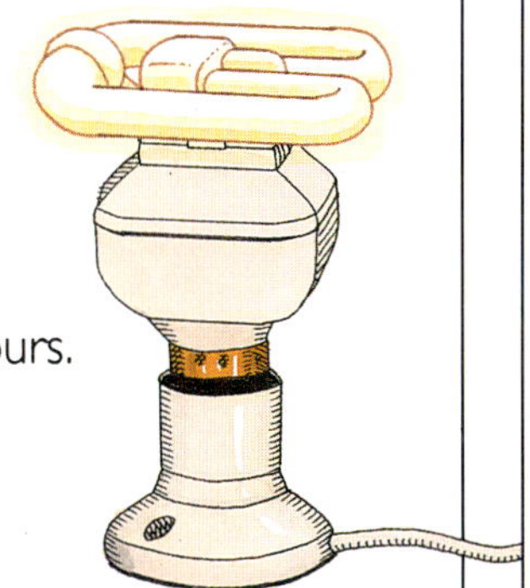

Recycling of domestic waste makes sense, but not if it involves driving many kilometres to put a few bottles in a bottle-bank. That would use far more energy in petrol than could ever be saved by recycling glass. Separating waste into different rubbish bins at home sounds more sensible. But often the prices paid for waste materials are too low to cover the costs.

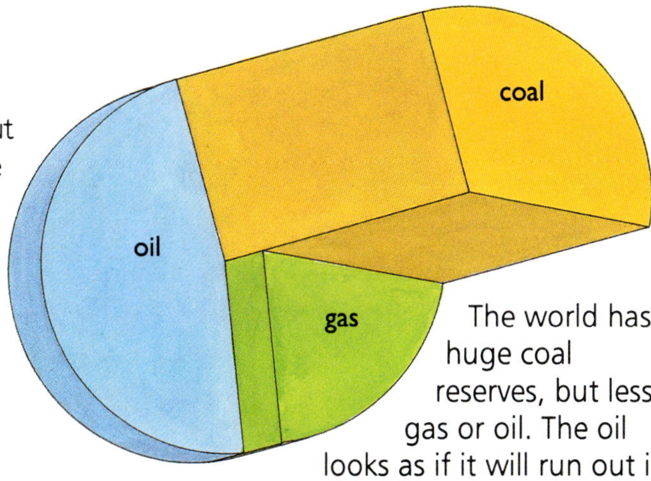

The world has huge coal reserves, but less gas or oil. The oil looks as if it will run out in only 20 years. This is misleading: oil companies do not explore for new oil if they have enough to be going on with.

Nuclear fuel that has already been used once can be reprocessed to extract plutonium and unused uranium. This process takes place in a reprocessing plant (above) where the used fuel is dissolved in nitric acid and waste products are chemically removed.

The solar printing press

The French engineer Abel Pifre showed this invention in Paris in 1882. Sunlight was shone on to a mirror and focused onto a steam boiler. The steam produced powered an engine which in turn worked the press.

THE DESTINY OF ENERGY

One day the Sun will run out of nuclear fuel and simply fizzle out, along with life on Earth. But that time is at least five billion years away. Long before then we shall have run out of fossil fuels, which we are now using far more rapidly than they were created. New energy resources will then be needed to keep civilisation going, and fortunately there are possibilities both here on Earth and up in space.

Ice caps

Our activities on Earth may be changing the climate. Gases such as methane in the atmosphere act like the glass in a greenhouse, allowing light in but preventing heat from escaping. These gases added by humans might increase temperatures by several degrees over the next century, melting the polar ice caps.

Building a solar station in space would be by far the biggest space construction project ever attempted. Because Earth's gravity is so strong, lifting thousands of tonnes of material into space would be very costly. So mining the Moon or Mars could be a better idea. It may even make sense to place the power station on the Moon.

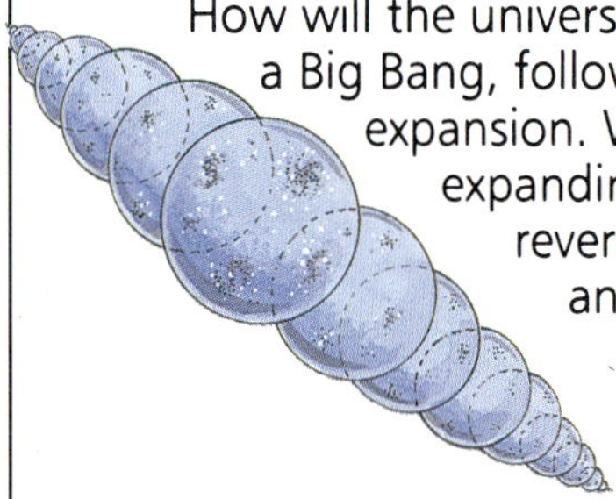

How will the universe end? It began with a Big Bang, followed by a rapid expansion. Will it go on expanding forever, or go into reverse, start shrinking, and eventually end in a Big Crunch? It all depends on how much mass there is in the universe.

Chemicals put into the atmosphere expose us to more ultraviolet radiation from the Sun, by damaging the protective layer of ozone (right) high in the stratosphere. These chemicals are being stopped, but it will be 2050 before the ozone recovers.

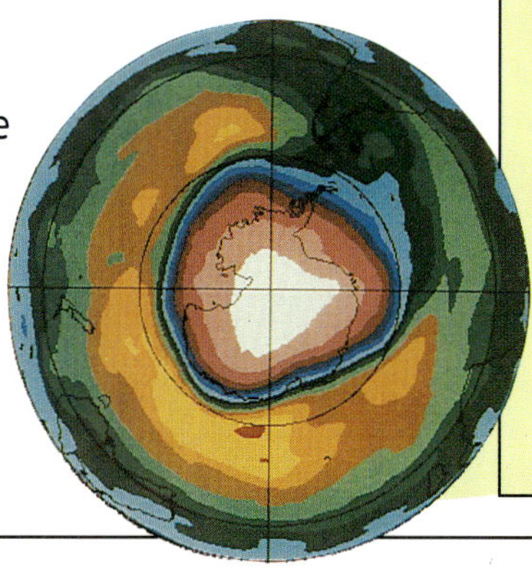

Ocean heat

Water deep in the ocean is much cooler than it is at the surface. Ocean thermal energy conversion (OTEC) plants make use of this difference. Warm water from the surface is used to boil a liquid, which drives a turbine and generates electricity. Then cold water from deep down is used to condense the vapour back to liquid, in a closed cycle. The system uses solar heat, but is not dependent on daylight, as the ocean acts as a store.

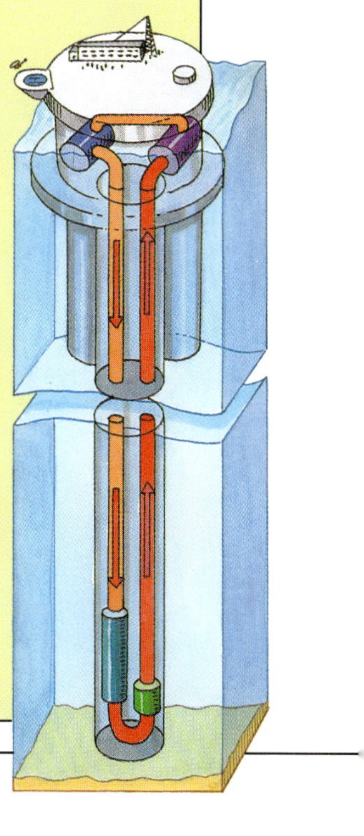

A better way of tapping solar energy might be in space, above the atmosphere. A solar satellite would consist of an array of solar cells, assembled in space, in orbit 37,000 km up. The power generated by the cells would be converted into microwaves and directed to Earth, to be converted back to electricity.

Futuristic energy

A lot of interesting thinking about future worlds is done by science fiction writers such as H.G. Wells, Aldous Huxley, or Arthur C. Clarke, author of *2001: A Space Odyssey*. It was Clarke who first thought of the geostationary communications satellite in 1945, long before the first real satellite went into orbit. His latest book imagines life on Mars.

Energy consumption varies enormously around the world, with the developed countries using far more than the developing countries. As a result, the known reserves in each part of the world vary greatly. This store is measured below. The former Soviet Union has the biggest reserves of coal and natural gas and the Middle East has the biggest reserves of oil.

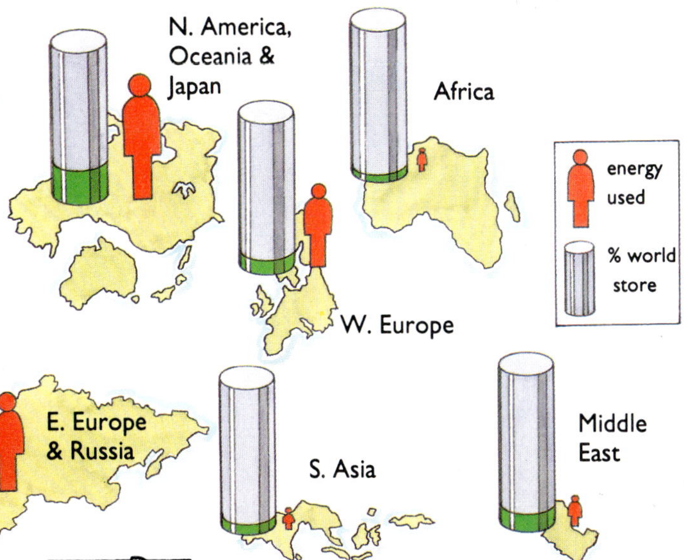

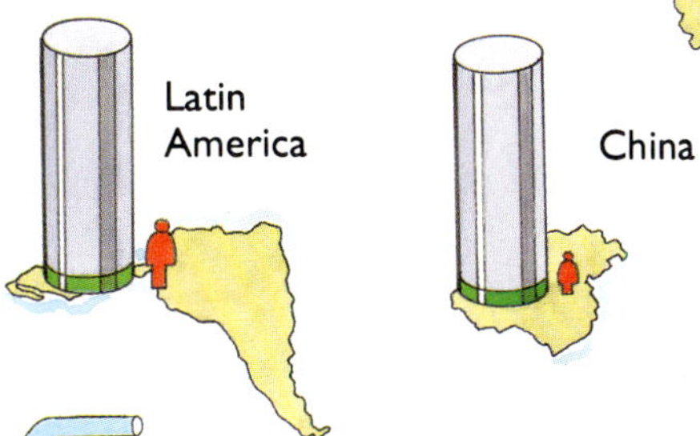

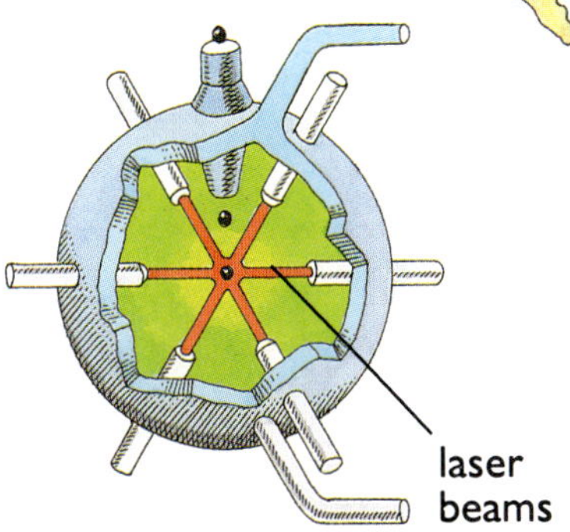

Nuclear fusion can be started with heat from high-power lasers. The lasers are focused on a minute fuel pellet, which is dropped into the reactor so that it does not touch the walls.

Fusion

In the future it may be possible to control nuclear fusion reactions, produced by combining two forms of hydrogen at very high temperatures. Scientists have created nuclear fusion in a tubular reactor. This is called a Tokamak. The most successful experiment of this has been in Princeton in the United States.

CHAPTER 5

ELECTRICITY & MAGNETISM

Electricity and magnetism have existed since the beginning of time. They exist in many forms in the natural world around us - the Earth is like a huge magnet and our bodies are full of tiny electrical signals. Over the last hundred years, we have discovered how to harness the powerful energy of electricity, together with the force of magnetism, transforming the world we live in.

Today communication, transport, industry and leisure rely on the power generated by electricity and magnetism. This chapter explores the scientific principles of electricity and magnetism. It aims to provide a complete picture of how we make, send and store electricity, and how it is used, with magnetism, in our lives.

CONTENTS

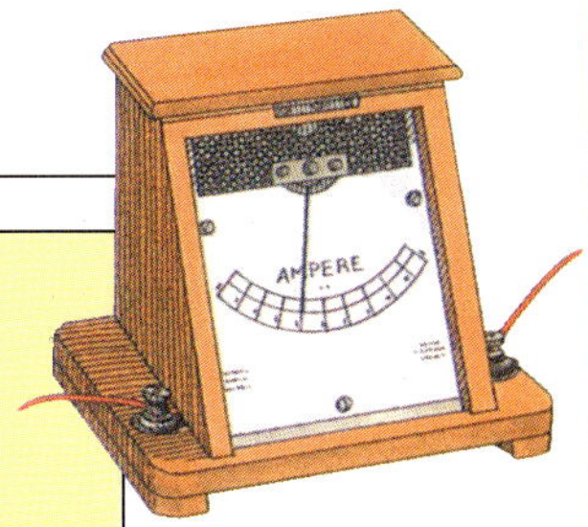

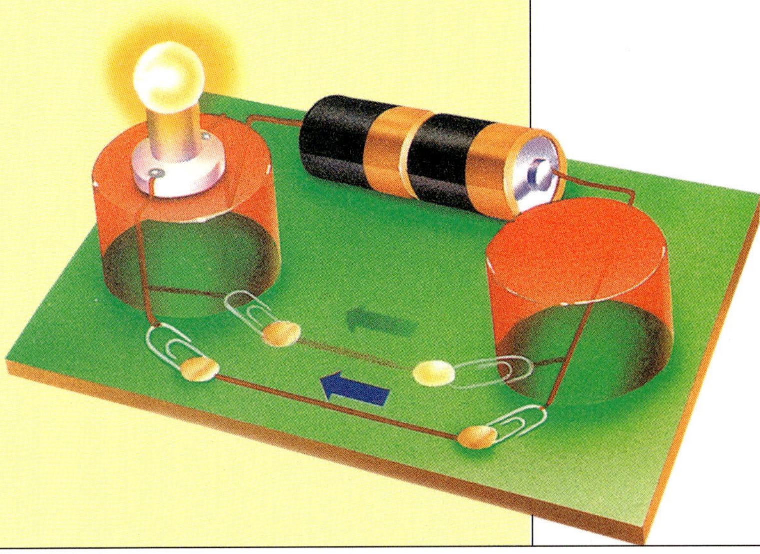

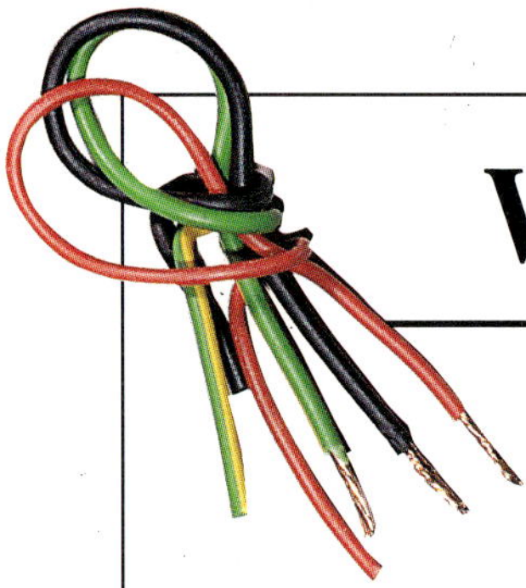

WHAT IS ELECTRICITY?

Electricity is an invisible form of energy which is stored in electrons and protons. These are the tiny particles in atoms (below) which make up all matter. Electricity is created when there is an imbalance of negatively charged electrons and positively charged protons. Current electricity is made up of moving electrons which travel through wires. In static electricity the electrons remain still. Electricity is a powerful and useful source of energy, but it can also be very dangerous.

Discovering electricity
Electricity was first discovered by the ancient Greeks, about 2,000 years ago. A Greek scientist called Thales noticed that a piece of amber (the hard fossilised sap from trees) attracted straw or feathers when he rubbed it with a cloth. The word "electricity" comes from the Greek word for amber – "elektron".

In 1600, William Gilbert (left), a doctor to Queen Elizabeth I of England, was the first person to use the word "electric". He carried out experiments and discovered that materials such as diamond, glass and wax behaved in a similar way to amber.

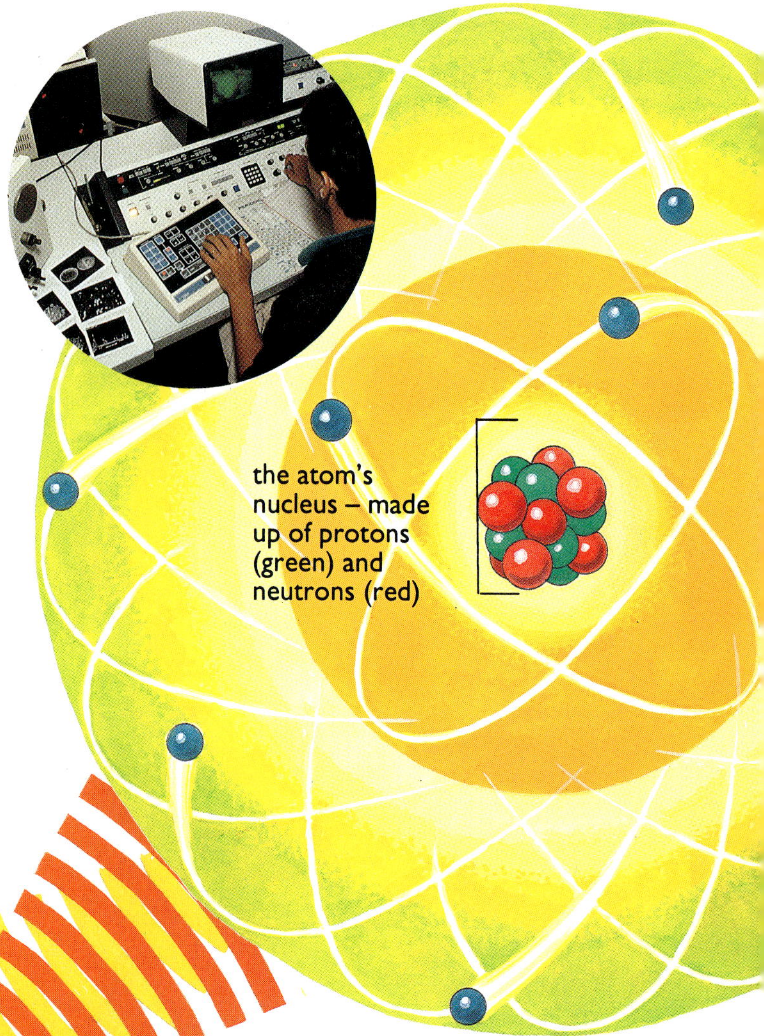

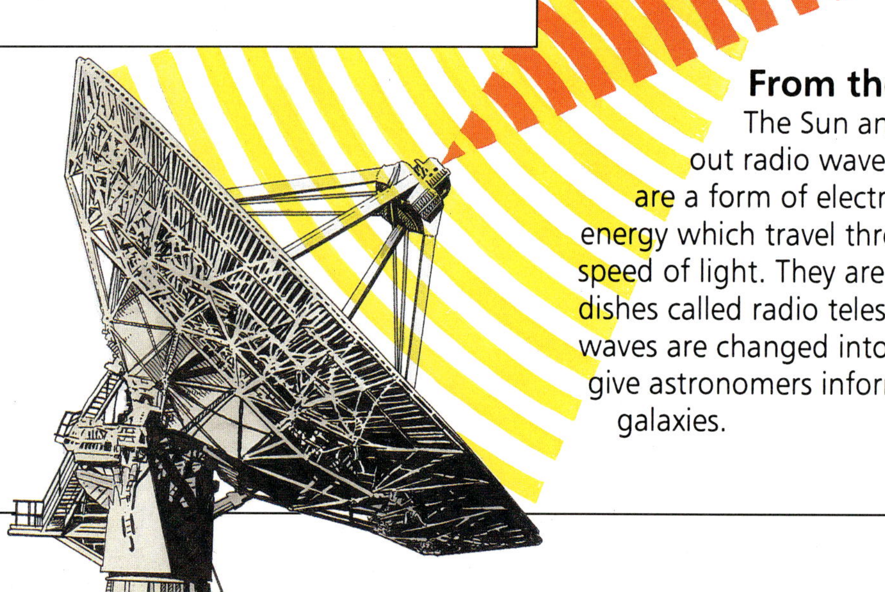

From the stars
The Sun and other stars send out radio waves through space. They are a form of electrical and magnetic energy which travel through space at the speed of light. They are picked up by huge dishes called radio telescopes. The radio waves are changed into electrical signals that give astronomers information about distant galaxies.

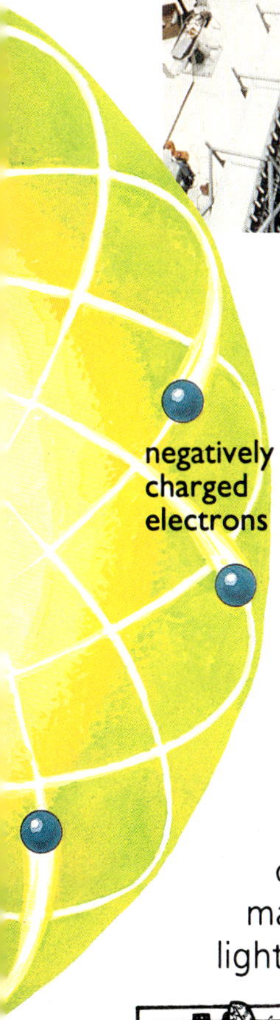

Electrons everywhere

A particle accelerator (above) is used for research into atoms. By smashing atoms together, scientists have discovered over 200 particles, even smaller than atoms. A beam of electrons in an electron microscope (above left) enlarges objects millions of times.

Switch on the light

In fluorescent lights, an electric current makes gas glow. Neon gas makes red light, sodium gas yellow light, and mercury gas makes blue light.

Investigating static electricity

Static electricity, used inside photocopiers and paint-spraying machines, can be generated by rubbing different materials together.

You can test materials for static charges, which are either positive or negative. Opposite charges attract things and like charges repel things. Experiment by rubbing different materials such as paper, plastic, metal, wood and rubber with a cloth. Do they attract or repel things? Make a chart of your results.

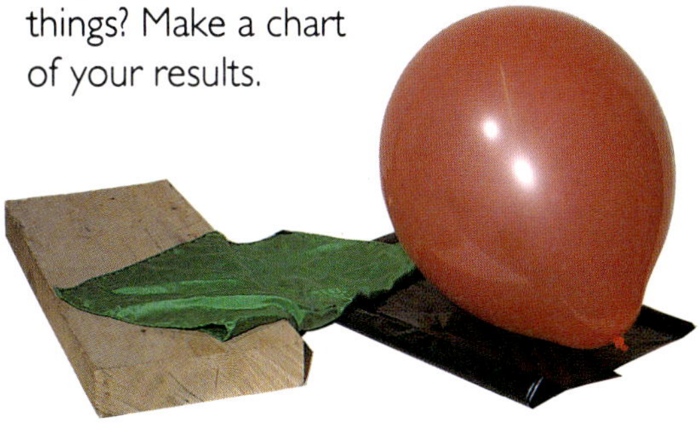

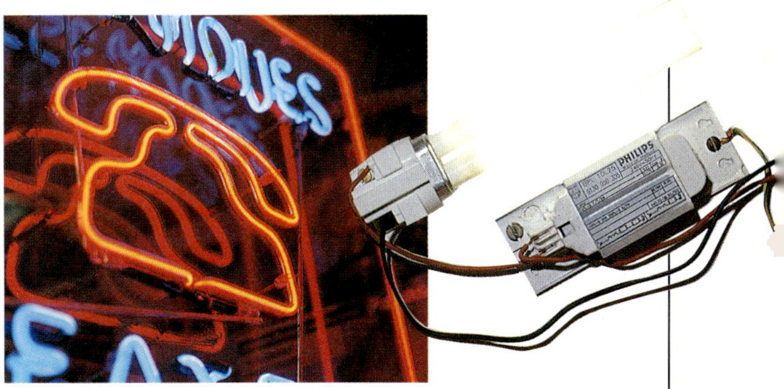

Electricity for life

Most animals rely on electrical signals which provide them with information about their environment and control the way their body works. A network of nerve cells collects the information and sends out instructions. Invertebrates such as an octopus (right) have simple nerve nets.

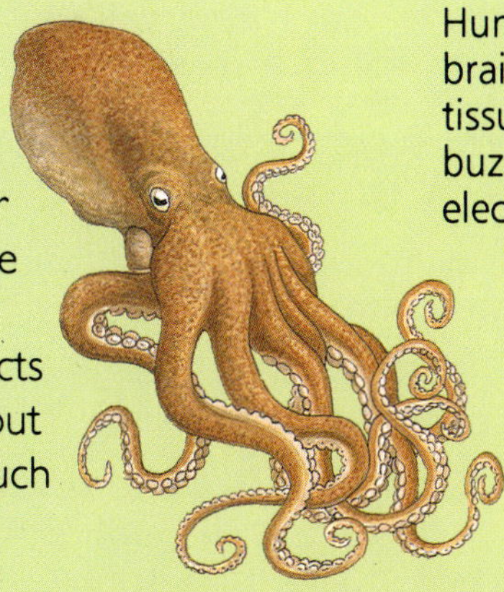

Humans have more complex systems. The brain has an intricate network of nervous tissue (below). Our brain buzzes with tiny electrical signals, which trigger our heart-beats, to make our muscles move and sustain our body processes.

WHAT IS MAGNETISM?

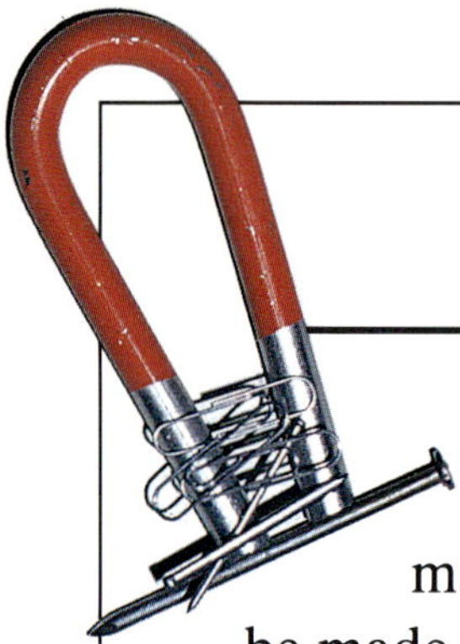

Magnetism is an invisible natural force given off by some pieces of metal or stone which have the power to attract or repel certain materials. Magnets occur naturally in rocks in the ground, but they can also be made from substances such as iron or nickel. Magnets attract iron, nickel, cobalt and most types of steel, but do not attract copper, aluminium, brass, gold, silver or lead. Some magnets are "permanent" magnets, because they only lose their magnetic power if they are dropped or become too hot. Every day we use magnets in televisions, computers and telephones. Huge magnets help to generate electricity in power stations.

Discovering magnets

About 2,000 years ago, near Magnesia, in modern-day Turkey, from where magnets take their name, people discovered rocks in the ground which were natural magnets. About 1,000 years ago, the Chinese noticed that certain rocks always pointed north and south when they were hung from a thread. They used these magnetic rocks as simple compasses to help them find their way around the oceans. The rocks were called "leading stones", or lodestones, because they led sailors along the right route.

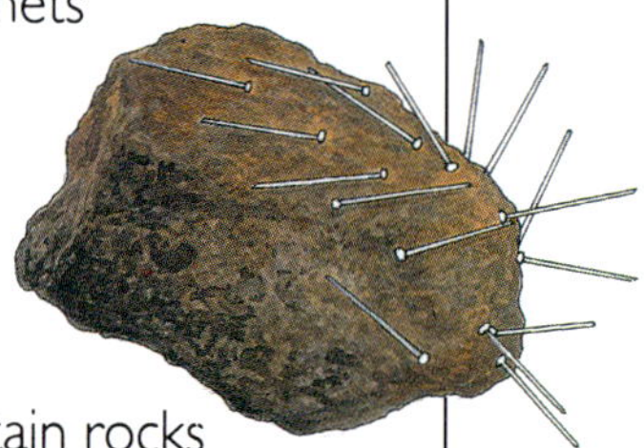

Working together

Some materials can be made to act like magnets when an electric current is passed through them. These are electromagnets. Electricity flowing through a coil of wire, wrapped around a metal core, produces a magnetic field. Electromagnets are not permanent magnets; when the flow of electricity is switched off, the magnetic field disappears. Electromagnets on cranes (right) pick up heavy scrap iron. When the electricity is switched off, the iron falls off.

The magnetic poles

The Earth is like a giant magnet with a magnetic north pole and a magnetic south pole. The Earth's magnetic field is strongest at these poles, which are in a different position from the Earth's geographic poles. The magnetic north pole (near Ellef Ringes Island in northern Canada) was first discovered by James Clark Ross (left) in 1831. The magnetic south pole was discovered off the coast of Wilkes Land in Antarctica in 1909, after one of the most outstanding sledge journeys of all time. Members of Ernest Shackleton's (right) first expedition to Antarctica, David, Mawson and Mackay, survived 122 days with rations for only 93 days. The expedition covered 2,028 km (1,214 miles) of unexplored territory on foot, pulling their sledges behind them.

Magnetic forces

Magnets are surrounded by an invisible force – a magnetic field – which attracts things within its field. Sprinkle iron filings around a magnet. More filings cluster together where the field is strongest, at the magnetic poles (far left). Like poles repel; unlike poles attract (left). Magnets only attract each other if their opposite poles are close.

Magnetic information

Today magnets are used in increasingly sophisticated ways. They can now "store" large amounts of information. Computer discs hold information as magnetic patterns. A magnetic strip on a credit card identifies the holder of the card. Smart cards have this strip but they contain microchips as well, so they can be used as bus tickets, or to pay bills over the telephone, and they can even "hold" people's medical records.

Seeing inside the body

Doctors use a technique called magnetic resonance imaging (MRI) to give them detailed 3D images of structures inside the body. The image is created by a computer from the effects of a huge magnet and radio signals on atoms in the patient's body. These images can be used to diagnose cancer, injuries and some diseases. Unlike X-rays, the patient is not exposed to harmful radiation. The technique also allows doctors to identify problems without having to operate.

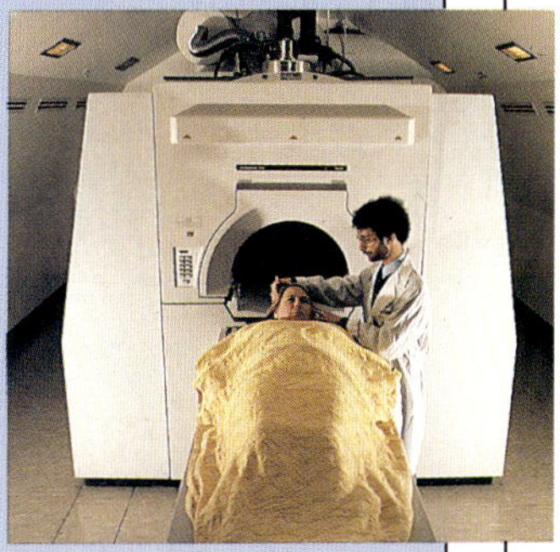

PLANET EARTH

There are many natural sources of electricity and magnetism on Earth which have existed since the beginning of time. In Greek mythology, lightning, which is a form of static electricity, was used by gods such as Zeus (above) to impose his authority over mortals. A magnetic field called the magnetosphere, surrounds the Earth, stretching over 60,000 kilometres (36,000 miles) into space. The Earth's magnetic poles move a few centimetres each year – over millions of years. Their positions have even reversed direction!

Finding your way

A compass needle is a tiny magnet, which always points to the Earth's magnetic poles. A map does not tell you which direction you are travelling in, but with the aid of a compass, you can find your way. To use a compass with a map, place the compass on top of the map. Turn the map around until the north arrow on the map points in the same direction as the compass needle.

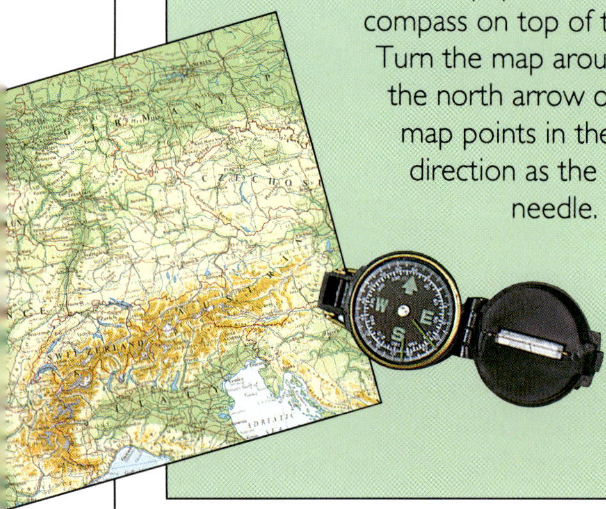

Magnetic Earth

Scientists believe that Earth's magnetic field is produced by the molten iron core at the centre of the Earth. This metal core has melted because of the very high temperatures there. As the Earth rotates (below), electric currents are created in the core. This produces the magnetic field. Scientists believe this works in a way similar to producing electricity in a power station (see pages 130-131).

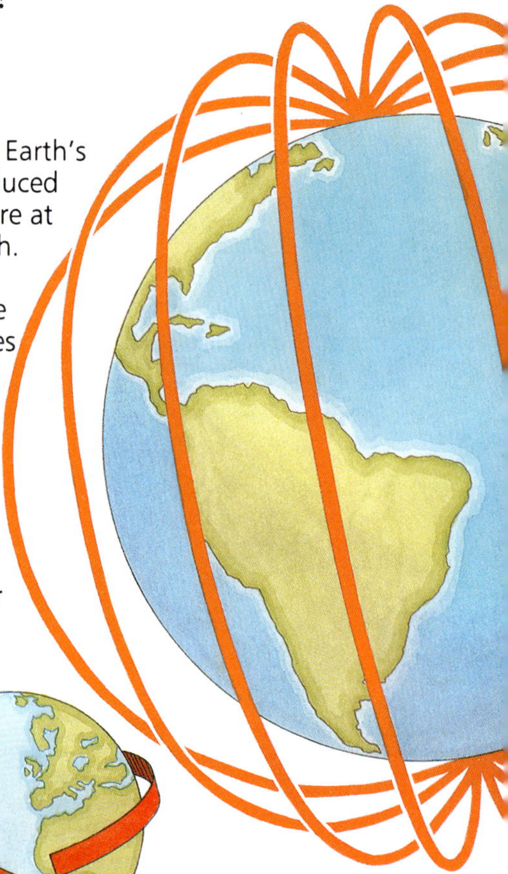

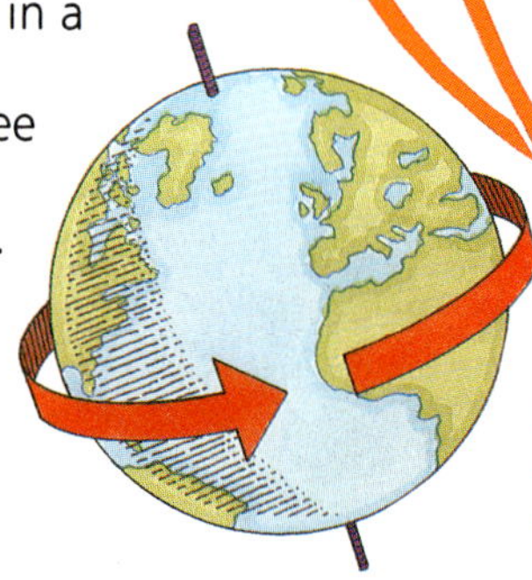

lines of force which make up the Earth's magnetic field

Clues to the past

Over millions of years, hot liquid rock rising and sinking beneath the Earth's continents has caused them to drift about the Earth's surface. This liquid rock has broken through the surface along ridges in the middle of the ocean floor. As the liquid cools down, magnetic material in the rock lines up with the Earth's magnetic field. The rocks have set in opposite directions, providing evidence that over time the Earth's magnetic field has changed direction (right).

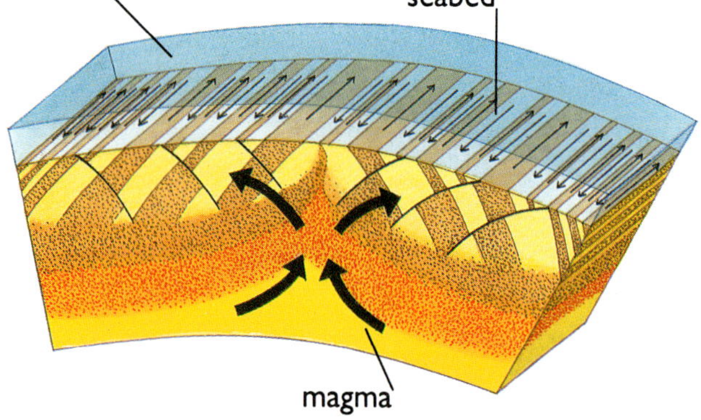

Electric fish

About 500 species of fish produce an electric field from special muscles with columns of wafer-like cells, which are a bit like tiny living batteries (see pages 134-135). Species such as the elephant nose fish give off almost continuous electric charges to help them navigate and communicate. Electric eels, rays (left) and catfish have large electric organs which can give off powerful bursts of electricity, enough to stun a person or kill a small fish. Sharks (right) pick up electrical signals from the muscles of fish. They can home in on their prey with deadly accuracy.

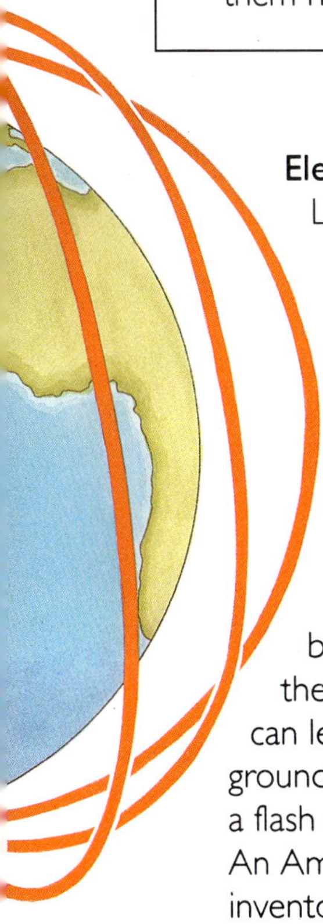

Electricity in the sky

Lightning is a huge spark of static electricity. It builds up inside storm clouds when small drops of water and ice rub against each other. Storm clouds build up either positive or negative charges as their particles are rubbed in different ways. When negative and positive clouds get near each other, giant sparks jump between them. These can leap to the ground, producing a flash of lightning. An American inventor called Benjamin Franklin (1706-1790, right) showed that a bolt of lightning was really a spark of electricity. In 1752, he flew a kite during a storm. Lightning flowed down the kite string, making a small spark on a metal key at the bottom of the string. This dangerous experiment led to the invention of lightning conductors – metal strips running from the top of a building to the ground. If lightning strikes the building, they carry the electricity safely to the ground. The top of a conductor (left) can be bent by the lightning's heat.

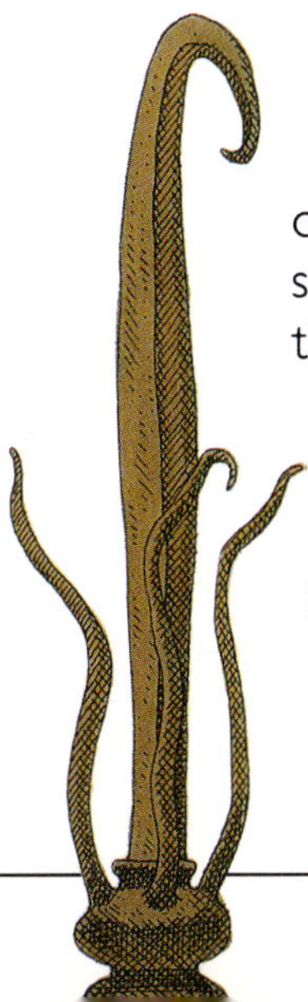

Animal migration

Many animals make long migratory journeys to find food or to avoid bad weather. They can sense the Earth's magnetic field which helps keep them on the right course. In Australia, compass termites protect their nests from the Sun's heat by building them facing north to south.

Force fields in space

Other planets in our solar system also have magnetic fields. Space probes sent out from planet Earth have discovered magnetic fields around the planets of Mercury, Jupiter, Saturn and Uranus.

The magnetic fields around Jupiter (left) are about 4,000 times greater than those around the Earth. These huge magnetic fields trap clouds of particles.

ON THE MOVE

Electricity is very useful to us because it can flow along wires to where it is needed, like water flowing along a pipe. This controlled flow of electric charge is called an electric current. A current can only flow if it is pushed along by a battery or by the force from a power station. The force which pushes electricity through wires is the voltage. The current is itself made up of billions of electrons. An electric current has to travel in an unbroken line, called a circuit. Different materials allow the flow of electric current through at different rates. This is called electrical resistance.

Giving their names

Electricity is measured in units which are named after the scientists who carried out experiments on electricity. Electric current is measured with an ammeter (left) in units called amperes or amps. The French physicist André Marie Ampère (1775-1836) was the first person to work out the mathematical values of electric currents.

An Italian physicist, Count Alessandro Volta (1775-1827), invented the first battery (page 134), the "voltaic pile" (right). This consisted of a pile of zinc and silver, or copper discs separated by pads moistened with a weak acid solution. The volt, a unit of electrical measurement, is named after him.

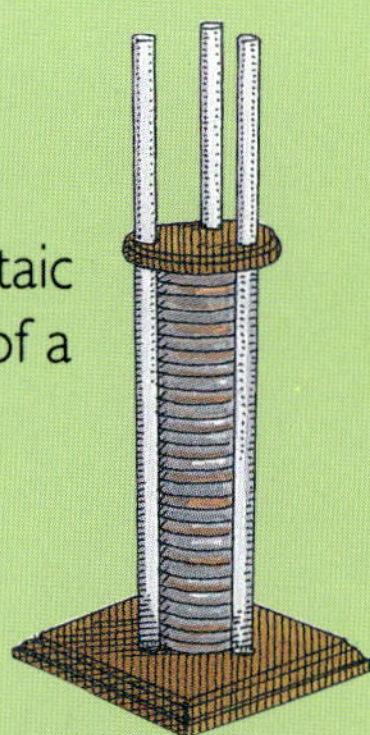

The Scottish engineer James Watt (1736-1819, right) gave his name to the watt, a unit of power. The German physicist George Ohm (1789-1854) worked out how to measure resistance – in units called ohms.

Dominoes

Individual electrons do not flow through a circuit from one end to the other. They pass on their electric charge by jumping across from one atom to another. In the same way, if you push a domino over, the one at the end of the row will eventually fall down. Each domino bumps into the next one until the whole line falls down.

Conductors and insulators

In some materials, such as metals, the electrons are free to move, allowing electricity to flow through them easily. These materials are called conductors. Other materials, such as most plastics, have electrons held tightly in their atoms, so they do not conduct electricity well. These are called insulators. Metal wires which conduct electricity are insulated with rubber or plastic to make them safe.

Build your own circuit

To make a simple circuit, join a wire to each side of a bulb holder. Screw in the bulb. Join one wire to the negative terminal of a battery and the other to the positive terminal. When the circuit is complete, the bulb will light up. Make a gap in the circuit to act as a switch (right). Push two paper fasteners through a card. Insert a steel paper clip under one fastener so it can slide over to touch the other. The paper clip acts as the switch. This is an open circuit.

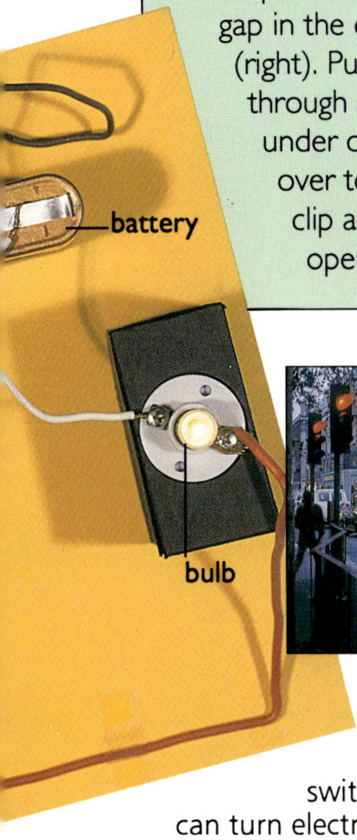

Measuring electricity

Electric current is measured in amps. One amp is 6 million million million electrons flowing past a point in a wire every second. The electric push of a current is measured in volts. The power of electricity depends on how much current is flowing and how hard it is being pushed. The faster and harder the push, the greater the power, measured in watts. This is calculated by multiplying volts by amps. Dividing the push by current gives ohms, the resistance of a circuit – how easy or hard it is for the current to flow through it.

Stopping at the lights

A gap in the circuit prevents the flow of electric current. A switch makes a gap in a circuit so we can turn electricity on or off to control the flow or current. This process is like the action of traffic lights. When the lights are green, the traffic flows. When they turn red, the traffic stops.

Holding back the flow

The flow of electric current through a wire depends on the wire's material, length and thickness. Electric charges flow more freely through thick wires than thin ones. A thin wire (above right) has high resistance, reducing the current's flow. A thick wire (below right) has lower resistance. It increases the flow. It is a better conductor.

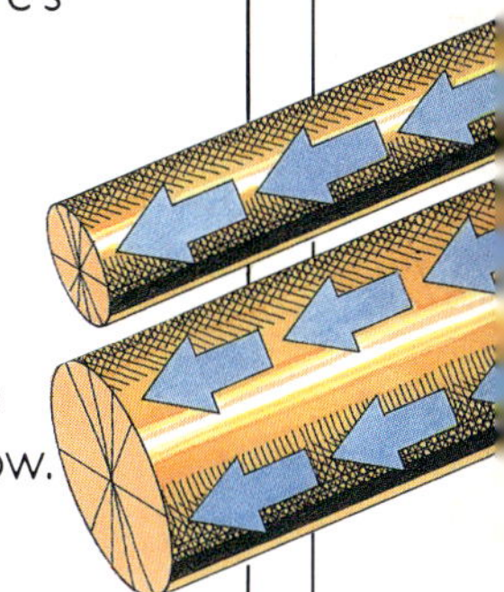

Resistance makes a light bulb work. (left). The wire filament inside the bulb is very thin. The electricity has to push hard to get through, making the filament so hot it glows white hot, giving out light. The wire is made of a metal (often tungsten) that can get very hot without melting.

A matter of death

Electricity can be dangerous. People often get electric shocks or even die, due to accidents with electricity. Take great care with mains electricity. Make sure you do not touch anything electrical with wet hands – water conducts electricity well and may give you a serious electric shock. Some countries still use the electric chair (right) to electrocute criminals.

Resistors are used in volume controls on televisions (right). When you turn up the volume, less wire is included in the circuit. More current flows around the shorter wire, making the sound of the television louder.

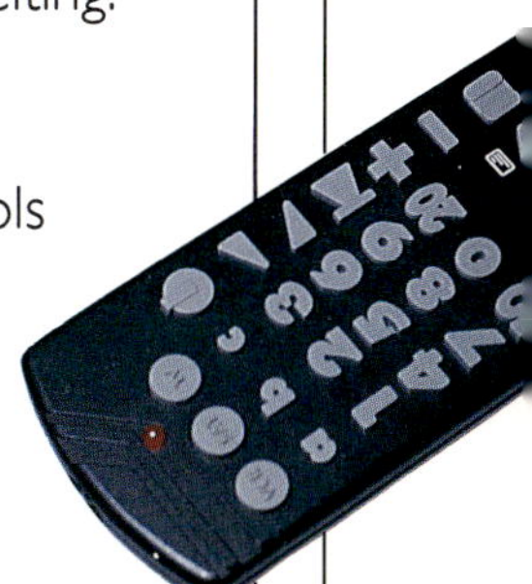

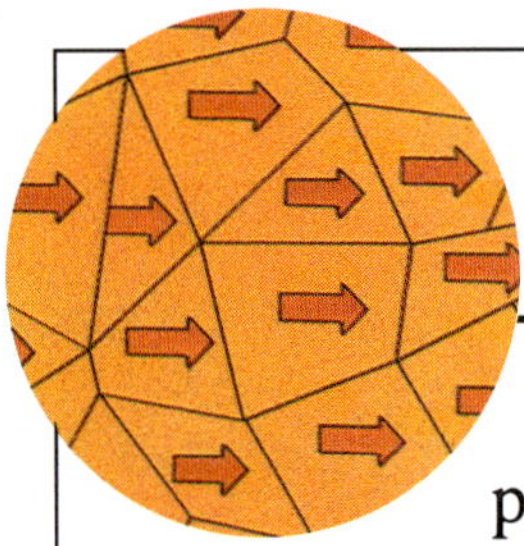

ELECTRICITY & MAGNETS

Electricity is used to make a magnetic field, and magnetism is used to produce electricity. In magnetic materials, the atoms are magnetic. These groups of atoms (domains) point in one direction (above). In non-magnetic materials, they point in different directions. Their magnetic fields cancel each other out. An electric current passing through non-magnetic materials makes the domains point in one direction, creating a magnetic field. The material is magnetic as long as the electrical current flows.

Making the connection
A Danish scientist, Hans Christian Oersted (1777-1857, left), first made the connection between electricity and magnetism. He discovered that a compass needle moved when electricity flowed through a nearby wire. The wire's electric current was producing magnetism, which made the compass needle move. Many everyday gadgets use magnetism which has been generated by electricity.

In 1831, an English scientist called Michael Faraday (1791-1867, below) thought, "If electricity can set up a magnetic field, a magnet should be able to make an electric current". He discovered that moving a magnet near a wire made electricity flow through the wire. He invented the dynamo, a machine which produces electricity from magnetism and movement. Many bicycles use a dynamo to power their lamps. The pedalling and turning of the wheels are used to turn a magnet within a coil of wire, producing an electric current.

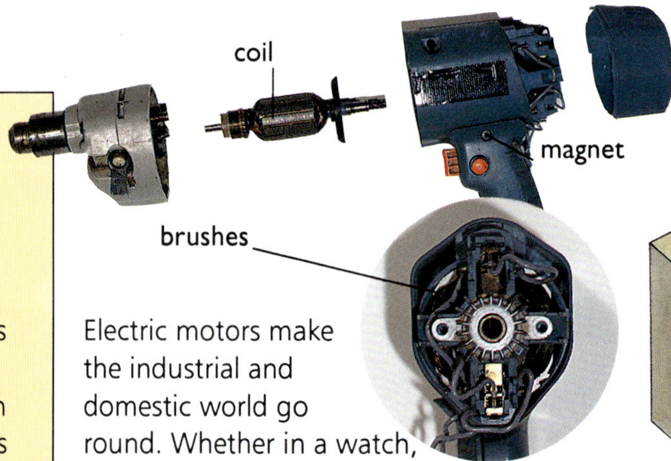

Electric motors make the industrial and domestic world go round. Whether in a watch, hairdryer, train or drill, the electric motor changes electrical energy into mechanical power. The diagram (right) explains how the different parts of a motor (above) work.

Electromagnets in medicine
If someone has a splinter in their eye which contains a magnetic material, surgeons can now use an electromagnet to remove it. This method is very safe because the powerful magnetic force pulls the splinter straight out from the eye. This micro-machine robot (right) is designed specifically to perform such delicate surgery on eyes.

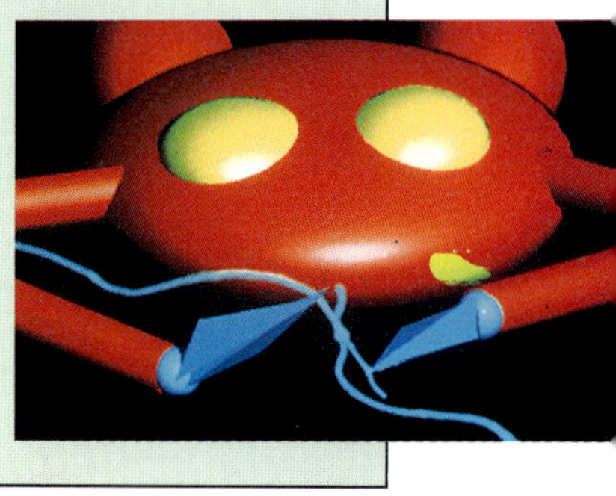

Separating metals

Electromagnets are used to sort metals in scrap yards or to separate steel cans from aluminium ones (right). When switched on, the electromagnet is a powerful magnet which picks up heavy magnetic materials. Most metals, including aluminium, are not magnetic. Once the scrap metal or cans have been sorted, they can be sent to a factory to be recycled.

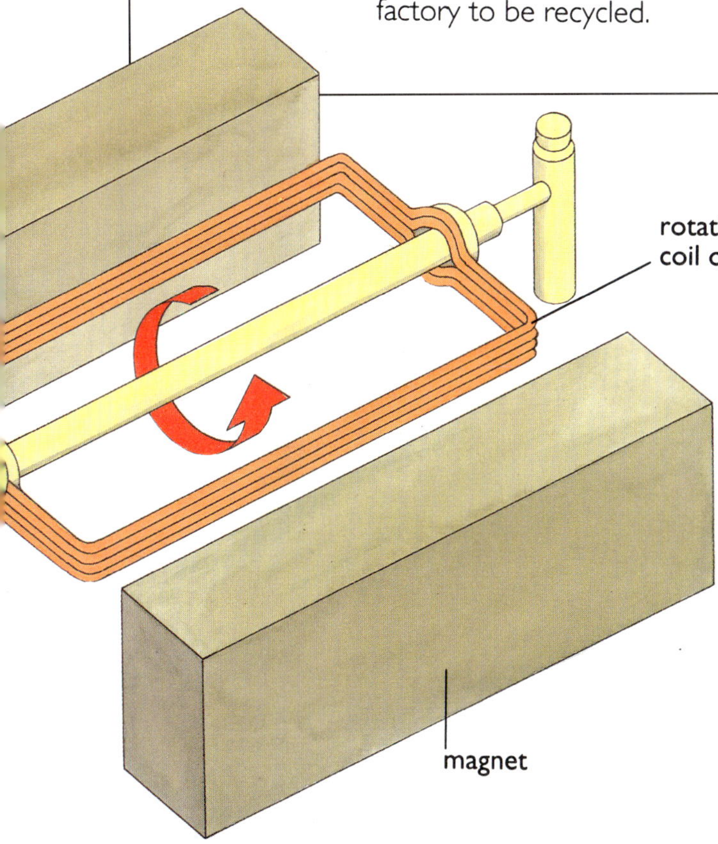

How it works

In an electric motor, a magnet is placed around a coil of wire to create an electromagnet (see page 122) which makes the coil move. A battery is connected to the coil. The current flows up one side of the coil and pushes the other side up. This movement is repeated so that the coil spins round between the magnets. Sliding contacts – brushes – touch the end of the spinning coil so the electric current can pass in and out of the spinning electromagnet.

First attempts

In the 1870s, the German company Siemens developed the first trains pulled by electric motors. A small-scale electric railway was demonstrated at the Berlin Trade Exhibition in 1879. The train picked up power from a rail laid down the middle of the track. Although electric trains did not catch on at the time, we now use them extensively, such as the tram (below).

Words and sayings

The words electricity and magnetism are often used in familiar sayings to convey different meanings and moods. For instance if you say "the atmosphere was electric" it means that it was an exciting, charged atmosphere, when anything could happen. "To electrify an audience" means to startle or excite, as if the people had been given an electric shock. If people are said to have "a magnetic personality", they ooze personal charm and attract people to them. Can you think of any other sayings like these?

MAKING ELECTRICITY

Most of the electricity we use today comes from power stations (left). A huge dynamo called a generator makes electricity from the energy of movement, produced by using coal, gas, or oil or by the energy from nuclear reactions, to boil water. Inside the generator, an electromagnet turns inside a coil of wire, producing electricity in the coil. The current flows first in one direction and then the other. This is called an alternating current, or A.C. for short. A direct current (D.C.) only flows in one direction.

The first generators

Electricity was only available on a large scale when efficient generators such as steam turbines were developed in the 1860s. At first, these were small units which generated electricity at places where it was needed. Big power stations which supplied electricity over wide areas were not built until the late 19th century.

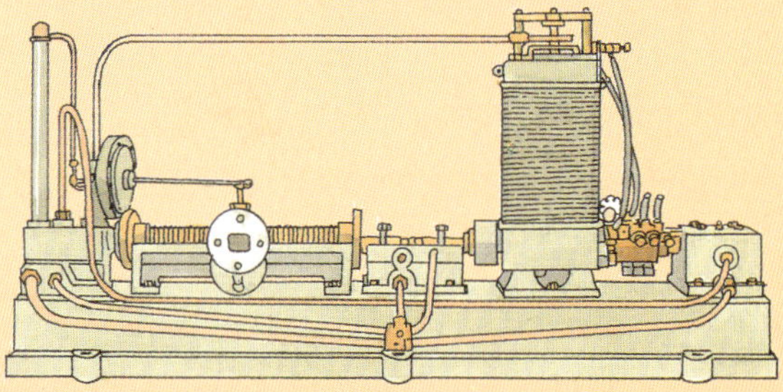

In the late 1800s the British engineer Charles Parsons (1854-1931, below) designed a quieter and more efficient turbine driven by high-pressure steam (above). The turbine blades, on the same shaft as the dynamo, made it spin at higher speeds to produce electricity.

Parsons' invention was taken up by the new electricity industry. The first large steam turbines were installed in a German power station in 1901.

Most modern power stations burn fuels such as coal (above), oil or gas to release the energy needed to make electricity. These are called fossil fuels because they are made from the remains of ancient animals and plants that have been preserved as fossils.

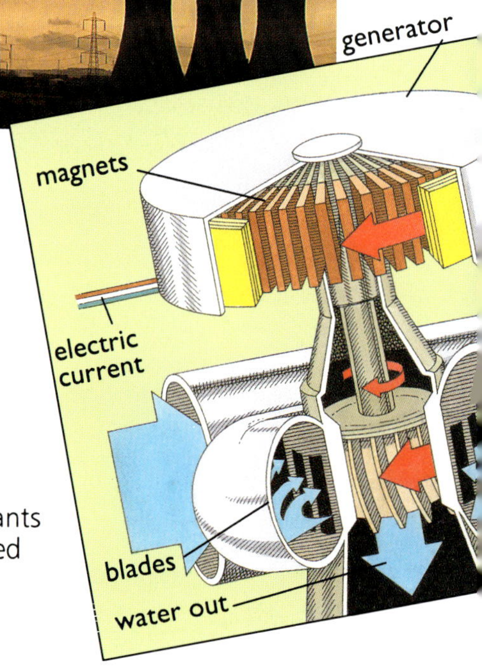

How a turbine works

Water-driven turbines (above) are used to generate electricity, known as hydro-electricity. A water turbine consists of fine-bladed fans running inside a tight-fitting case. Water is fed into the turbine at such a high pressure that it forces itself past the successive rows of fans, driving them round. The movement of the water turns the turbine. All the fans are connected to a single shaft which runs directly to a generator.

Fuel cells

A fuel cell converts chemical energy directly to electrical energy. Inside the fuel cell, hydrogen and oxygen combine to make electricity and water. Fuel cells (below) are silent, clean and efficient. There are no moving parts to wear out. Fuel cells are now being tried out as the power source for some buses.

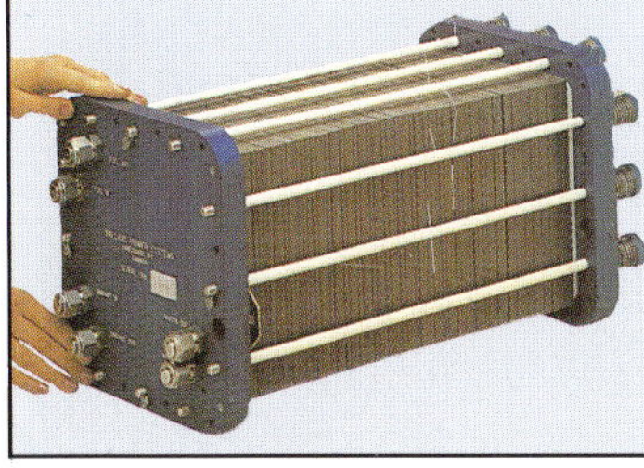

In a hydro-electric power (HEP) station (above), flowing water is used to turn the turbines. Most HEP comes from big dams built across large rivers. The water falls from the top of the dam to the bottom. The water pressure drives the turbines which power the generators to produce electricity.

Electricity and the environment

Power stations, that burn coal or oil, release a lot of a gas called carbon dioxide into the air, polluting the air. Carbon dioxide builds up, forming a blanket that traps heat given off by the Earth. This causes the Earth to warm up – the greenhouse effect (below) – and causes global warming.

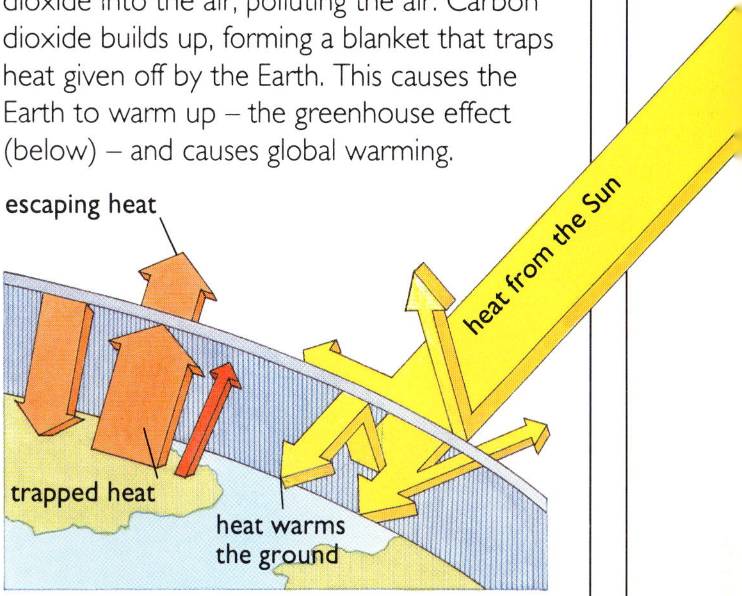

Power stations discharge a gas called sulphur dioxide. This mixes with water in the air to form sulphuric acid, making rain acidic. Acid rain can kill wildlife and flora. Its acidity eats into building stone, causing it to crumble, as in this statue in Wells Cathedral in Britain.

Electricity from rubbish

A few power stations burn rubbish to turn water into steam, which is then used to generate electricity. At Wolverhampton in Britain, a power station (right) has been built to use the energy from burning tyres. More power stations like this would conserve other fuels, such as coal or oil, which are rapidly running out.

The Sun

The Sun could provide an endless supply of energy, but this is expensive to channel. In the Solar One power station in California in the United States (below), nearly 2,000 mirrors are used to reflect light on to a central tower, heating the oil inside. This can turn water into steam which is then used to generate electricity.

SENDING ELECTRICITY

Power stations send electricity through thick cables. These are usually carried high above the ground by tall metal towers called pylons. In towns and cities, the cables are buried below ground, though this system is more expensive to install and maintain. The power flows through the cables at up to half a million volts (to reduce power loss). The voltage is then lowered by transformers at substations, to a level which can be used safely in homes and offices (above). A modern mains circuit in a house carries between 110-240 volts.

A.C. or D.C?

In 1888, Croatian-born American inventor Nikola Tesla (1856-1943) patented a system of generating and distributing electricity using alternating current.

The main advantage of A.C. over D.C. is that the voltage can easily be changed by a transformer. Tesla's induction motor (below) is still widely used as a type of electric motor.

Transforming power

Transformers at a power station (above left) increase the voltage to about 225,000 –400,000 volts. This reduces the resistance from the cables when the electricity is sent over long distances (see page 127). A transformer consists of two linked electromagnets, with a different number of turns in the coils around each electromagnet.

Electricity for all?

Today, in the developed world, people take an electricity supply for granted. Electricity has transformed domestic and working life (far right). But most of the electrical inventions we use today only date back about 70 to 100 years. Electric lights only became widely available in the 1930s. Up until the 1950s, a television set (below) was a rarity. With the development of electric motors in the 1930s, electrical appliances, such as small heaters and food mixers, appeared. But they were only owned by the wealthy, who made servants operate them because they were dangerous!

How much electricity?

Make a chart of how much electricity you use in one day. Start from the moment you wake up. What about the alarm clock? Your radio? How do you make your breakfast? What about brushing your teeth or running the tap? Does the weather make a difference? Will it help if you look through the TV listings?

The grid

A system of pylons and cables (above left) may connect all the power stations in a country into one huge network called a grid. Therefore, if one power station breaks down, interrupting the electricity supply, electricity from another power station in the grid can be sent to replace it. This helps to avoid power cuts. The grid can also be international, with countries linked by cables capable of transmitting electricity, even across the sea.

In developing countries, one television is often shared by a whole village (right). Electric lights may be used for a short time relying on small, local generators. Power can also be created by burning animal waste.

Switch on the light

Before 1900, electric lights were mostly arc lamps, where an electric spark jumped across a small gap between the ends of two rods. Then the American inventor Thomas Edison (1847-1931, left) and the English chemist Joseph Swan (1828-1914) invented light bulbs. These were cheaper, more reliable and less glaring than arc lamps. Edison tested all sorts of materials, even bamboo stems, but his first bulb used a cotton filament. It glowed for about 13 hours. Modern bulbs last about 1,000 hours. Special long-life light bulbs can last 8 times longer, using the same amount of electricity.

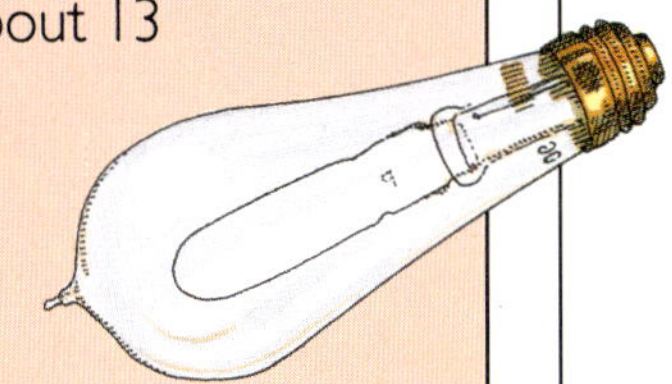

Power on the move

Countries can trade in electrical power. If a country has a surplus of electricity, it exports this to another country. In the spring, as the snows melt on the mountains and the rivers flow faster, Switzerland generates enough hydro-electric power to export some (below). But in autumn and winter, when the water is frozen, it needs to import electricity from neighbouring countries.

STORING ELECTRICITY

Storing electricity efficiently is a problem that has yet to be solved by scientists. Small amounts can be stored in batteries and capacitors, such as those found in electrical appliances like radios and washing machines. But it is extremely difficult to store large amounts of electricity in this way. With more and more cities being polluted by exhaust fumes from combustion engines, an efficient, pollution-free battery becomes a global necessity.

Giant sparks

In the 1930s, an American scientist, Robert Van de Graaff (1901-1967), developed a machine to collect and store huge amounts of static electric charge. A continuous moving belt passes charged brushes, and transfers electricity to a storing device at the top of the machine. This transfers it to the outside of a large metal sphere, which is insulated by the column below. A Van de Graaff generator (left) can produce up to an incredible 20 million volts!

Dinorwig, Wales

In Europe's largest pumped storage station (above), water is pumped uphill at times when demand for electricity is low. When demand is higher, the water is allowed to run down again to generate electricity.

The first batteries

In 1780, an Italian scientist, Luigi Galvani, discovered that dead frogs' legs twitched if touched with a metal scalpel when pegged to iron railings with brass pins. He thought the legs must be making electricity. Volta (right) believed that the electricity was produced because the salts insides of the frogs' legs connected the metals in a circuit. Both were right. Animals do create electricity, but it is also made by metals reacting together. Volta invented the first battery (see page 126), using chemicals.

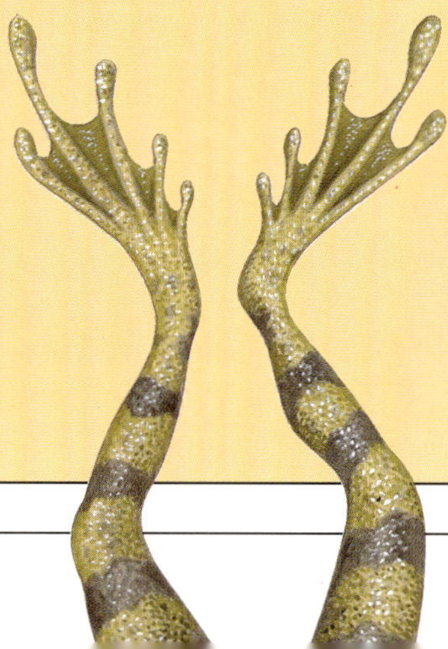

Batteries all around

Batteries come in all shapes and sizes, from the tiny round batteries inside watches, to the cylindrical or square batteries in toys or torches, or the heavy batteries in cars or other vehicles. But all batteries work in the same way, storing chemical energy and changing it into electrical energy. Batteries have a much lower pushing power than mains electricity, so they are not so dangerous. Batteries can also be carried from place to place. When the chemicals inside many batteries are used up, the batteries no longer work. It is dangerous to keep "flat" batteries because the chemicals may leak and cause damage.

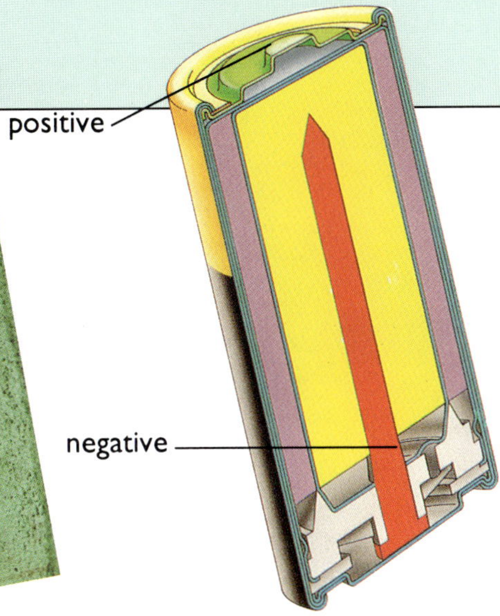

How a battery works

Chemical reactions inside the battery (above) build up negative charges at one terminal and positive charges at the other. This is why battery terminals are identified by plus and minus signs. When the battery terminals are joined in a circuit by a metal wire, a path is made from one terminal to the other. The electrons flow through the wire from the negative terminal to the positive.

Capacitors at work

In a capacitor, two plates are separated by a small distance, capable of storing small amounts held in place by electrical forces. Variable capacitors (below) in radios allow you to change stations. Turning the knob on a radio changes the capacitance (the ability to store charge), causing the radio to pick up signals of a different frequency.

The amount of energy stored can be changed.

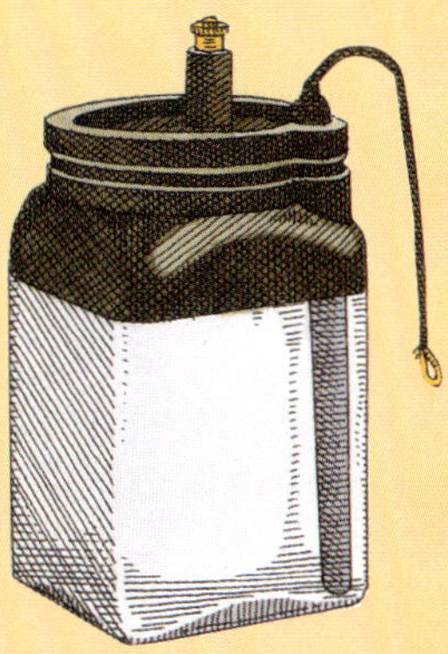

During the 1860s, George Leclanché (1838-1882) developed a battery which did not use dangerous acids.

The dry cell batteries we use today – in torch batteries for instance – are based on the Leclanché model (left).

Lemons into batteries

Make a simple battery from a lemon, two pieces of metal and two wires! Stick the metal pieces into the lemon, making sure they do not touch. Connect a piece of wire to each piece. Put the wires on your tongue and you will feel a tingle. Your tongue is conducting electricity produced in the lemon. A chemical reaction takes place between the pieces of metal and the juice inside the lemon. This makes electricity in a similar way to a battery.

ELECTRICITY AT WORK

Without the power generated by electricity and magnetism, the industrial world would grind to a halt. Mass production of consumer goods relies on milling machines, drills and lathes to produce parts for products which can be welded together. They are assembled on conveyor belts and lifted in loads by cranes. From metalworking to mining, the electric motor provides power which can be controlled with precision and safety. Agriculture, medicine and office work have been revolutionised by sophisticated electronic devices.

Life or death?
Hospitals in war zones (below) or disaster areas have to make do with unreliable supplies of electricity. Without advanced electrical life-saving equipment, or even basic lighting, doctors and nurses have to continue operating on the sick and wounded.

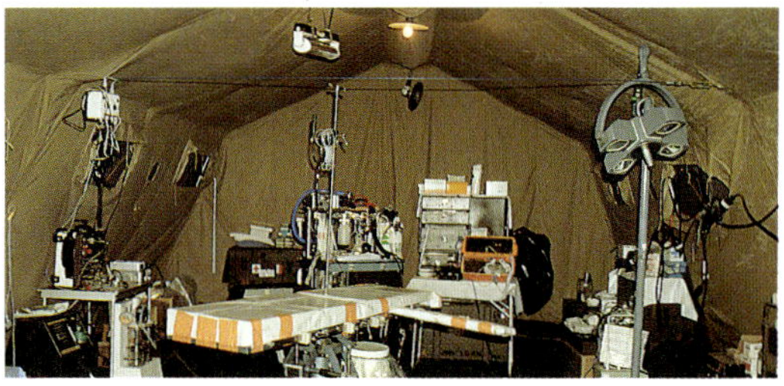

Electrolysis
In a battery, chemicals react to produce an electric current. But an electric current can also be used to cause chemical reactions, splitting chemicals into the substances they are made of. This is called electrolysis. It is used to purify metals such as aluminium (above). This is an important metal found in a rock called bauxite. Electrolysis allows us to extract the pure metal from the bauxite.

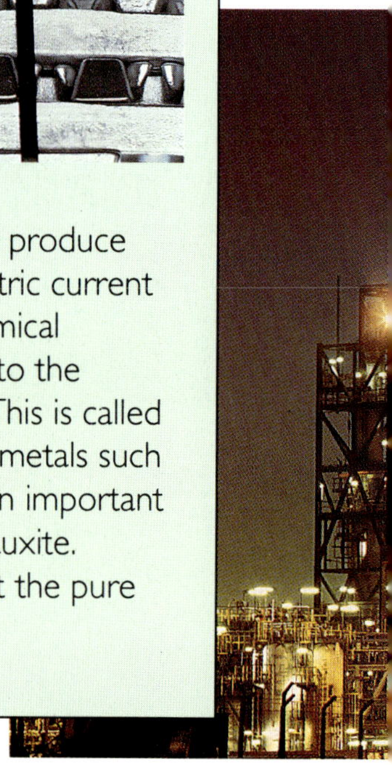

Hotting up
In electric arc welding, intense heat is created by a strong electric current leaping across a gap between two conductors (see page 126). Pieces of metal melt in order to join together. A robot arc welding machine (below) is able to work with great precision.

Electricity and farming
Electrical power and electrical machinery play an important part in the lives of farmers, their crops and their animals. Electric machines help with work such as milking cows, drying grain after harvest and moving heavy loads. Computers control the amount of food, heat and fresh air many animals receive. Electricity has also made the growing season much longer for greenhouse crops. It is now possible to create ideal growing conditions, no matter what the weather is like outside. Electric clocks control the artificial lighting to change day length and so influence flowering times.

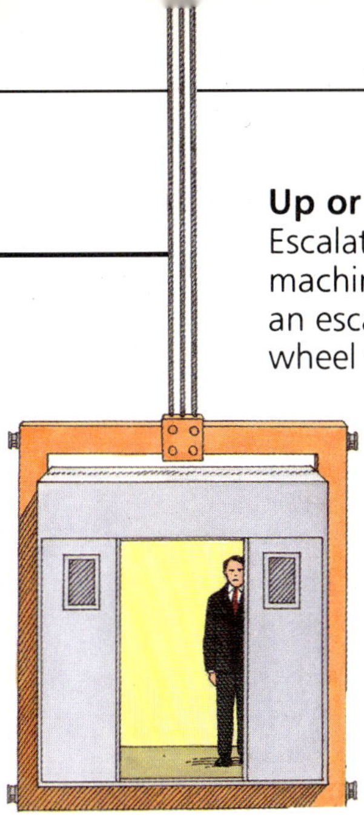

Up or down?

Escalators and lifts (left) are both lifting machines powered by electric motors. In an escalator, the motor powers a drive wheel which moves a chain connected to the stairs. In a lift, the motor drives a pulley which raises or lowers the lift by means of cables attached to the lift car.

Night and day

Industry never sleeps. This oil refinery (below) continues to work through the night, powered by constant supplies of electricity.

Humphrey Davy

The English chemist Humphrey Davy (1778 -1829) and his assistant Michael Faraday (see page 128) were amongst the first scientists to use electrolysis. Using this technique, they discovered many new elements, such as pure potassium, sodium and calcium. To make pure potassium, a silvery metal, Davy passed a current through potash, which is found in the ashes of burned plants.

Electroplating

Electrolysis is also used to give a thin metal coating to another piece of metal. This is called electroplating. If the metal is to be coated with silver, it is attached to the negative terminal of an electricity supply and dipped in a liquid containing positive silver particles. When the current flows, the silver moves to the negative terminal and coats the metal. Tin cans are made by electroplating tin onto steel.

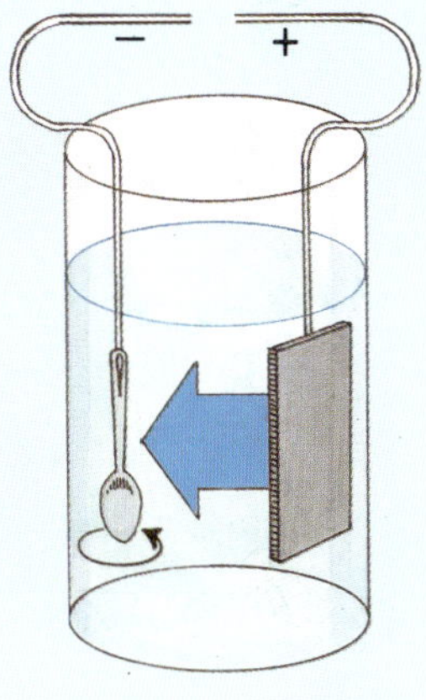

Electric mist sprays give moisture to plants and electric soil warming and irrigation encourage good root growth. Young chicks grow quickly in the carefully controlled warmth of an electronically heated incubation room (below).

Electricity in films

In the silent film *Modern Times* (1936, right), Charlie Chaplin explored the extent to which electrical machinery has taken over our lives. In the film, Chaplin's lovable character of the little tramp with the funny walk struggled to cope with different machinery. Electricity was a vital component of films about Frankenstein's monster, which was brought to life with the energy from a lightning bolt.

TRANSPORT

Without electricity, people would find it very difficult to get about, especially in the developed world. Motor vehicles use electric sparks to explode the petrol which drives their engines, and electric cars run on battery power. Across the world, electric trains (left), electric trams and trolley buses rely on electrical power, while electro-magnetic trains "float" above the track. Diesel-electric engines pull many trains and also power many huge cargo ships and ocean liners. Aeroplanes and ships use sophisticated electronic navigation to find their way.

Car computers

Traffic computers, powered by batteries, are becoming more commonplace on car dashboards (below). They can display maps, warn of roadworks and traffic jams, plan the best route for a journey and even give the driver spoken directions. The information is received from radio beacons which feed data into a control centre.

Solar-powered cars (above) or planes (left) use solar cells to convert sunlight into electricity.

Aircraft and ships rely on electronic navigation for direction (below). Computer-controlled equipment allows aircraft to fly on automatic pilot without manual control. The equipment picks up signals from a chain of radio beacons on land. Satellites use this information to calculate accurately the position of the aircraft.

Pedal power?

The Sinclair Zike (below) is an electrically powered bicycle. Batteries in the frame produce electricity to drive the Zike. The battery can be recharged, and is turned on or off with a simple switch on one handlebar.

The right track

The first mainline electric trains ran on the Baltimore and Ohio railroad in the US in 1895. Electric trains take power from overhead cables or a rail next to the track. They do not need to carry fuel, but they travel near power lines. Electric track is expensive to build and maintain. Diesel-electric trains use a diesel engine to run a generator, which produces electricity to drive motors linked to the wheels. Today, trains can achieve remarkable speeds, particularly those in France and Japan.

The French Train à Grande Vitesse (TGV, right) reaches over 483 kph (290 mph) and the magnetically levitated (Maglev) train has reached speeds of more than 402 kph (241mph).

In a nuclear-powered submarine (left), an atomic reactor provides heat energy to drive turbines which generate electricity. The submarine can travel a long way without refuelling. This is an expensive source of power, and the safety of nuclear power is under question. An experimental Japanese ship, *Yamato 1*, uses electro-magnetic power to drive the ship.

Green electricity?

Pollution in cities such as Los Angeles, United States, where most people drive (below), can be a serious health hazard. However, electrically powered vehicles do not emit harmful gases into the atmosphere. But most of the electricity (except solar power) is still made in power stations that burn fuels and cause pollution. Electric cars are one step towards reducing pollution. To date, however, a satisfactory battery-powered car with good performance has yet to be developed.

Batteries forever

Some batteries do not need to be thrown away when they go "flat". Instead, they can be recharged to start up their chemical reactions again.

Electric wheelchairs are run on rechargeable batteries. A car battery is also rechargeable. While the car is running, the battery builds up a store of electric current with which the engine can be restarted.

COMMUNICATION

Since the invention of the electric telegraph in the early 19th century, electricity has made it possible to talk or send information to people almost anywhere in the world. Electronic equipment converts sounds or pictures into electricity, which travels around the world at the speed of light. Telephones, faxes, televisions and radios change this back into sounds or pictures. Computers can communicate directly with each other in seconds, using electronic mail, or E-mail.

On the line

Alexander Graham Bell (1847-1922), a Scots-born scientist, invented the telephone in 1876. He realised that varying electrical signals can make a flat sheet vibrate to produce sound waves. The telephone turned them into electrical signals at one end and back into sound waves at the other end.

Samuel Morse (1791-1872) worked out a way of sending pulses of electric current along wires to form a coded message. A code of dots, dashes and spaces represented numbers and letters. This came to be known as the Morse Code after its inventor. Morse's first permanent telegraph line opened in 1844 between Baltimore and Washington in the United States.

Radio and television

In a radio or television station, sound waves or light waves are first changed into electrical signals. A transmitter then changes the electrical signals into radio waves, which are beamed into the Earth's atmosphere by an antenna or aerial. The antennae of a radio or television set pick up radio waves from the air. The radio changes them first into electrical signals and then into the sound waves that you hear. A television set changes the radio waves into electrical signals and then into sound waves and light waves.

radio mast sending signals to a satellite in space

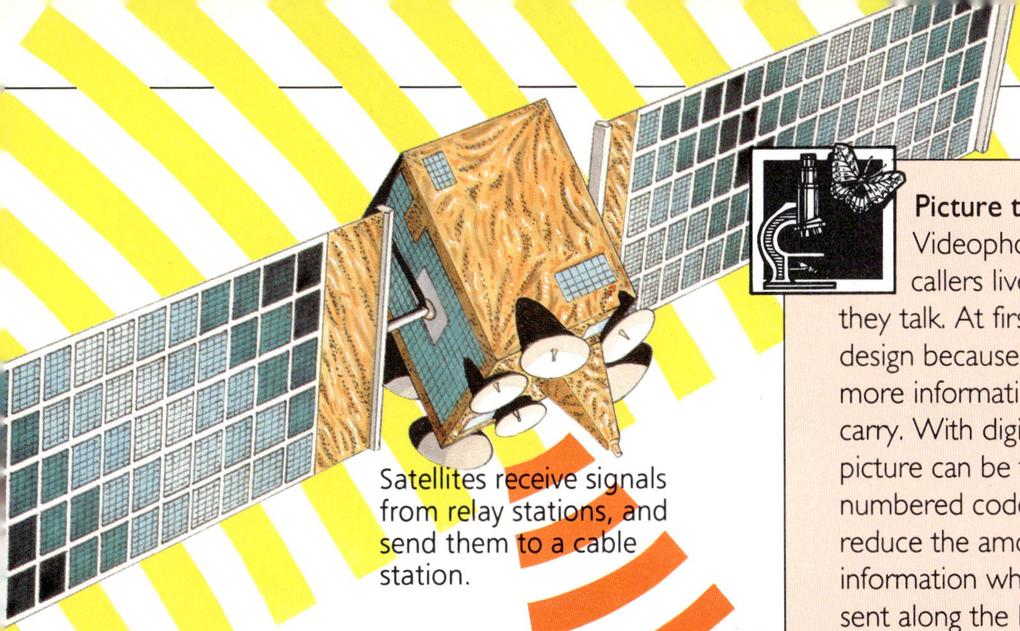

Satellites receive signals from relay stations, and send them to a cable station.

Picture this

Videophones (below) show telephone callers live pictures of each other while they talk. At first, they were difficult to design because moving pictures contain more information than a telephone line can carry. With digital electronics, a picture can be turned into a numbered code, to reduce the amount of information which is sent along the line.

Satellite communication

Hundreds of communication satellites, or Comsats, are now orbiting the Earth. They receive radio signals from huge, dish-shaped aerials on the ground and beam the signals back to an aerial in another part of the world.

Some television channels are transmitted by electrical signals that flow along a special cable to people's homes. This is called cable TV (left). It can transmit live reports across the world. Viewers with cable TV were able to see live international reports from the Gulf War.

From live bands (left) to high-quality recordings, music has been revolutionised by electricity. Using a numbered and shortened code, it is now possible to send compact discs (CDs, below left) of high-quality music over the phone. The Digital Compact Cassette recorder (DCC, below right) plays cassettes that have been recorded as coded numbers. The sound is of a very high quality.

Electric art

Electronic art computer programs for both drawing and painting are now becoming more sophisticated. You can reproduce different painting materials, such as oils or charcoals, smear oils together, blend watercolours and even create your own brushes by choosing the number of bristles. Paintings on a computer screen can be endlessly improved and re-touched, but it needs a lot of computer memory and a good colour printer.

TOMORROW'S WORLD

From "intelligent" computers and miniature robots to virtual reality (left), new developments in electricity and magnetism herald exciting advances in the future. The communications possibilities of computers, linked in global networks, open up an enormous potential for people to share ideas and information world-wide. Advances in technology have discovered new ways of generating electric power, such as that from nuclear fusion. Although these could solve some pollution problems, caused by the way we generate electricity today, there are many questions over safety.

Insect robots

As well as complex robots, scientists are also working on much simpler models which will carry out tasks by just reacting to situations instead of thinking. These "insect" robots would be only about 30 cm (12 ins) long and weigh less than a bag of sugar. Genghis (right) is brought to "life" by one of the researchers who helped create him. Simpler robots would be cheap and easy to build, and could explore new planets before human astronauts. Closer to home, insect robots could also carry out useful tasks such as housework.

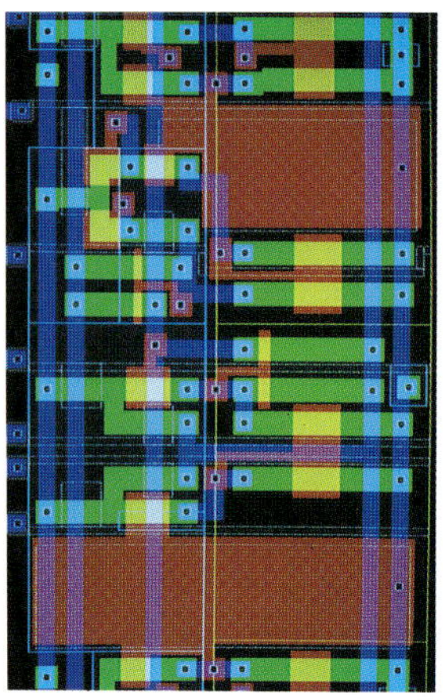

Clever computers

Intelligent computers may be developed from the "neural nets" (left) which scientists are working on today. These computers tackle problems in a similar way to human brain cells, or neurons, which are linked in a network in the brain. Neural nets will be very important in the design of seeing and hearing systems for intelligent robots.

Fission or fusion?

At the moment, nuclear power stations split apart dangerous materials such as uranium and plutonium to release energy. This is called nuclear fission. In the future, nuclear power stations could force together safe materials such as hydrogen and helium to release the energy stored in them. This is called nuclear fusion. Fusion power would be less polluting than conventional power stations. It only needs small amounts of fuel to produce huge amounts of energy.

Global community

In the future, satellite links and vast networks of optical fibres will connect houses and businesses around the world. Optical fibres are made of glass fibres and send information as pulses of light.

Although the world powers are eager to outdo each other in their atempts to discover ways of establishing networks in space, they collaborate on projects such as the US/Russian Space Co-operation Phase (left). This co-operation extends to the use of solar technology here on Earth, as shown above in the picture of houses using solar heating panels.

When some materials, such as tin, are cooled to very low temperatures they have no resistance to the flow of electric current. They are called super-conductors because they conduct electricity very well. They would make ideal materials for electric cables (right) because they would waste no power, but the cooling system is expensive to run. We need to find ways of making them work at high temperatures.

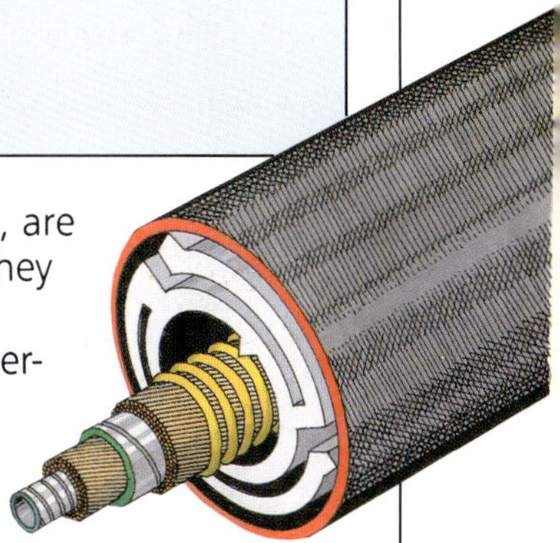

At Princeton in the United States (left), a nuclear fusion experiment produced a short burst of energy for a few seconds. The reaction took place in a Tokomak, a magnetic machine. It uses a powerful magnetic field to hold atoms of hydrogen together long enough for them to start fusing together. This is done at extreme heat.

Keeping track

Electronic security cameras (right) are being used increasingly to fight crime and reduce overcrowding in prisons. In some countries, people who have committed minor crimes have an electronic tag strapped to their wrist instead of going to prison.

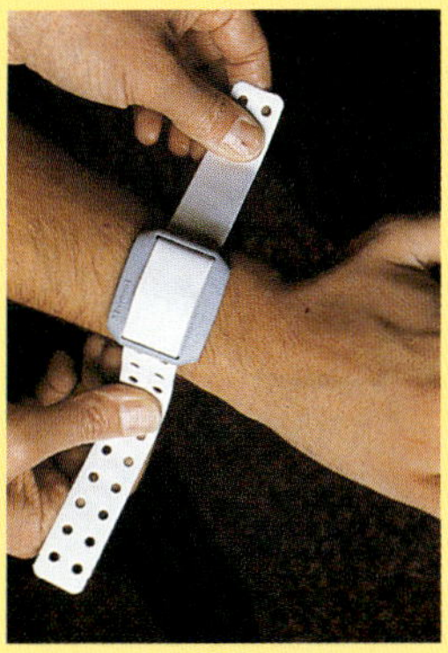

The tag transmits a radio signal to a receiver in a person's home. If the person moves too far from the receiver, the signal becomes too weak for the receiver to detect it and it sets off an alarm.

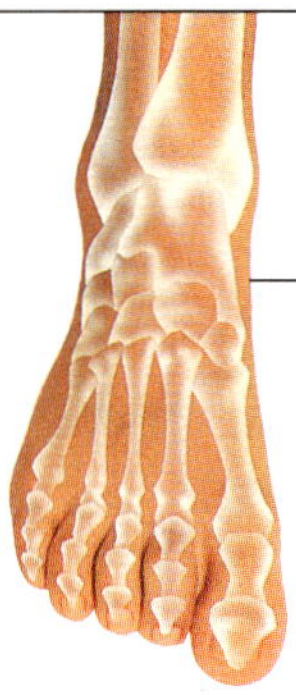

CHAPTER 6

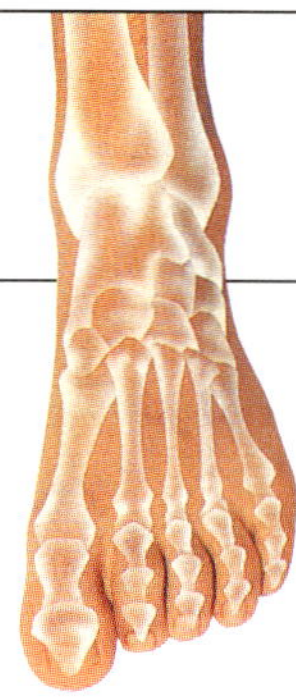

THE HUMAN BODY

Each of us possesses one of the most complex devices in the universe - a human body. Yet few of us have read the owner's manual. This chapter provides a biological background to the body, its structures and systems. It includes information about human history and different ways of life around the world.

It describes how the human body has featured in many works of literature, and has formed the basis for words and phrases in many languages. It shows that the body has also been a springboard for the progress of science through the ages, and records some of the milestones in that process.

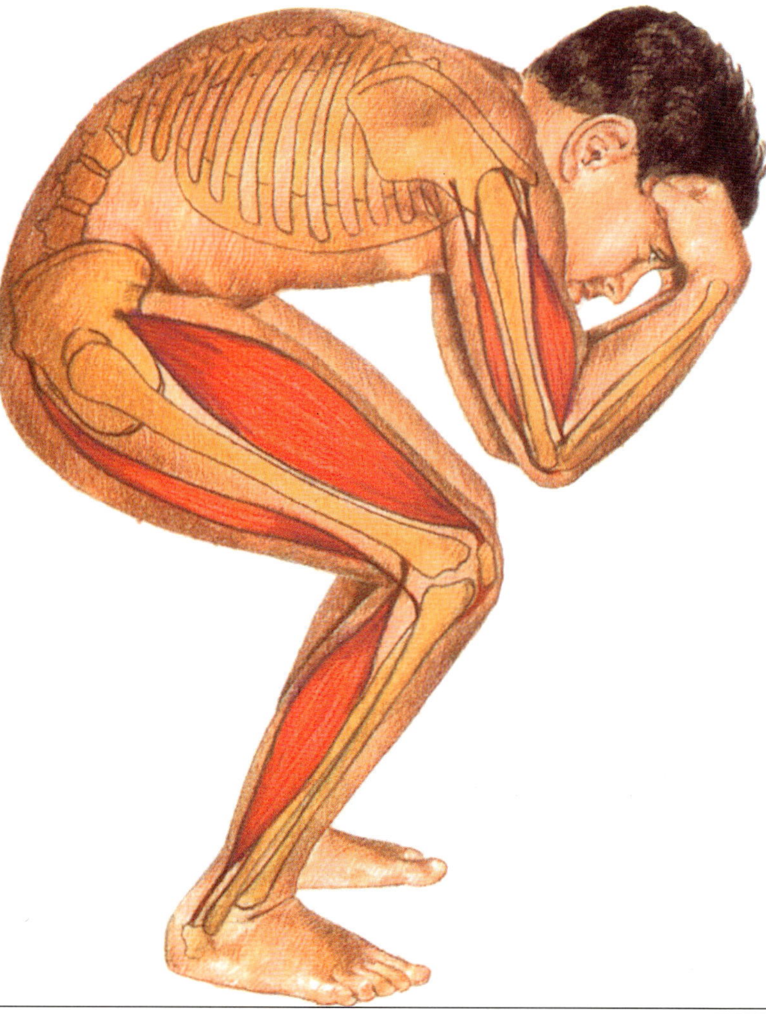

CONTENTS

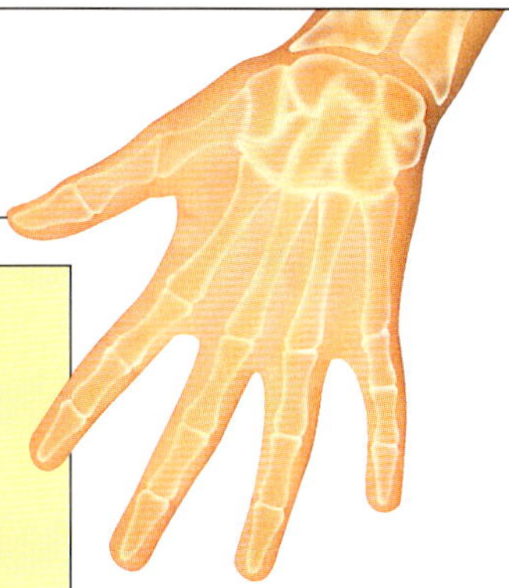

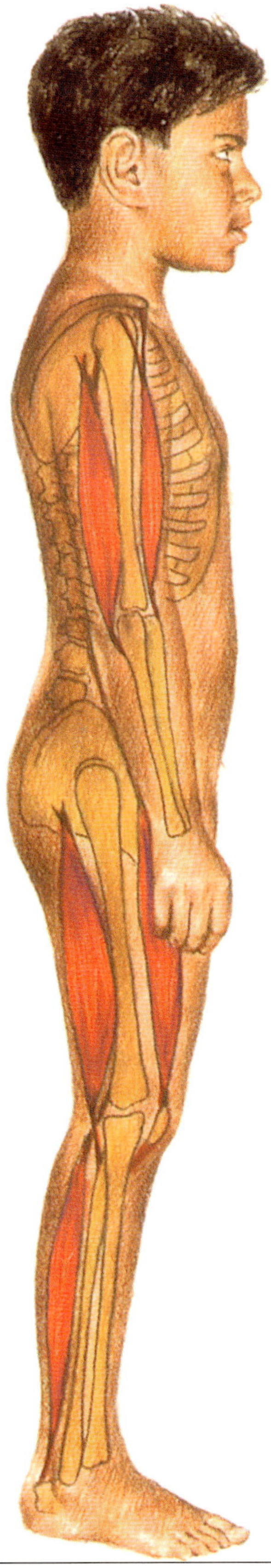

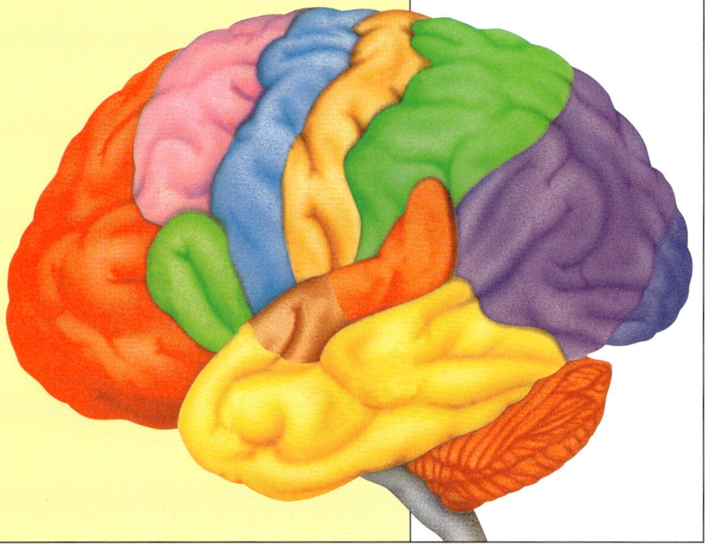

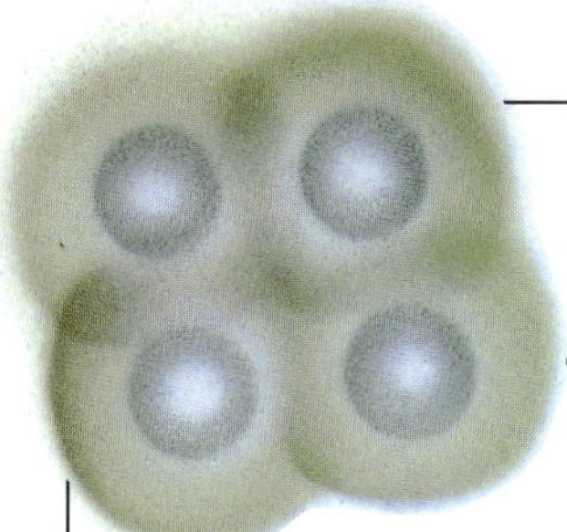

STRUCTURE AND SYSTEMS

The human body, and especially the brain that controls it, are extremely complicated and truly amazing. Even so, scientists now understand much of the body's structure, or anatomy, and how the body works. Like all living things, the body is made up of tiny units called cells. There are many different types of cells in the body, doing different jobs. Cells combine with others of the same type to form tissues. Various tissues combine to form the body's main parts, the organs, and the organs combine to make working systems.

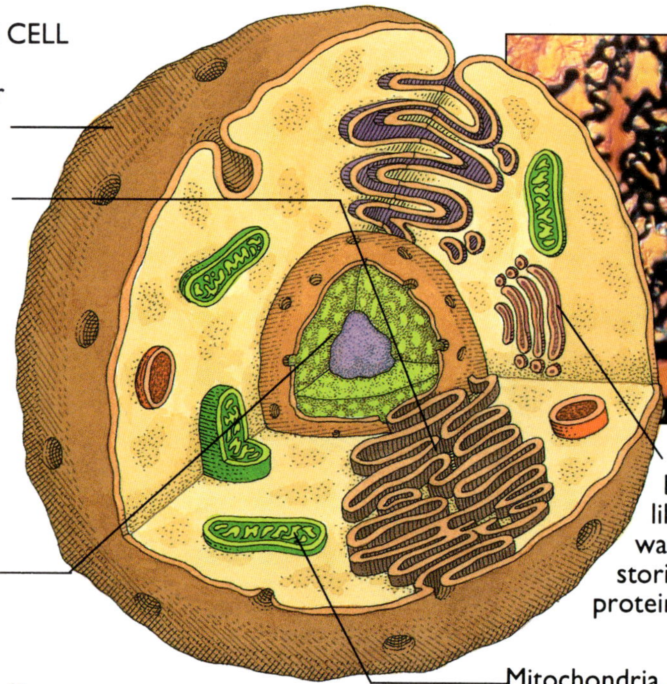

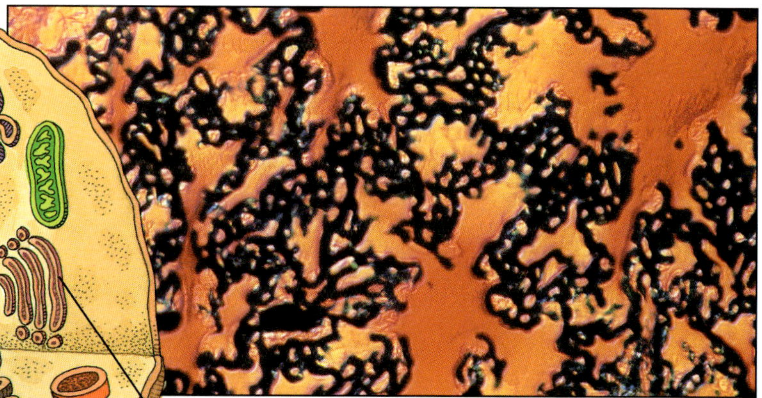

Inside a cell

A cell contains even smaller parts known as organelles, such as ribosomes, above. Each is like a mini-organ, with a special job to do. The nucleus is the cell's control centre and contains the genetic material, DNA (see page 171).

Tissues

There are four basic types of body tissue: skin tissue, muscle tissue, nerve tissue and connective tissue (above), which includes bone, cartilage and fat.

Body organisation

The basic building-blocks of the human body, and of all other living things, are cells. These microscopic objects are the smallest units capable of the vast range of chemical and physical processes that we call life. There are about 100 million million cells in the body, of more than 20 main kinds, such as muscle cells and skin cells. Each has a special shape, adapted for the job it does. A group of cells and the substances in which they live make up a tissue.

Ancient beliefs

In ancient times, people had only the vaguest ideas about how the body worked. Traditions and religions often forbade them to cut open, or dissect, the body to study its parts. One of the first great body-scientists was the Roman physician Claudius Galen (AD 129-201). Galen was medical officer for the gladiators who fought bloody battles in the arenas of Ancient Rome. He wrote many books, and his reputation was so great that doctors followed his ideas – even the many wrong ones – for 1,500 years afterwards.

Organs

An organ is a part of the body with a particular job to do. Some organs are located in body cavities. The heart and lungs are found in the chest cavity, which is separated from the abdominal cavity by the diaphragm. The stomach, intestines, liver, kidneys and reproductive organs are located in the abdominal cavity, as shown below. Other organs are found throughout the body, such as bones and muscles.

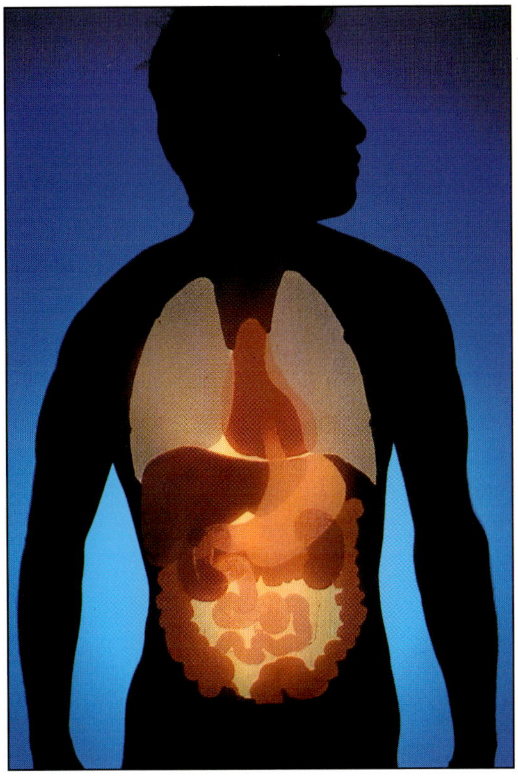

Systems

The organs combine into systems, which are the body's main working units. For example, the lungs and the air passages that lead to them make up the respiratory system (see pages 152-153). The heart, arteries, veins and other blood vessels, and the blood itself, make up the circulatory system (see pages 156-157). The brain and nerves combine to form the nervous system, which controls body processes (pages 166-167). The human body has a dozen of these main working units, explored within this book.

Bodywords

In Ancient Greece and Rome, physicians believed that the parts of the body were made from different mixtures of four fluids, or humours. These were blood (sanguis), phlegm (pituita), black bile (melanchole) and yellow bile (chole). They were connected to the four essences that made up all matter: air, water, fire and earth. These old beliefs gave rise to many words we still use today. A person in a sad mood is said to be melancholic, because these feelings were thought to be caused by an excess of black bile. Words such as phlegmatic, bilious and sanguine have similar origins.

Looking into the body

In the 1600s, the microscope was used with great skill by a Dutch scientist, Anton van Leeuwenhoek. By the late 1600s, great anatomists such as Marcello Malpighi were using the microscope to look into the body and discover cells and other tiny parts. Their work laid the foundations of micro-anatomy. Doctors today use scans of various kinds to look inside the body. Unlike ordinary X-rays, which show only bones, these scans show all the soft parts of the body, such as muscles and nerves. A Magnetic Resonance Image (MRI) can reveal the structure of the brain, spine and facial tissues (below).

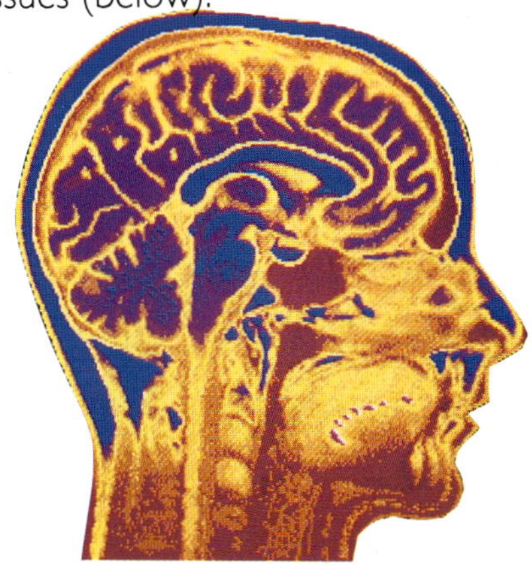

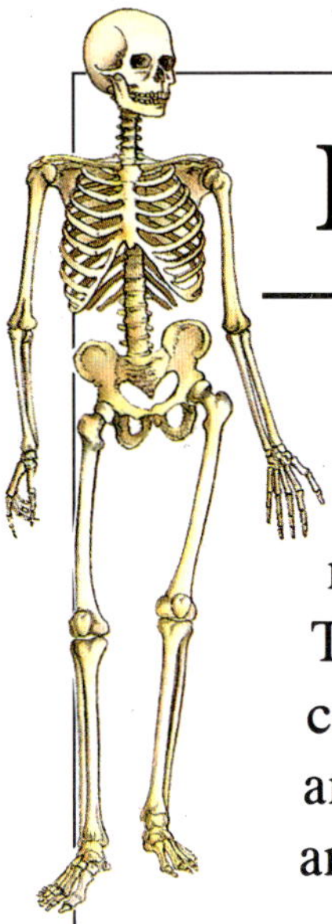

BONES AND JOINTS

The human body is supported by the hard, strong framework of the skeleton. A single bone is stiff and unbending. But the body can bend and move because most of the bones are linked to each other at flexible, movable joints. Living bones are not dry and brittle, like bones in museums. They are one-third water; the rest is composed of crystals of minerals such as calcium, and a protein called collagen. Bones have a good supply of blood and nerves, and are just as alive and active as the muscles and other soft parts around them.

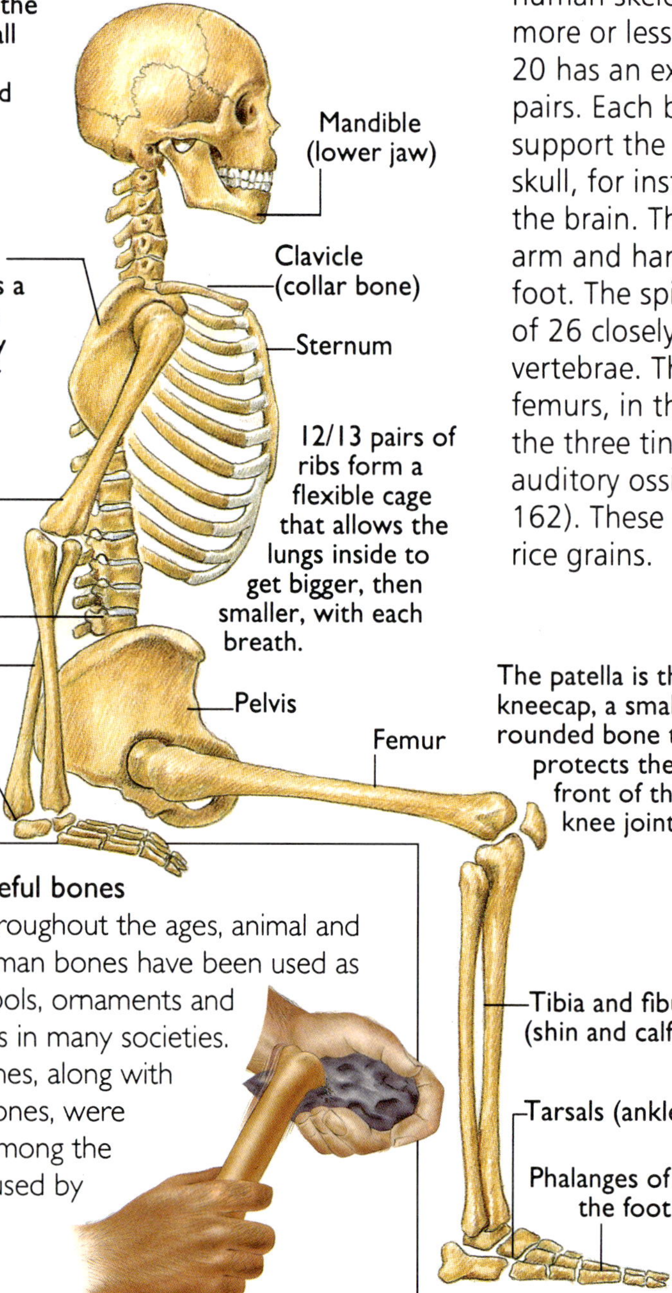

The skeleton

There are 206 bones in the average human skeleton. A few people have more or less. For example, one person in 20 has an extra pair of ribs, making 13 pairs. Each bone is shaped to protect and support the soft parts around it. The skull, for instance, encloses and protects the brain. There are 32 bones in each arm and hand, and 30 in each leg and foot. The spine or backbone is a column of 26 closely-linked bones called vertebrae. The biggest bones are the femurs, in the thighs. The smallest are the three tiny bones known as the auditory ossicles, in each ear (see page 162). These bones are about the size of rice grains.

Useful bones

Throughout the ages, animal and human bones have been used as tools, symbols, ornaments and decorations in many societies. Animal bones, along with chipped stones, were probably among the first tools used by prehistoric humans.

False colour X-ray of hand of a two-year old.

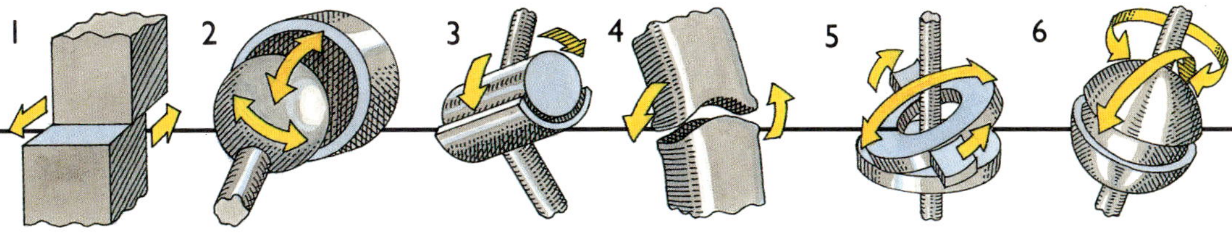

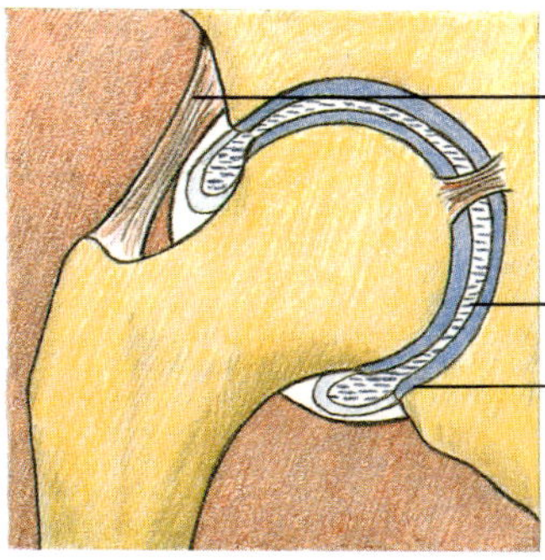

Bones and X-rays

Inside a joint, above, two bones are connected, yet are still able to move. In X-ray photos, bones show up as white shapes. X-rays can detect broken (fractured) bones, or abnormalities as the skeleton grows and matures. Compare the X-ray below, of an adult human hand, with the one on the opposite page. These X-rays illustrate how the bones in the hand and wrist grow and strengthen during childhood.

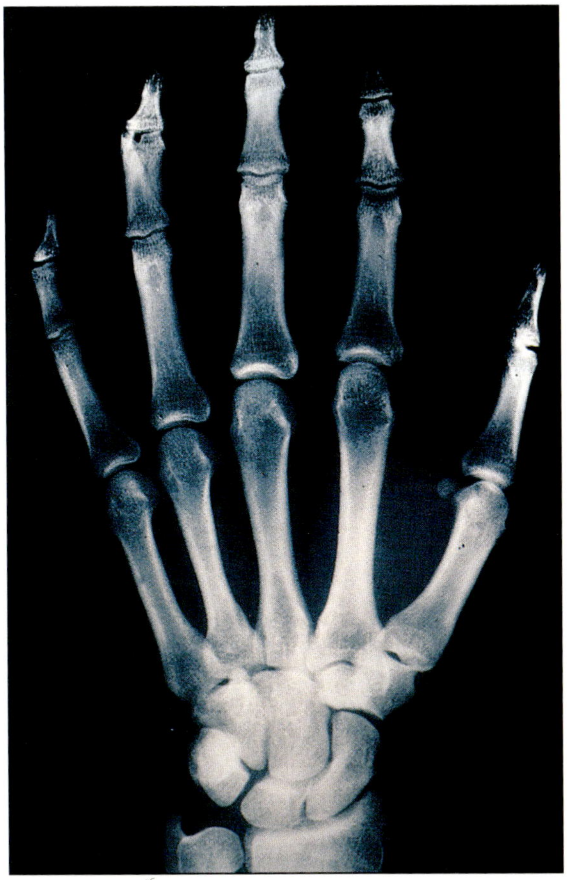

Types of joints

There are many different types of joints in the human body. Amongst the most important are the plane joint (1) which allows small gliding movements between the vertebrae of the spine, and the ball-and-socket joint (2), found in the hip and shoulder, which allows the limbs to rotate. The hinge joint (3) is found in the knee and elbow, and the saddle joint (4) in the base of the thumb. A pivot joint (5) allows the neck to move freely, and ellipsoid joints (6) connect the lower arm to the wrist, and the lower leg to the ankle.

The short and the tall

There are wide variations in the size of a human body, both within one group of people, and between different groups around the world. These variations are based on the sizes of the bones. One of the tallest human groups, the Dinkas, and the smallest, the Pygmies, both come from Africa. Most Pygmies are between 1.2 and 1.4 metres tall. The tendency in developed regions such as Europe and North America is for people from all ethnic groups to become bigger, due to better health care and diet. A bone expert can tell at a glance whether a skeleton comes from a man or a woman, a large child or a small adult.

Two adult Pygmies stand beside a Western man of Caucasian origin.

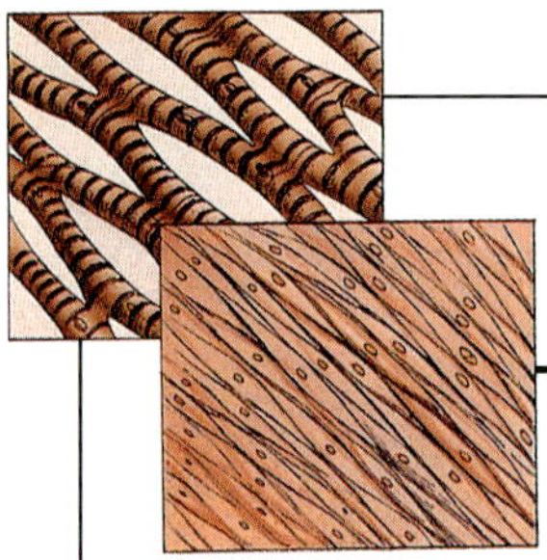

MUSCLES AND MOVEMENT

All the body's movements are powered by muscles. Muscle tissue is specialised to contract, or get shorter. The body has three main kinds of muscles. One is the skeletal muscles, attached to the bones of the skeleton, which you use to move about. There are more than 600 skeletal muscles, from the huge gluteus in the buttock, to tiny finger and toe muscles. The other kinds of muscles are cardiac muscle in the heart (top left above) and smooth muscles in the stomach, intestines and other internal organs (left above).

Inside a muscle

A skeletal muscle has a bulging central part known as the body. This tapers at each end into a rope-like tendon, which anchors the muscle to a bone. As the muscle contracts, the tendons pull on their bones and move the body. The muscle body is divided into bundles of hair-fine fibres called myofibres. These long cells contain proteins that slide past one another to make the cell shorter in length.

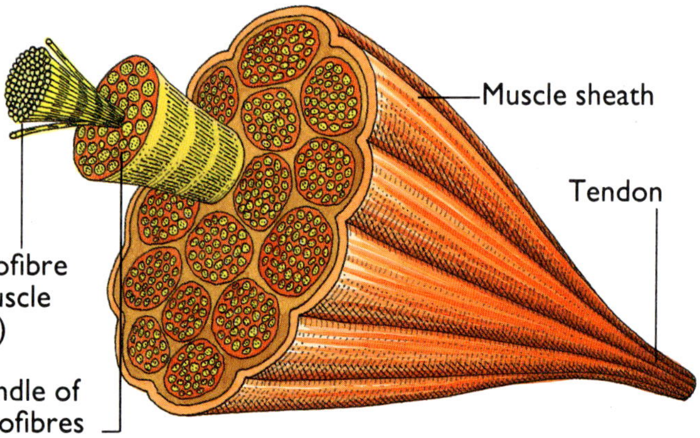

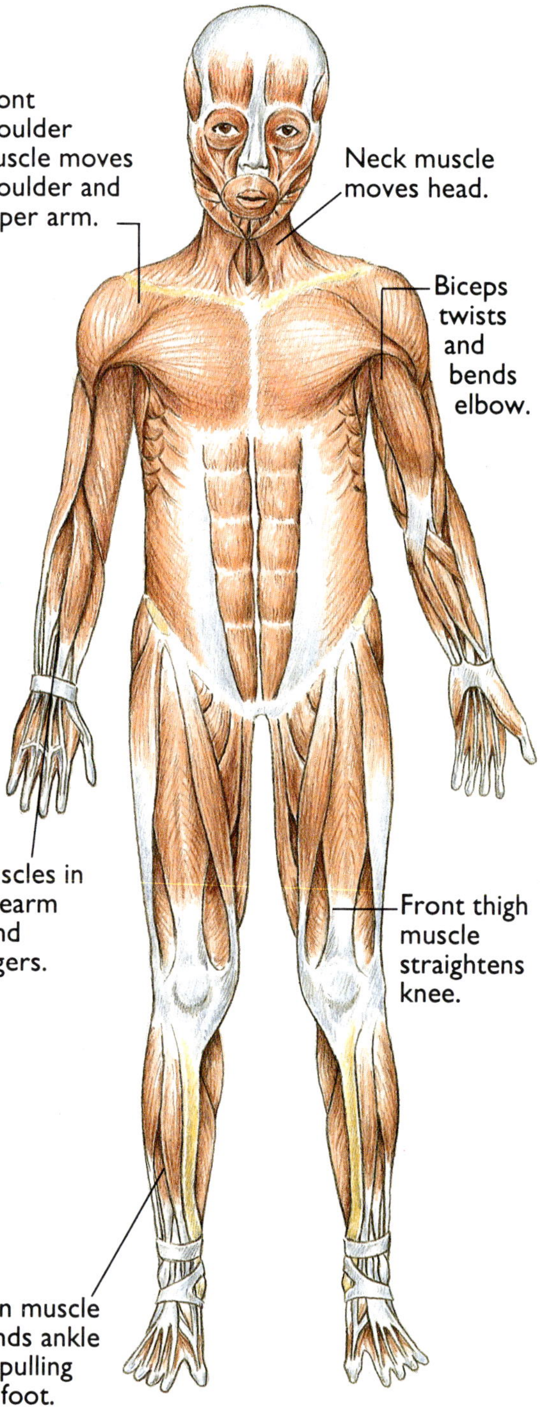

Changing fashions

Bulging muscles have been in and out of fashion through the centuries. A few hundred years ago, plump bodies were seen as desirable. Today some men and women like to look slim. Other people work hard at body-building, training and lifting weights in the gym. They strive to increase the thickness of their muscle fibres through special exercises and diet.

Stories of the strong

Legends from many different cultures tell of well-muscled, strong men and women. Some are heroes, others are villains. Hercules of Ancient Greece had to undertake 12 "herculean" (very difficult) tasks or labours. In the Bible, the boy David fought and killed the giant Goliath with his slingshot. Samson was a hero who fought the Philistines, but he lost his strength when Delilah tricked him into having his hair cut. Blinded and chained, he pushed the columns of the Gaza Temple and brought it crashing down on himself and his captors, as pictured right.

Master of art and science

During the Renaissance period, from about the 14th century, there was a rebirth of fascination in the beauty of the human form, and a scientific interest in the structure and workings of the body. Foremost in this field was the genius of art and science, Leonardo da Vinci (1452-1519). He performed amazing dissections of the body, especially the muscle system, and drew them with unparalleled skill and mastery, as shown here.

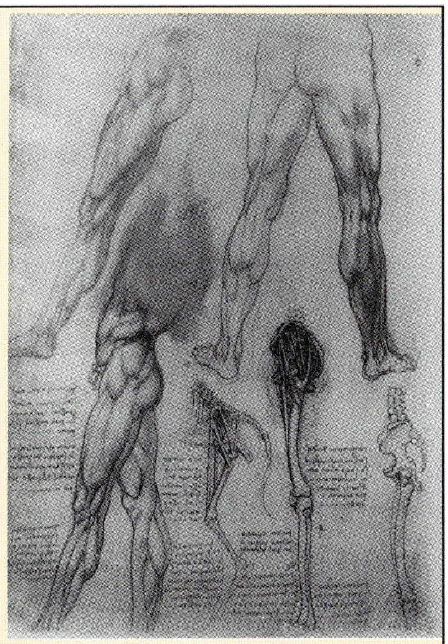

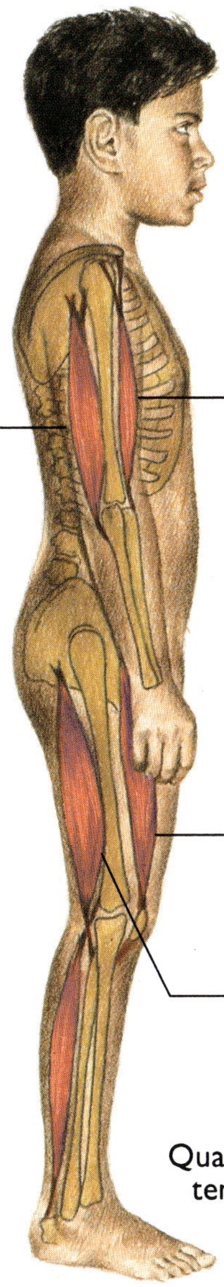

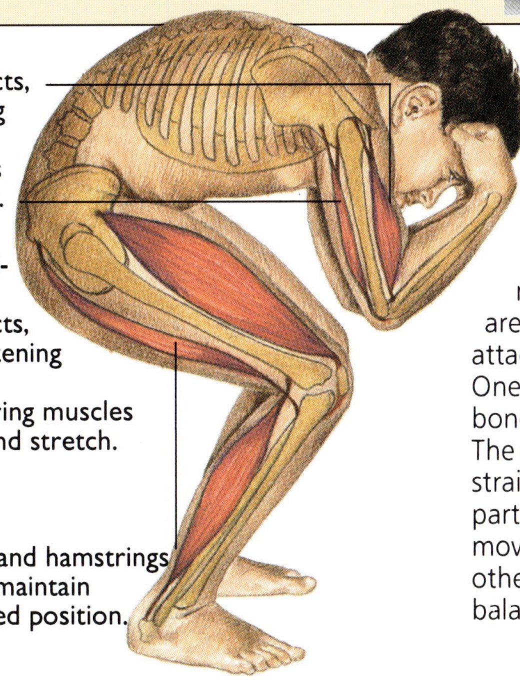

Muscle pairs

A muscle contracts to pull on its bone. But it cannot do the reverse – actively get longer and push the bone the other way. So many of the body's muscles are arranged in opposing pairs, attached across the same joint. One partner of the pair pulls the bones one way, bending the joint. The other pulls the other way and straightens the joint, while its partner relaxes. Even a simple movement also involves many other muscles that keep the body balanced.

LUNGS AND BREATHING

Nearly all living things, apart from some microbes (tiny organisms), need a supply of oxygen. Oxygen is necessary for the chemical reactions inside a cell known as cellular respiration. These reactions break up nutrients from food, such as sugars, and set free the energy for driving the cell's life processes. The human body gets its oxygen supplies from the air, which is one-fifth oxygen. We breathe air into our lungs, where oxygen is absorbed into the blood and sent around the body. The nose, throat, windpipe, and the two lungs are all involved in breathing; together they are called the respiratory system.

A new chemical element
Oxygen was discovered to be a chemical element, and vital in breathing, by a series of experiments carried out by scientists such as Joseph Priestley (1733-1804), Carl Wilhelm Scheele (1742-86) and Antoine Lavoisier (1743-94, below). Lavoisier named the substance oxygen and discovered it was necessary for burning, and for living things to breathe. This was proved when scientists put animals into glass jars and sucked out the air. This sounds cruel today, since we know that the animals would suffocate and die. But those early experiments helped to explain why life depends on oxygen.

Nasal passage
Breathed-in air flows through the nose, where small hairs filter out bits of dust and floating particles. Sneezing also clears dust particles from the nose.

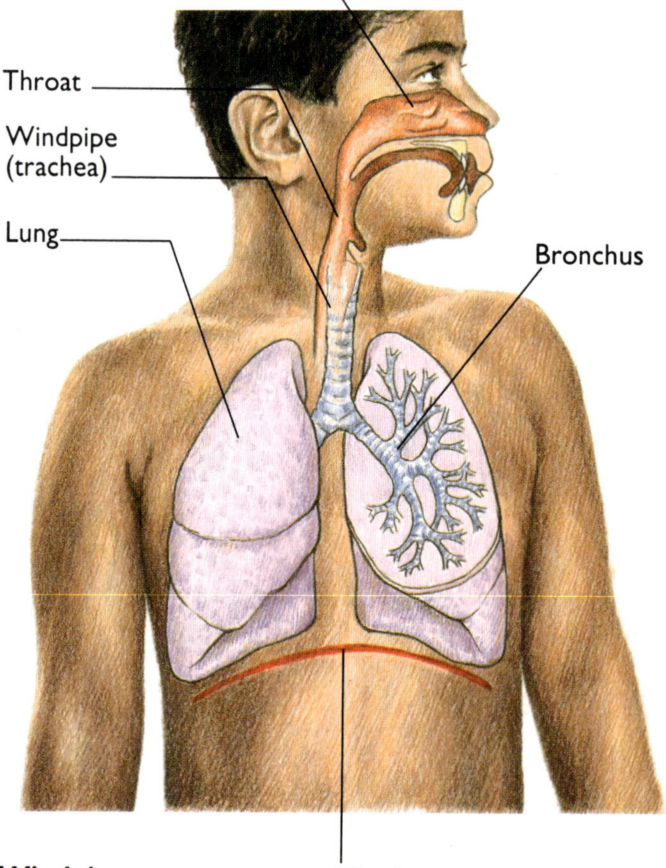

Windpipe
The windpipe divides into two main airways, the bronchi. Their insides are lined with a sticky fluid, mucus, that traps dirt, and tiny hairs that propel the dirty mucus to the top of the windpipe, where it can be swallowed.

Diaphragm
The chest is filled by the two lungs, the heart and the main blood vessels. The diaphragm is a dome-shaped muscle sheet that forms the base of the chest and the roof of the abdomen. It is the main breathing muscle.

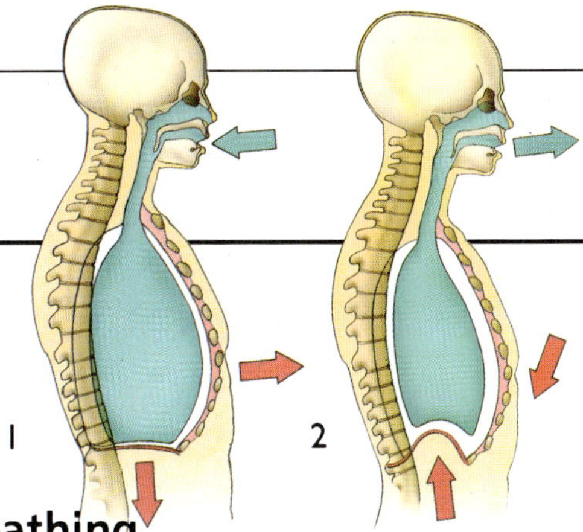

Breathing

Breathing not only obtains vital oxygen. It also gets rid of carbon dioxide. To breathe in, the diaphragm muscle contracts, pulling down the base of the lungs. The intercostal muscles around the ribs also pull the front of the chest up and out. These movements expand the lungs, sucking in air (1). To breathe out, the diaphragm relaxes. The lungs spring back to their smaller size, pushing out air (2).

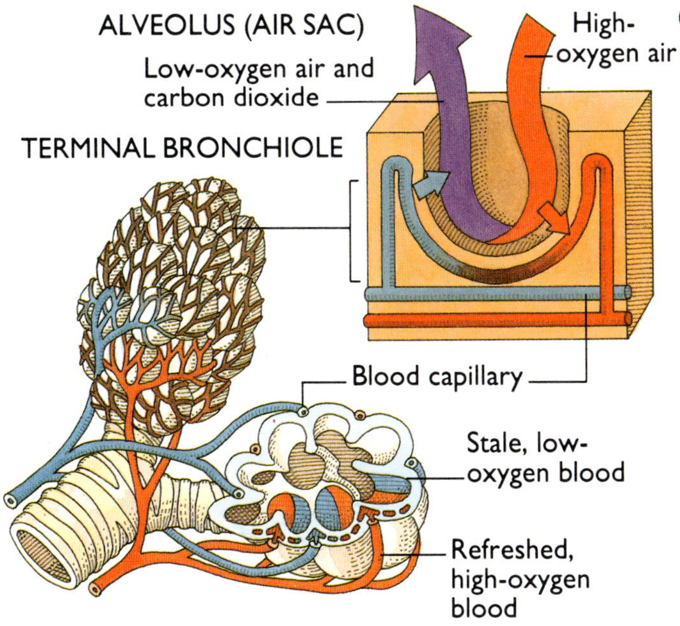

Inside the lung

The main bronchus (airway) of each lung divides more than 15 times. These airways become smaller, until they form thousands of hair-thin air tubes called terminal bronchioles. The bronchioles end at microscopic air sacs known as alveoli. In the alveoli, oxygen seeps from fresh, breathed-in air, through the very thin linings, into the blood flowing through capillaries (tiny blood vessels) on the other side. Blood distributes the oxygen around the body, and carries carbon dioxide back to the lungs, where it is breathed out as stale air.

Recycled breath

Exhaled or breathed-out air contains less oxygen and more carbon dioxide than normal fresh air. But there is still enough oxygen to keep the body going for a couple more breaths. When first-aiders carry out mouth-to-mouth resuscitation (below), they breathe their own air into the patient's lungs. Great escapologist Harry Houdini (1874-1926) is said to have re-breathed his exhaled air a few times, during the daring escapes he staged underwater.

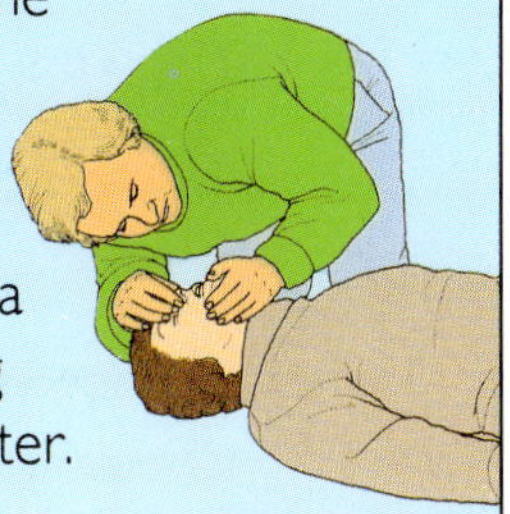

Cooling the fire

For thousands of years, people wondered why we breathe air. The Ancient Greeks such as Plato and Aristotle believed that nutrients from food were burned in the heart to make a "vital flame" that brought warmth and life to the body. They thought that the breathed-in air helped to keep the fire controlled.

Exercise is good for you

Aerobic means "with oxygen". Aerobic exercise makes the body's muscles increase their demands for oxygen, because they are using up more energy, thereby making the lungs and heart work harder. In general, this type of exercise improves the health of the lungs, heart and blood system. In anaerobic ("without oxygen") exercise, the muscles work for short bursts, without immediately increasing their need for oxygen.

DIGESTION

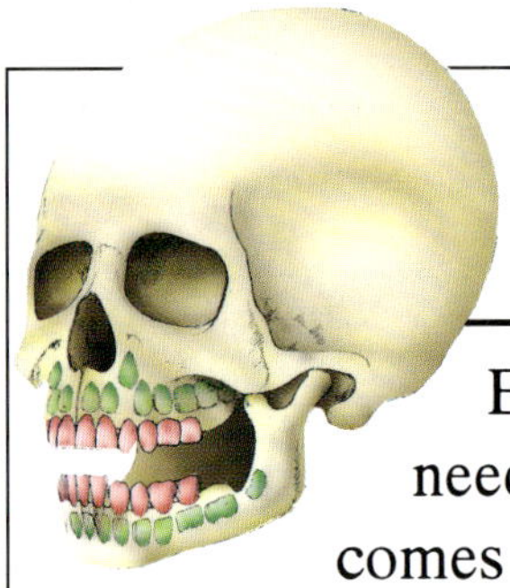

Energy makes things happen. Every living thing, and every machine, needs energy to power its inner processes. The human body's energy comes from its food. Food also supplies the raw materials and building-blocks for bodily growth and repair. The set of organs that gets food into the body, breaks it down or digests it, and absorbs it into the blood, is called the digestive system. It includes the mouth and teeth, gullet, stomach and intestines.

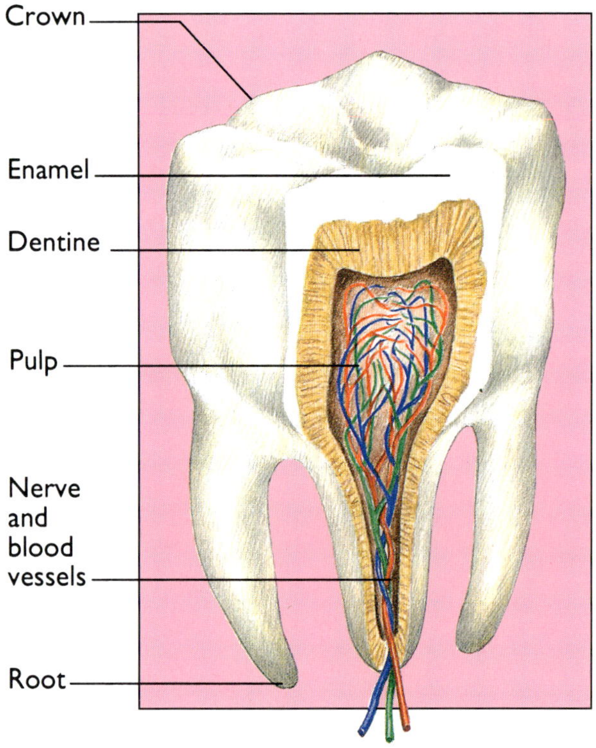

Teeth

Prehistoric people did not have knives and forks. Like wild animals, they used their teeth to cut off and chew mouthfuls of raw food. Today, we have cooking and cutlery, but teeth are still important – especially for thorough chewing, which helps the body to digest food more effectively. A tooth is covered with pale enamel, the hardest substance in the body. Under this is dentine, a shock-absorbing barrier. Inside the tooth are a good supply of blood vessels, and the nerves that warn of toothache. Babies grow a first set of milk teeth, 20 in number (in pink, above left). From about the age of six years, these fall out naturally, and are gradually replaced by 32 adult or permanent teeth. The main types of teeth are shown on the left below.

Grinders
Premolars and molars crush and chew food. An adult has four premolars and six molars in the upper jaw, and the same in the lower jaw, shown here.

Chisels
Incisors at the front of the mouth cut and snip food. An adult has four incisors in the upper jaw and four in the lower jaw.

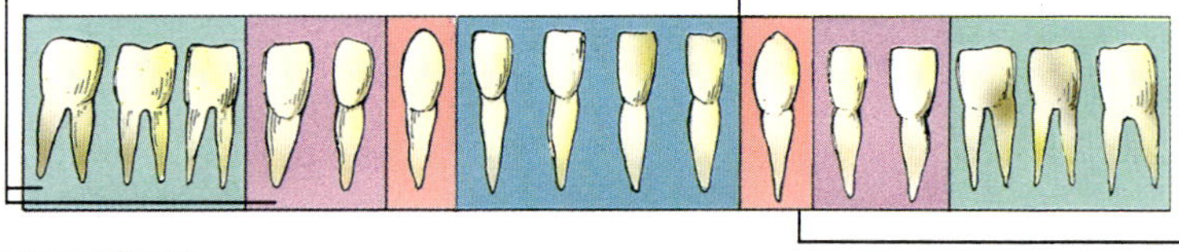

Spears
Canines, next to the incisors, spear and slice food. An adult has two incisors in the upper jaw and two in the lower jaw.

The balanced diet

The science of foods and their effects on the body is called nutrition. There are many differences in foods around the world. Some people eat mainly potatoes, others rice and others wheat. Yet all these foods contain lots of carbohydrates for energy. A good, healthy diet contains balanced amounts of the substances shown here, plus vitamins and minerals.

Fibre or roughage for digestive-system health:
Fruits, leafy vegetables, unrefined breads and cereals and pastas, beans and lentils

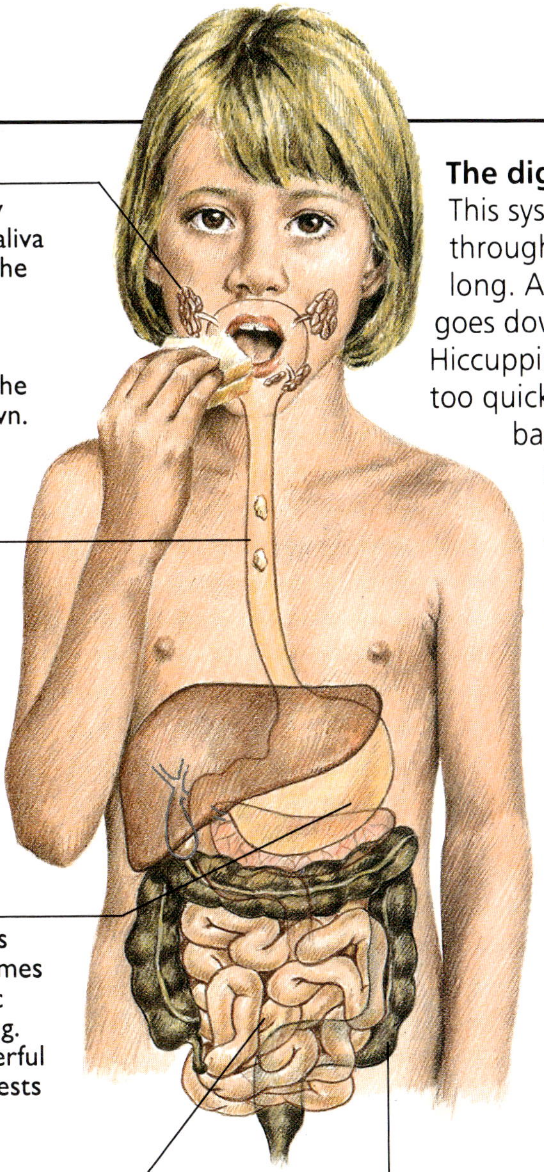

Moistening food
Three pairs of salivary glands make watery saliva (spit). This moistens the food for chewing. Digestive chemicals known as enzymes in saliva start to attack the food and break it down.

Pipe through the chest
The gullet is a muscular tube that pushes swallowed food down through the chest, into the stomach. Normally the gullet is squashed flat by the pressure inside the body.

Acid bath
The stomach contains strong digestive enzymes and also hydrochloric acid, made by its lining. This mixture of powerful chemicals further digests the food, for several hours.

Long but narrow
The small intestine contains more enzymes which complete the food's digestion. Nutrients are absorbed through its velvety lining, into the blood that flows through the lining.

Short but wide
The large intestine forms the undigested and left-over contents into semi-soft masses. It stores these until the body is ready to expel them through the ring of muscle at the end of the tube, the anus.

The digestive system

This system is like a long tube coiling through the body, about seven metres long. After the mouth and throat, food goes down the gullet into the stomach. Hiccupping may occur if we eat or drink too quickly. The stomach is like a storage bag that expands as it fills with a meal, and squeezes the food into a thick soup. The food passes on to the small intestine, where most of the nutrients are absorbed. The large intestine takes up much of the water from the left-overs.

Curious cuisine

Most people in developed regions buy their food from shops. In other regions people hunt and gather food from the wild. Traditional foods vary around the world. Honeypot ants are a delicacy for Australian Aborigines. Mosquito pie is eaten in parts of Africa.

The honeypot ant has sugary fluid in its swollen body. It is a "living larder" for its nest members.

Fats for growth, repair, healthy nerves and energy:
Dairy produce, nuts, plants and their products and oils, meat, poultry, fish

Carbohydrates (sugars and starches) for energy:
Breads, potatoes, pastas, rice, cereals and fruits

Proteins for body-building:
Meat, fish, eggs, cheese, peas, beans and other vegetables

HEART AND CIRCULATION

The body has an efficient transport network to carry supplies and products to where they are needed. It is known as the circulatory system, because its fluid, blood, circulates, or flows round and round, through tubes known as blood vessels. Blood contains three types of cells. Red cells carry oxygen; white cells fight disease (see page 160), and platelets cause blood to clot (see page 161). All these cells float in the liquid part of blood, called plasma. On its endless journey blood distributes nutrients, oxygen and other substances, and collects wastes and by-products.

The blood network

The human body contains between four and five litres of blood, which travels round in an endless one-way circuit. Large, muscular, thick-walled vessels called arteries carry blood from the heart. They branch into smaller tubes, which divide further to become capillaries. A capillary's wall is so thin that oxygen and nutrients can easily seep through to the cells beyond, while carbon dioxide and other wastes seep from the cells into the blood. The capillaries join together to make larger tubes, which come together to form large, thin-walled veins. The main veins take blood back to the heart.

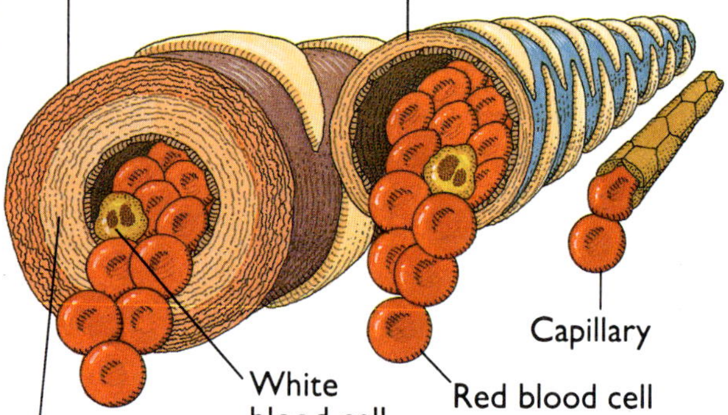

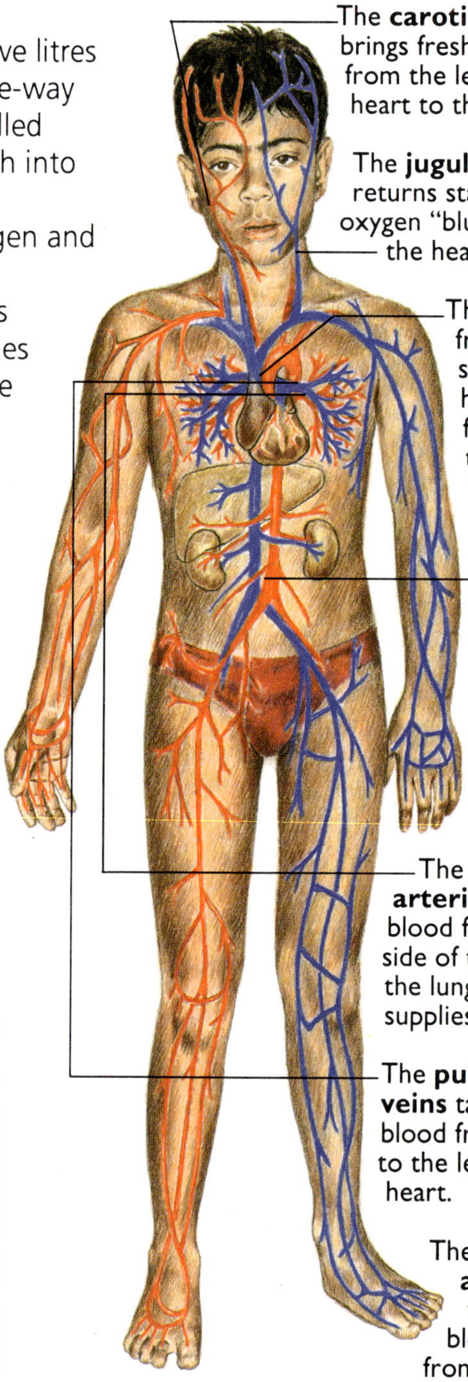

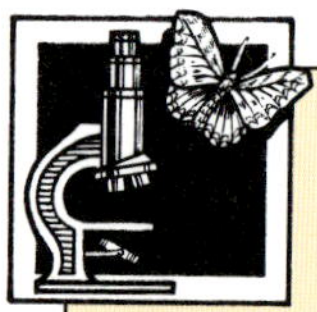

Harvey's heart

The English physician William Harvey (1578-1657) realised that the heart was a pump, which forced blood around the body. His discoveries began the modern age of scientific medicine.

Blood groups

In the 1900s, Karl Landsteiner (1868-1943) and other scientists discovered blood groups. They showed that blood from certain groups could not mix safely with blood from other groups. Today blood transfusions are commonplace and safe, replacing blood lost through injury or an operation. Blood can only be stored for a few months, so it is important for people to keep giving fresh supplies.

Romance and reality

The heart is a symbol of love and romance. Cards with hearts and romantic messages are exchanged on February 14, the anniversary of St. Valentine, an early Christian martyr (below). Literature is full of references to the heart as the seat of love, courage and emotions. But the heart is simply a muscular pump, though an amazingly reliable one. True, it does flutter, miss a beat or speed up during passionate moments. But this is under the control of the brain.

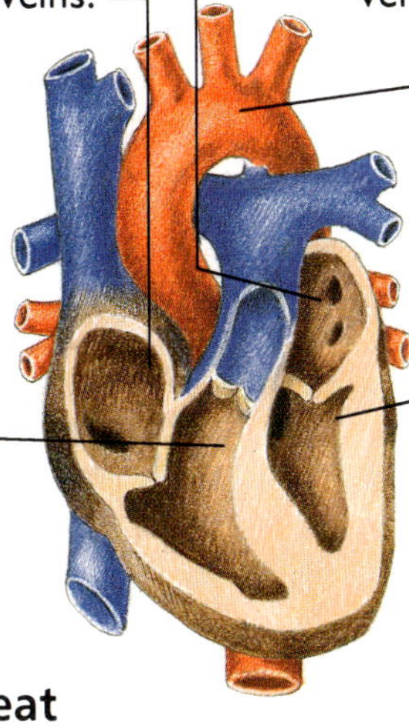

The heart has two sides, each with two chambers. The right atrium (upper chamber) receives blood from the main veins.

The left atrium receives blood from the lungs along the pulmonary veins, and pumps it into the left ventricle.

Aorta

Blood is pumped into the right ventricle. This sends out blood to the lungs to get oxygen.

The muscular heart wall is thickest in the left ventricle. This chamber must pump out blood through the aorta to the whole body.

The pulse

When the body is active, the muscles need more oxygen and nutrients. So the heart pumps faster and harder. With each beat, a bulging pressure wave of blood passes out along the arteries. This is known as the pulse. When you are resting, your pulse rate is about 70-75 beats per minute. After strenuous exercise your pulse rate may more than double.

The heartbeat

When you are at rest, the heart squeezes once a second. Blood oozes into the atria (1), and is pumped through the heart valves into the ventricles (2). The ventricles' muscular walls contract to pump out the blood (3). The cycle starts again (4).

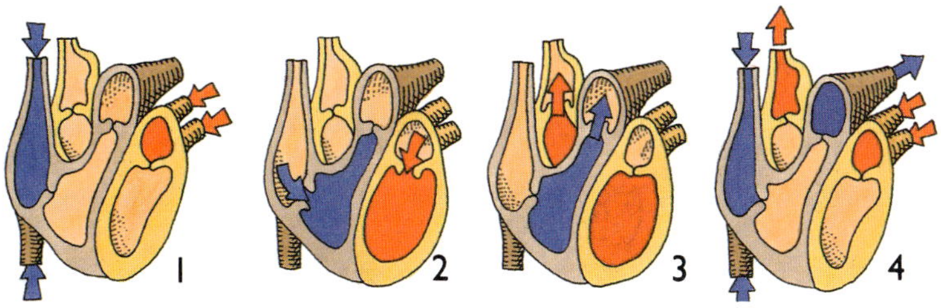

Fingers on the pulse

You can hear a person's heartbeat by placing your ear on his or her chest, slightly to the left of centre. Find the pulse of the radial artery in the inside of the wrist, or of the carotid artery in the neck under the side of the jaw. Feel gently with your fingers, not your thumb, since this has its own small pulse that may cause confusion.

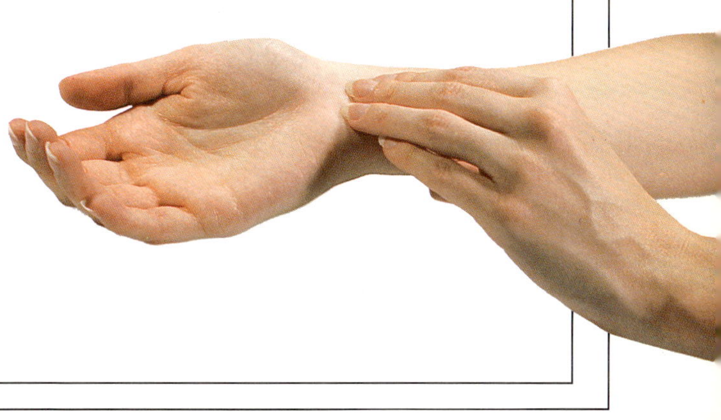

WASTES AND HORMONES

The body's life processes produce dozens of wastes and by-products. These are collected by the endlessly circulating blood, and dealt with mainly by the liver and kidneys, the chief organs of the excretory (waste-disposal) system. In addition, blood circulates special body chemicals called hormones. These control various internal processes such as digestion, fluid balance, growth, and maturing from a child into an adult woman or man.

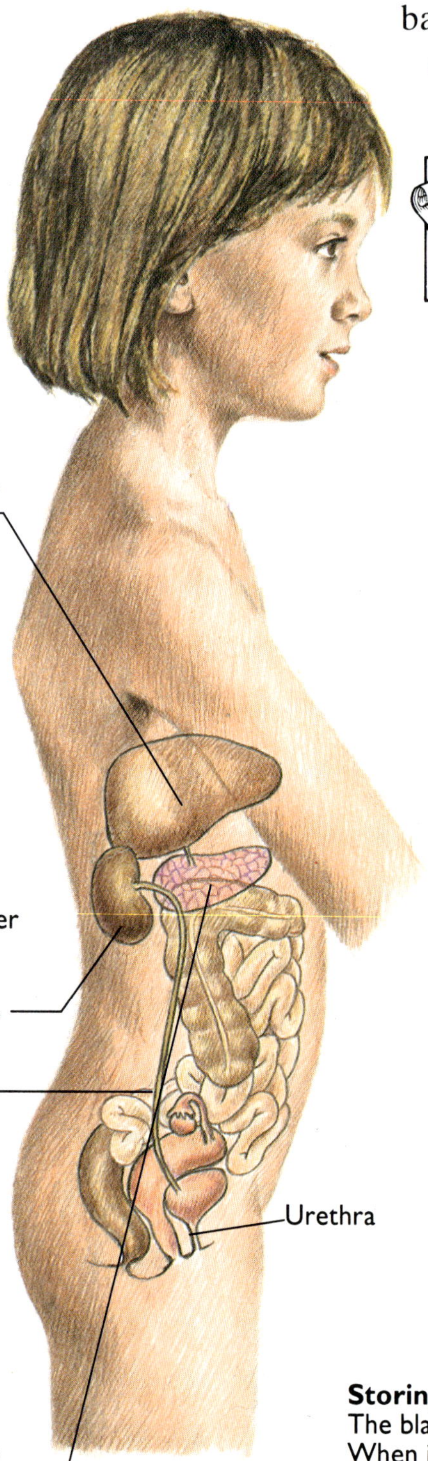

Processing foods
The liver is the largest organ in the body. It has a rich blood supply from the stomach and intestines, and receives digested nutrients. It makes toxic (poisonous) substances safe, stores some vitamins and carbohydrates, and converts nutrients into useful forms.

Filtering blood
The kidneys are blood-filters. Inside each kidney, one million microscopic filter units called nephrons take waste products such as urea from the blood, along with excess water. These wastes-and-water form the liquid urine, that trickles down the ureters to the bladder.

Doing two jobs
The pancreas has two distinct roles. One is to make strong digestive enzymes. These pour along the pancreatic duct into the small intestine, to digest food. The other role is to produce hormones such as insulin.

Testing urine
During the Middle Ages many physicians believed that a patient's urine could show exactly what was wrong with him or her. The urine in a glass tube was held up to the light and examined carefully. This process, called urinoscopy, continued for several centuries until physicians realised it was not very accurate. Today urine is still examined and used to detect diabetes and other diseases, but this is usually done by chemical tests in the laboratory.

Dealing with wastes
The body makes several types of wastes. Digestive left-over wastes are expelled through the anus. Some blood by-products are processed and altered in the liver. The unwanted substance carbon dioxide is breathed out through the lungs. The main wastes in the blood are removed as a fluid called urine, by the urinary system. This system is made up of the two kidneys, the bladder, the ureter tubes which link the kidneys and bladder, and the urethra that empties the bladder to the outside.

Storing urine
The bladder is a balloon-like storage bag for urine. When it holds about 200-300 millilitres, stretch sensors in its walls send messages along nerves to the brain, signalling that it needs emptying.

Master gland
The pituitary just under the brain makes several hormones and similar chemicals that control other hormonal glands around the body.

Energy regulator
The thyroid gland is shaped like a bow tie in the lower neck. It makes thyroxine, that affects processes such as the way the body uses energy.

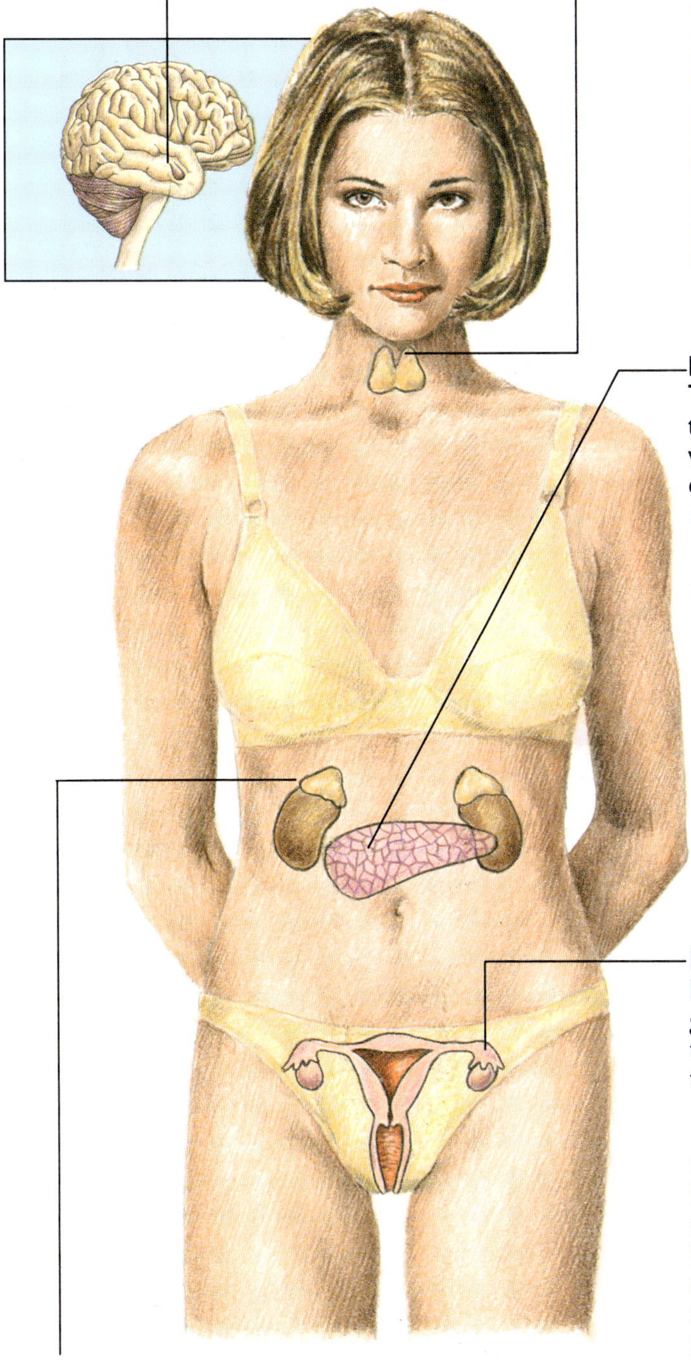

The long and the short of it
Stories about very tall or short people exist in many cultures. Such stories are often exaggerated into legends of giants or tiny humans. In real life, adult humans have grown to more than 2.7 metres tall or less than 70 cms short. Humans may have been even bigger or smaller in the distant past. Such extremes are often due to too much or too little growth hormone, made by the pituitary gland.

Insulin factory
The pancreas produces the hormone insulin, which controls the way cells take in and use energy-containing sugars.

Chemical control

Hormones are the body's chemical messengers. Each is made in a certain gland. The hormone circulates in the blood and affects specific cells and tissues, making them work faster or slower, or releasing their products. Along with the brain and nerves, hormones help the body to function as a coordinated whole.

Female sex glands
In a woman, the ovaries produce the eggs that can grow into babies if fertilised. They produce hormones that help to control the process of maturing from girl to woman, and the monthly menstrual cycle.

Male sex glands
In a man, the testes are small egg-shaped glands hanging below the abdomen in a skin bag, the scrotum. They produce the sperm for reproduction. They also produce hormones that help to control the maturing from boy to man (see page 170).

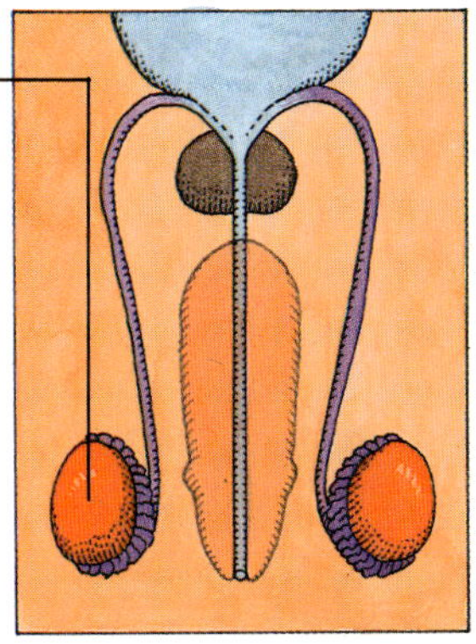

Adrenal glands and kidneys
The adrenal gland on top of each kidney makes a hormone connected with the balance of body water and salts, and adrenalin, that prepares the body for emergency action. The kidneys produce renin, which regulates fluid content and blood pressure.

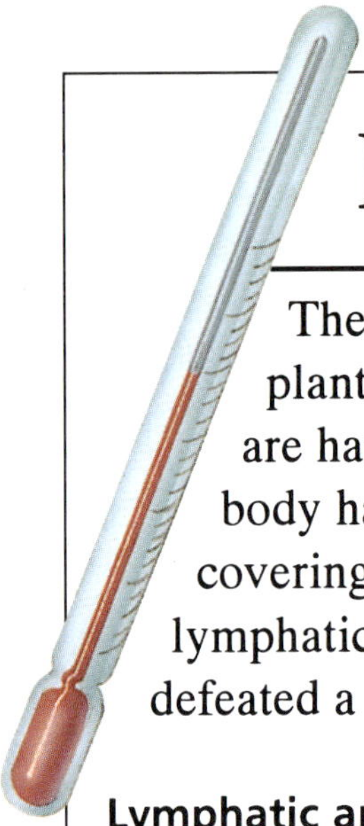

BODY DEFENCES

The world is full of "germs". They are in the air we breathe, in the soil, on plants and animals, even on our skin, and in some of the food we eat. Some are harmful microbes, such as the bacteria and viruses that cause diseases. The body has several lines of defence against them, including the outer covering of skin, and two systems with scattered parts, the lymphatic and immune systems. In some cases, once the body has defeated a type of germ it is always protected, or immune, against it.

Lymphatic and immune systems

Lymph is the body's "other blood". Lymph fluid collects in the spaces between cells, is channelled into tubes called lymph ducts, and flows through lymph nodes, where it is filtered and cleansed. Travelling around the body, lymph distributes fats and digested nutrients, and collects wastes, which are returned to the blood and filtered out by the kidneys. Lymph, and the blood itself, carry the germ-fighting white blood cells that form the basis of the immune system. These cells recognise germs and make chemicals called antibodies that kill them.

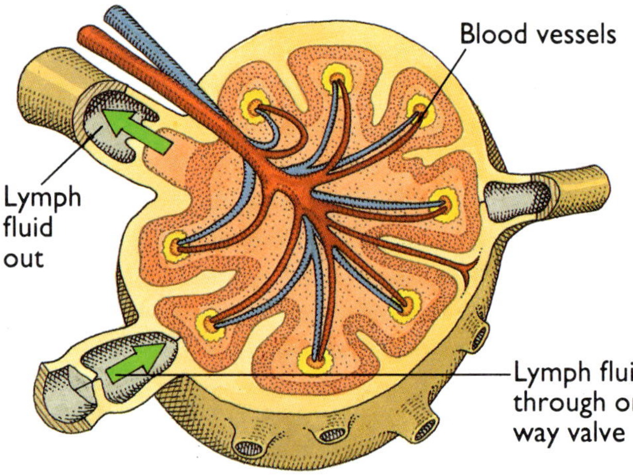

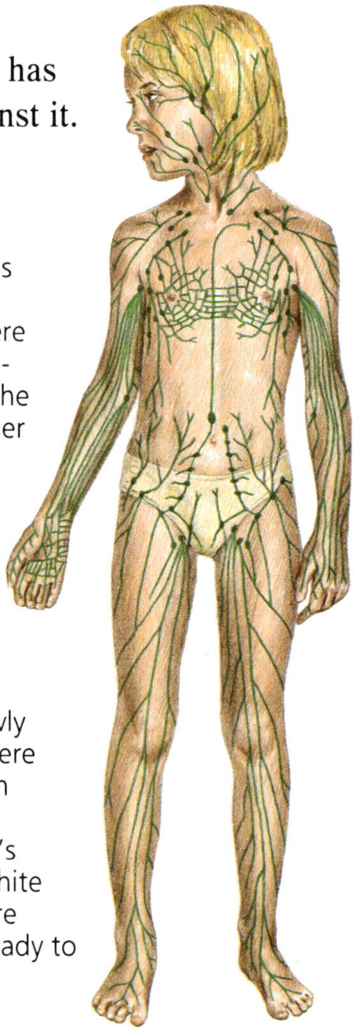

The lymph network

The lymphatic system is body-wide, like the circulatory system. There are collections of bean-sized lymph nodes in the armpits, groin and other places. The lymph ducts finally come together into large tubes that empty into main veins, near the heart.

Lymph node (left)

Lymph fluid flows slowly through the node, where cells are added, broken down and recycled according to the body's needs. In particular, white cells from the blood are stored and multiply, ready to fight germs.

Vaccination

Blood and lymph contain billions of germ-killing white blood cells. The body can be tricked into defending itself, by injecting it with disabled versions of real germs. These prepare the body so that if real germs invade, they are killed at once. This process, vaccination, was introduced by a British doctor, Edward Jenner (1749-1823, right). In 1796 Jenner successfully vaccinated a patient against the disease smallpox.

Deadly rhyme

"Ring-a-ring-a-roses, A pocket full of posies, A-tishoo, A-tishoo, We all fall down." This nursery rhyme originated at the time of the Great Plague, which swept Britain in 1665. As the plague spread, people carried posies of flowers, hoping the scent would prevent the disease. If they fell ill, one of the first signs was sneezing, and death would soon follow. Plague pits were dug (right) to dispose of the bodies and to try to prevent further spread of the disease.

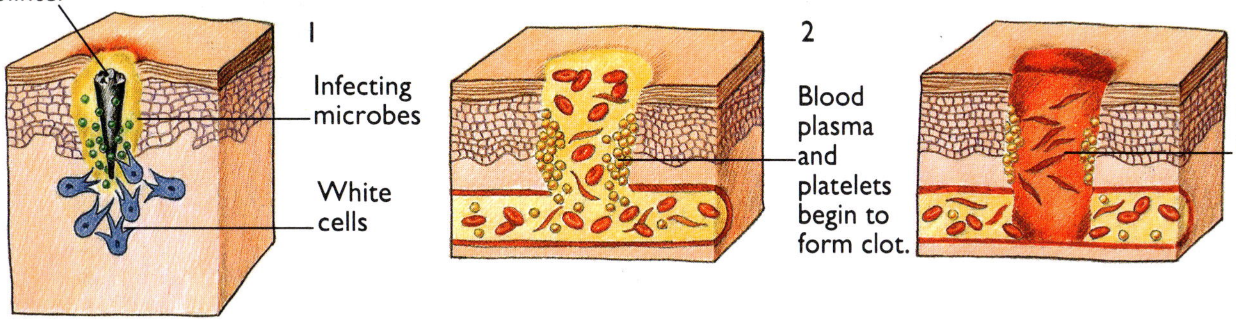

Sealing wounds

Small cuts and wounds happen all the time, inside the body and outside on the skin. At a wound, no matter how small, blood undergoes a chain of chemical changes. If the skin is punctured, for example by a splinter (above), the blood becomes thicker and sticky, and white cells gather to attack any germs that may try to get in (1). As the splinter is removed, tiny cell fragments that normally float in the blood, known as platelets, become stuck in the stickiness and make a gooey barrier. This process is known as coagulating or clotting (2). The clot goes hard and seals the wound, to stop blood and body fluids leaking out, and to prevent dirt and germs getting in (3). Gradually the skin or other tissue grows back and heals itself.

Healers through the ages

Different societies have many types of healers or shamans. In prehistory, shamans may have worn the skins of animals during ceremonies (left). Modern medicine relies on factory-produced drugs, chemical tests, advanced surgery and complicated equipment. There is no doubt that it has been amazingly successful. But there has been renewed interest in traditional medicines that use natural products, and place more importance on the mind and soul.

AIDS

One of today's greatest health challenges is AIDS, Acquired Immune Deficiency Syndrome. A microbe called HIV (Human Immunodeficiency Virus) infects the body and attacks the immune system, so the body cannot protect itself against other microbes. Millions of people around the world have HIV. Drugs slow the course of this fatal disease, but a cure is yet to be discovered.

A human cell infected with HIV

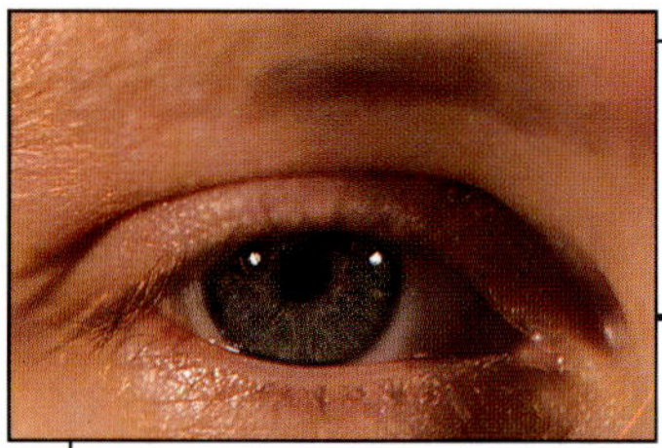

SIGHT AND HEARING

An animal needs to sense the world around it, in order to find food and drink, locate shelter and mates, and detect and move away from danger. The organs specialised to do this form the sensory system. They are closely connected to the nervous system. The human body's five main senses are sight, hearing, smell, taste and touch. Our sense of balance is also vital. This involves the semicircular canals in the ears, and information from the skin about touch, from stretch detectors in the muscles in joints about body position and from the eyes about head position.

Inside the ear
The ear detects patterns of sound waves travelling through the air. The outer ear flap funnels sound waves into a 25-millimetre-long tube, the outer ear canal. At the end of this tube is the eardrum, which vibrates as sound waves bounce off it. The vibrations pass along a chain of three tiny bones, the ear ossicles, and into the fluid inside the cochlea. There the vibrations are transformed into electrical signals known as nerve impulses, which flash along nerves to the brain.

Eustachian tube
The Eustachian tube leads between your ear and throat. It opens during swallowing and yawning, to equalise air pressure within the ear.

Sense of balance
The semicircular canals are involved in balance. They are filled with fluid. As the head tilts, tiny hair cells in the fluid move, sending signals to the brain.

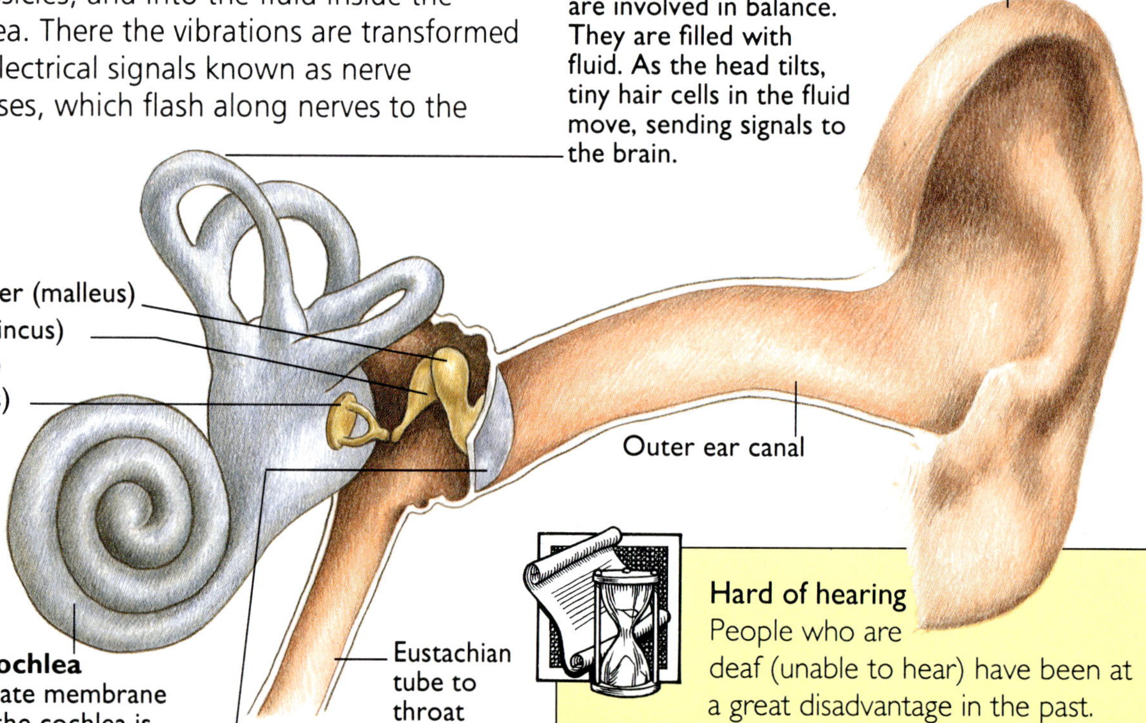

The cochlea
A delicate membrane inside the cochlea is covered with microscopic cells that have hairs sticking from them. The vibrating fluid in the cochlea shakes the hairs and generates nerve impulses from the cells.

The eardrum
This disc of tightly-stretched, skin-type tissue is about as big as the nail on the little finger. Like skin, it can heal itself if slightly cut or torn.

Hard of hearing
People who are deaf (unable to hear) have been at a great disadvantage in the past. Ear trumpets, that collect sound waves and concentrate them into the ear, have been used for centuries. A Victorian version is shown here. Today deaf people learn lip-reading, and sign language with the hands. Modern electronic hearing aids can also help some deaf people.

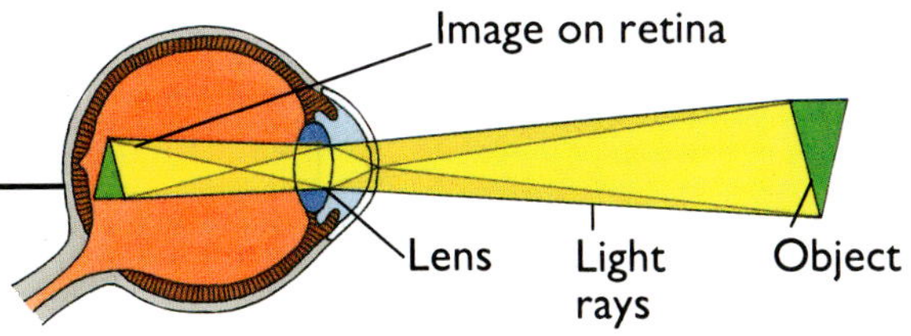

Inside the eye

The eye is a sphere about 25 millimetres across, filled with clear jelly. It is specialised to detect patterns of light rays and transform them into tiny electrical signals, nerve impulses, which flash along nerves to the brain. At the front of the eye is a clear domed part, the cornea. Behind this is a coloured ring, the iris, with a hole in the centre, the pupil. Behind the pupil is a clear bulging disc, the lens, which bends the light rays. Light rays pass through the cornea, pupil and lens, into the interior of the eye. They shine on a very thin layer lining the inside, the retina. This contains more than 120 million cells known as rods and cones, because of their shape. The rods and cones turn the colours, patterns and brightnesses of light-ray energy into nerve-signal energy, and send the nerve impulses along the optic nerve to the brain for analysis.

The world upside down?

Because of the way a lens works, the image it shines onto the retina is upside down. But a baby's brain has no concept of up or down. It learns to turn the images "right side up" almost from the very beginning, as a natural part of sight.

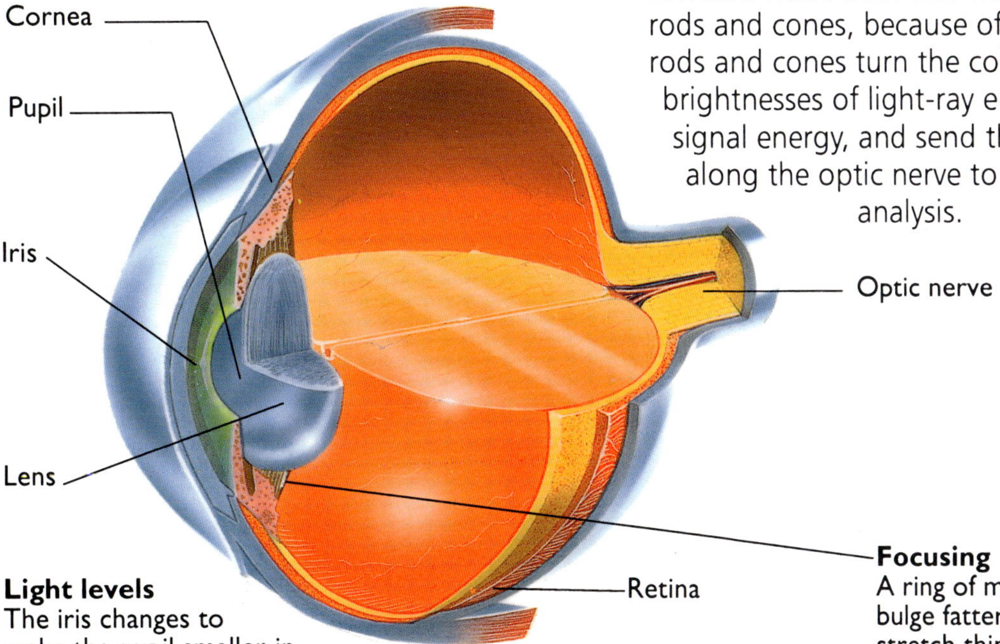

Focusing
A ring of muscles makes the lens bulge fatter for near objects, and stretch thinner for faraway ones, to focus light rays clearly on the retina.

Light levels
The iris changes to make the pupil smaller in brighter conditions. This protects the eye's delicate interior from being damaged by too much light.

Better sight

Spectacles and contact lenses change the path of light rays, so that people whose eyes cannot focus properly are able to see clearly and sharply. The first spectacles were in use by the 13th century. The system of Braille allows blind people to read, by running their fingers over tiny patterns of raised dots on the page. It was invented in 1824 by Louis Braille (1809-1852), a blind French student, when he was 15.

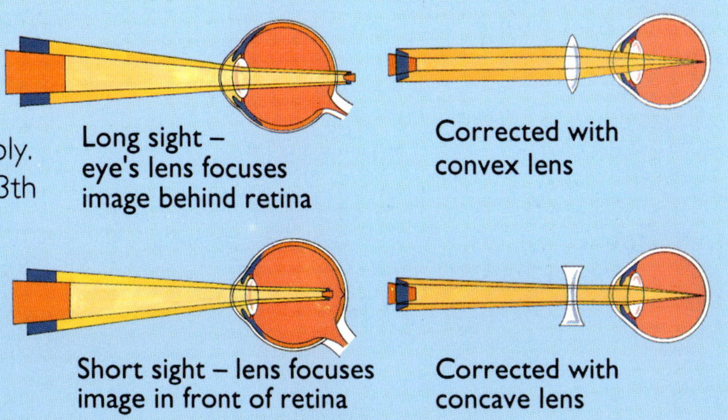

SMELL, TASTE AND TOUCH

The human body's main senses are sight and hearing. However, our sense of smell is also important, helping us to identify things at a distance, unlike taste and touch. Taste is similar to smell, but detects flavour substances in foods and drinks, rather than odour substances floating through the air. Both these senses check that foods and drinks are not bad or rotten, as revealed by unpleasant odours and flavours. The skin also has a warning function, signalling if the body is in danger from extreme heat, cold or pressure.

Inside the nose and mouth

Air carrying odour substances passes through the nasal cavity as you breathe in and out. The odours land on a batch of toothbrush-like olfactory hairs, in the roof of the cavity. Microscopic cells attached to the hairs send nerve impulses to the brain when they detect certain odours. Similarly, flavour substances from foods are detected by tiny, onion-shaped groups of cells known as taste buds. These are scattered over the tongue, among the larger lumps and bumps known as papillae. The taste bud cells send nerve impulses to the brain when they recognise four main flavours: sweet, salt, sour and bitter.

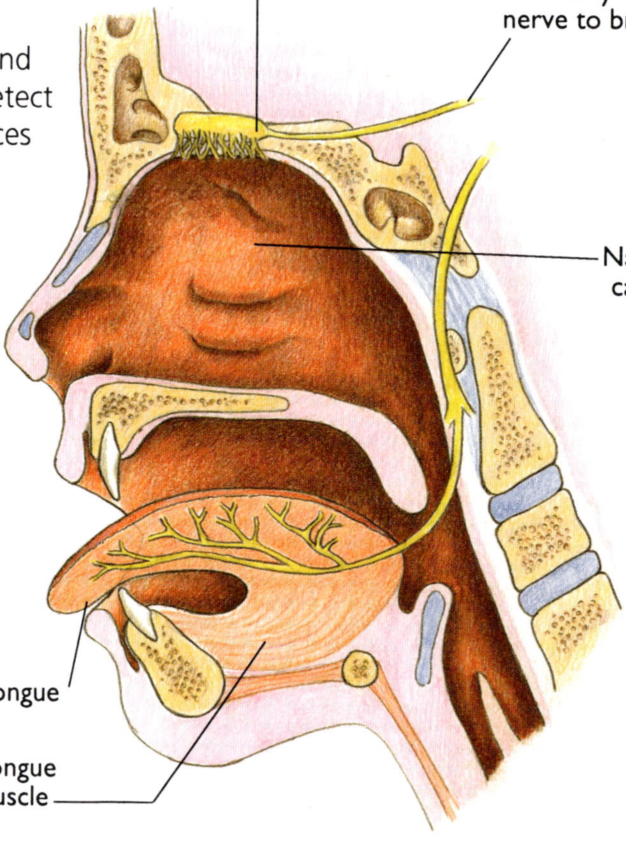

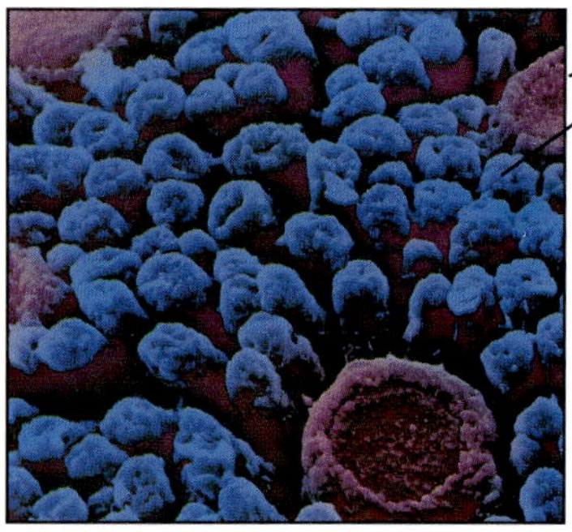

Testing smell and taste

Test your senses of smell and taste by trying this experiment with a friend. Prepare small samples of sweet, sour, salt and bitter foods. See if you can tell which sample is which when you are blindfolded. Then try the experiment again, holding your nose. How successful are you this time at detecting different tastes?

Taste buds

An average person has about 10,000 taste buds. They are located mainly on the tongue, among the tiny projections known as fungiform papillae that appear in pink in the magnified false-colour image on the left above. Conical papillae (blue) form a rough surface that helps in the chewing of food. There are also taste buds on the insides of the cheeks, on the roof of the mouth, and on the upper throat.

Sweaty lies

When people are nervous, they tend to sweat. This reduces the skin's resistance to small, harmless amounts of electricity. The polygraph or "lie detector" measures the electrical resistance of the skin. It has been used to test whether people are calm and probably innocent when questioned, or nervous and perhaps guilty.

Skin colour

Groups of people who have traditionally lived in certain parts of the world have different skin colours. Where the Sun's rays are strong, skin makes more of its natural dark colouring substance, melanin. This protects the tissues beneath from the Sun's potentially harmful UV (ultra-violet) rays. Over thousands of years, evolution has produced dark skin, compared to the light-coloured skin of people who live in temperate regions.

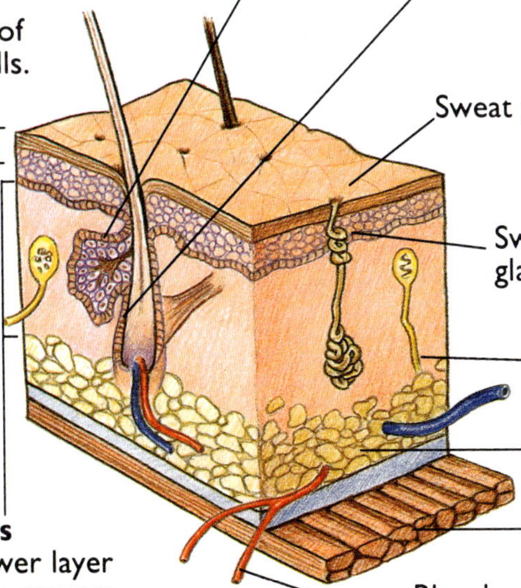

Sensors
In addition to the cold and light touch receptors shown, the skin contains sensors for heat, pain and pressure.

The skin

The skin is the body's supple, protective coat. It helps to keep out too much heat, cold, water, germs and harmful rays, and keeps in body warmth and fluids. Its surface consists of microscopic skin cells, dead and hardened with the substance called keratin. Every day, millions of these cells are worn away as the body moves, wears clothes and washes. They are replaced by cells below multiplying and moving upwards. Under this layer are microscopic sensors that detect touch, pressure, pain, heat and cold. Under the dermis is a layer of fat, which absorbs shocks, and helps insulate the body from heat and cold.

Washing is fashionable

Thorough personal hygiene, with daily washes, is relatively recent. In the past, the nearest running water was the local river. Rich people used perfumes to mask their body odours. By the last century, people knew that some germs caused disease. They began to wash more often, sometimes helped by a maid (right).

NERVES AND REACTIONS

Along with hormones (see pages 158-159), nerves control and coordinate the whole body, and make it respond to information about the outside world obtained by the senses. The nervous system has two main parts. One is the central system, consisting of the brain and spinal cord. The other is the peripheral system. This includes the thin interconnected nerves snaking all through the body, which link the central system to the organs and tissues. There are more than 50,000 kilometres of nerves in the body.

Automatic nerves

The nerve network shown here deals mainly with information for the conscious brain – things you are aware of, and can control. Running alongside it is another nerve network, mainly in the chest and abdomen. This is the autonomic network. It deals with vital processes such as heartbeat, regular breathing, digestion, waste disposal and blood pressure. It is controlled by the brain, but works automatically, in the subconscious.

Body artist

During the Renaissance period, Andreas Vesalius (1514-64) followed Leonardo da Vinci as a great artistic anatomist. Born in Brussels, he became medical professor at Padua in Italy at the age of 23, where he dissected and studied human bodies, and drew beautifully accurate pictures of what he saw. He corrected the traditional teachings of Galen (see page 146), which offended many people. Vesalius' book *De Humanis Corporis Fabrica* (*On the Structure of the Human Body*), in 1543, began the era of scientific anatomy.

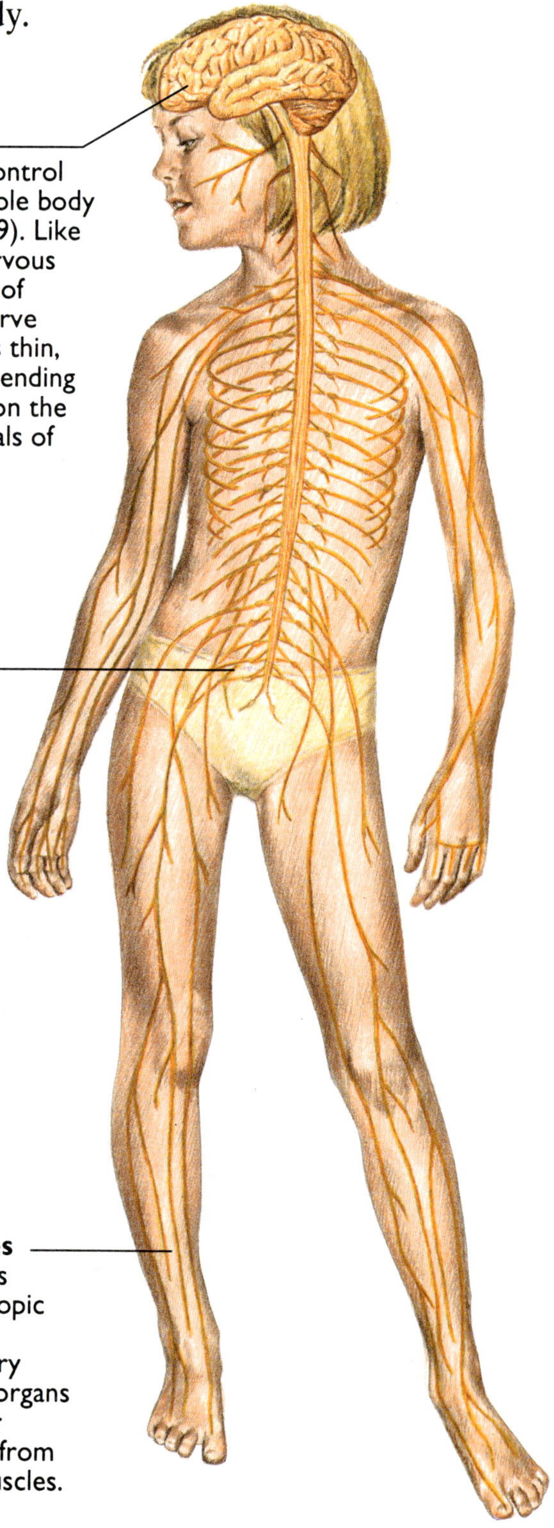

Brain

The brain is the control centre for the whole body (see pages 168-169). Like the rest of the nervous system, it is made of interconnected nerve cells. Each one has thin, wire-like parts extending from it, that pass on the tiny electrical signals of nerve impulses.

Spinal cord

This thick bundle of nerves merges into the lower brain. It is sited inside a tunnel in the vertebral bones, where it is protected from knocks. Spinal nerve roots branch out to the various organs and parts.

Peripheral nerves

Each nerve contains bundles of microscopic nerve-cell "wires". Sensory nerves carry signals from sense organs to the brain. Motor nerves take signals from the brain to the muscles.

Madness and bedlam

Brain disorders are some of the most unsettling of all illnesses. In epilepsy, the brain is overcome by random nerve impulses firing through the nerve-cell network. These make the body jerk or convulse, in a fit or seizure. In past times, people with certain brain disorders were labelled as "mad" and locked away in asylums such as Bethlehem, or Bedlam (right). Now, drugs and other medical treatments can help many problems.

Fast reactions

Quick reactions help the body to play fast-moving sports, and also to survive and minimise injuries. If a finger touches a flame, the skin's pain sensors send nerve impulses along sensory nerves to the spinal cord, which relays them to the brain. In case the brain does not react in time, the cord also sends impulses straight back along motor nerves, telling the arm muscles to jerk the finger away. This is known as a reflex action.

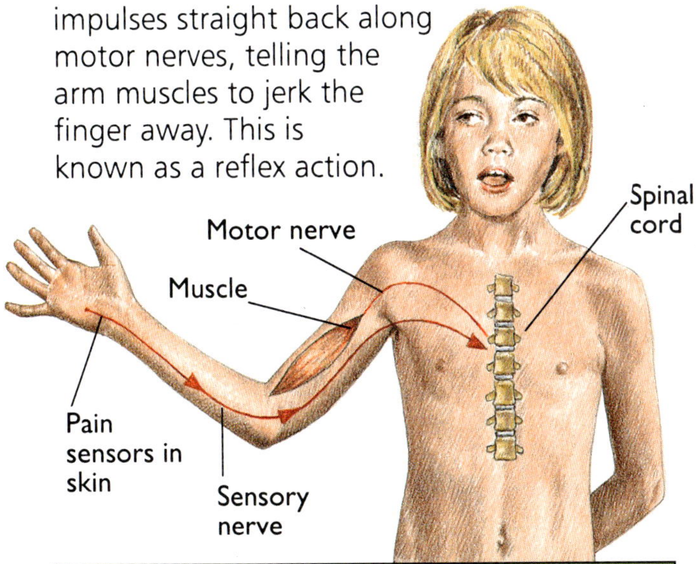

Skilful coordination

The Ancient Greeks had a great tradition of strength and skill in sports such as running, jumping, spear-hurling, discus-throwing (below), boxing and wrestling. They needed fast reactions and good coordination – activities involving not only the muscles, but the nervous system that controls them. The Greeks held their original Olympic Games every four years from as long ago as 1000 BC. Gradually, the games were enlarged to include more running events, and even theatre and music performances. The games were supposed to celebrate the ancient Greek gods, but the winners came to be treated as gods themselves. In AD 394, the games ended. The modern Olympics began in 1896 and carry on the tradition.

Statue in the Olympic Stadium, Athens, Greece

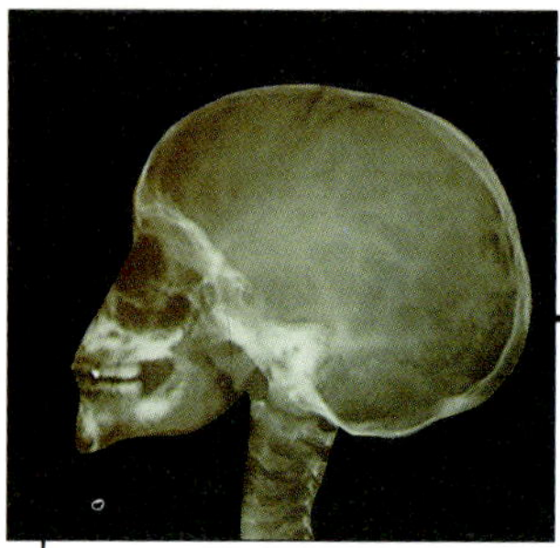

CONTROL CENTRE

The brain is the control centre of the body, and the place where consciousness and the mind are based. Some 100 billion nerve cells, each one connected to up to half a million others, make up an unimaginably complicated network for nerve impulses. Much of the brain's activity does not take place consciously. The "automatic brain" controls heartbeat, breathing, digestion, temperature and many other body processes, without your conscious involvement. Certain areas of the brain are concerned with specific functions.

Thalamus
This egg-shaped part is a relay station between the cortex and the rest of the brain. It filters out or redirects many nerve impulses, so that the "thinking" cortex can concentrate on what is important.

Hypothalamus
Small as a fingertip, the hypothalamus regulates basic urges and desires such as hunger, thirst, heartbeat, breathing, blood pressure, body temperature and sexual activity.

Cortex
This wrinkled sheet of "grey matter", 2-4 millimetres thick, is the outer wrapping for the two cerebral hemispheres that make up nine-tenths of the brain. The cortex deals with thoughts, memories, learning, sensations and body control (see opposite).

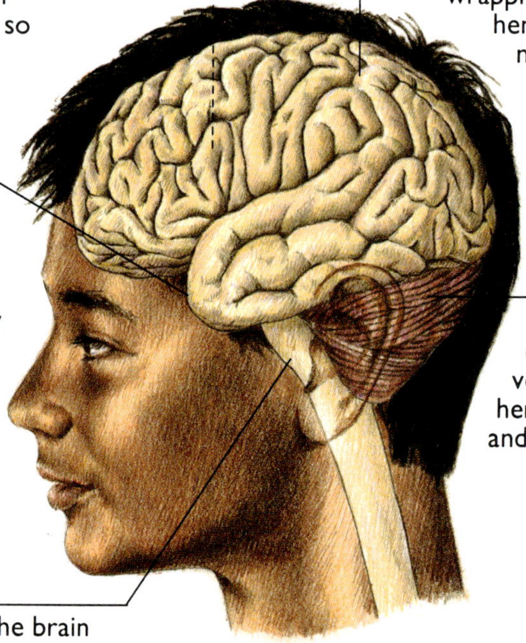

Cerebellum
The wrinkled lobes of the cerebellum look like a mini-version of the cerebral hemispheres. They coordinate and organise muscle actions.

Medulla
The lowest part of the brain narrows and merges with the spinal cord. It is involved in automatic processes such as pulse rate, digestion, breathing and chewing.

Reading head bumps

In the 19th century, phrenology was a popular and important "science". A phrenologist was an expert at reading the lumps and bumps on the human skull, which were supposed to reveal the person's intelligence, friendliness, reliability, truthfulness and emotional behaviour, and other aspects of the personality. Phrenology is now seen as fake by modern scientists.

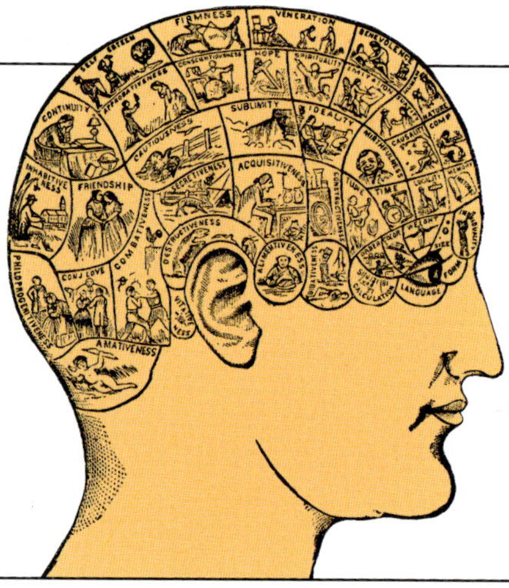

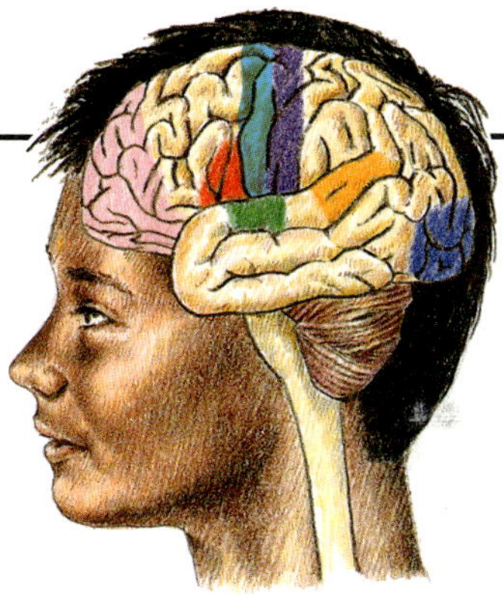

Brain areas

Different areas of the brain's outer cortex are the centres of various kinds of mental activity.

- Reading and understanding
- Hearing
- Speech
- Body motor centre
- Awareness
- Visual
- Body sensory centre

"You are getting sleepy ..."

One mysterious but scientifically recognised feature of the mind-and-brain is hypnosis. This is also called mesmerism after one of its pioneers, Austrian physician Franz Mesmer (1734-1815). The hypnotised person will do many things asked of him or her, and can be "put to sleep". Hypnotism has become a useful technique in treating various mental disorders, easing pain, and controlling obsessions and habits such as gambling and smoking.

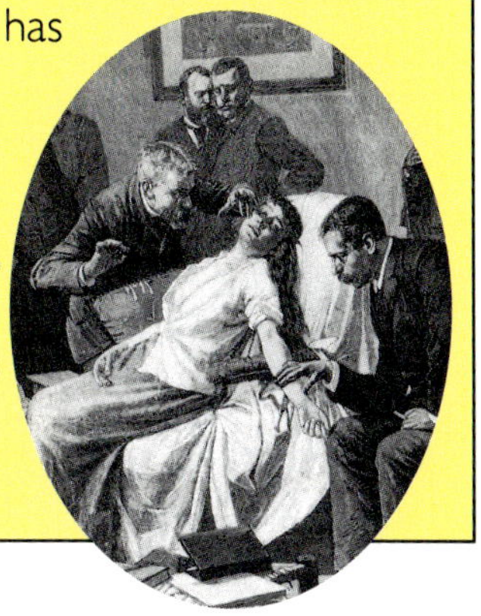

Animal brains

Humans are the most intelligent animals on Earth. This is due partly to our large brains, and especially the area of the cortex. More accurately, it is linked to the size of the brain and its cortex, in proportion to the whole body. In general, animals that we consider to be "intelligent" have large brains in relation to their body sizes. The average human brain weighs 1.2-1.4 kilos.

In various mammals, different proportions of the cerebrum are taken up with hearing, seeing and so on, depending on how important those functions are to the animal. Smell is a very important sense for rats and ground shrews, but is less important to chimpanzees. Chimpanzees and other intelligent primates have a much larger proportion of non-specific brain.

Rat Chimpanzee Ground shrew

- Motor
- Smell
- Hearing
- Sensory
- Seeing
- Non-specific

Head-hunters

Until recent times, some groups of people used to sever and preserve the heads of their enemies, to commemorate victory in battle. Some have even eaten their enemies' brains in an attempt to gain extra courage and wisdom. These traditions were carried out in parts of South America, Papua New Guinea and Indonesia, shown in the illustration on the right. They are now exceptionally rare.

REPRODUCTION

The reproductive systems of women and men are the parts specialised for producing babies. Mating (sexual intercourse) and pregnancy are a natural part of the life cycle, found in all animals. Parents have young, who grow up and have young of their own, and so on. The biological basics of human reproduction are much the same as in our mammal relatives, such as monkeys.

MALE REPRODUCTIVE ORGANS

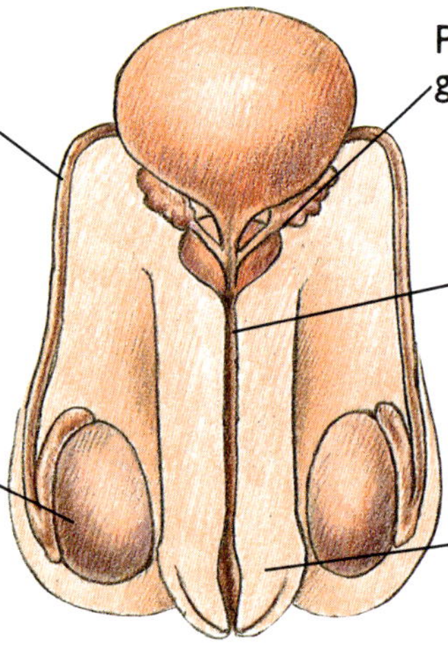

In the male, the testes are glands that make millions of sperm cells. During sex, the man's penis becomes longer and stiffer, and is inserted into the woman's vagina. Sperm come along the urethra and out into the vagina. They swim through the womb and into the egg ducts, towards a ripe egg.

FEMALE REPRODUCTIVE ORGANS

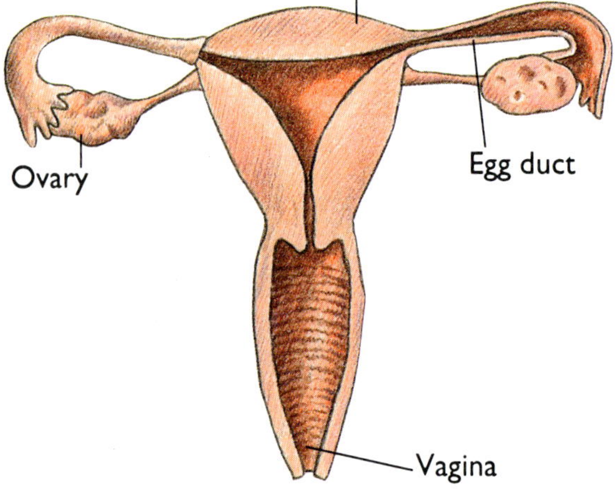

Every four weeks, one of the woman's ovaries releases a tiny ripe egg cell which travels down the egg duct towards the womb. The womb is ready to nourish the fertilised egg. If there is no fertilised egg, the womb lining breaks down and flows out of the vagina as the monthly blood loss or period.

Families big and small

In times gone by, and in some countries today, parents have lots of children. As soon as they are able, the children must work to bring back money for the family. In other parts of the world, parents have only one or two children, and may practise birth control (contraception) to prevent the possibility of having any more. This may be due to personal preference, or lack of money and jobs, or because of their countries' official encouragement for small families.

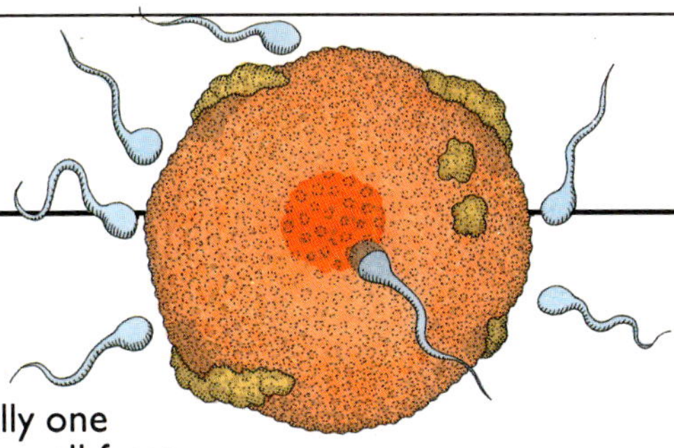

Usually one sperm cell fuses with the egg cell to fertilise it.

Fertilisation

An egg cell cannot develop into a baby unless it is fertilised by a sperm cell from the male. The head of one sperm merges into the egg cell (above), and their genetic materials or DNAs come together. The DNAs contain all the instructions, in the form of a chemical code, to make a new living, breathing human body.

The egg cell begins to divide 24 hours after fertilisation.

The secret of life

In 1953, American biologist James Watson (1928-) and English biochemist Francis Crick (1916-) worked out the structure of DNA. Its shape is a double helix, like two intertwined spiral staircases. The strands can separate and copy themselves, as cells divide. The sets of DNA are in the nucleus of the cell, tightly coiled into X-shaped structures called chromosomes. Watson and Crick's discovery explained how general features are passed on from parents to children (right), yet each child (apart from identical twins) is always slightly different.

Embryo at six weeks

Foetus at four months, with the umbilical cord that connects it to the mother's placenta

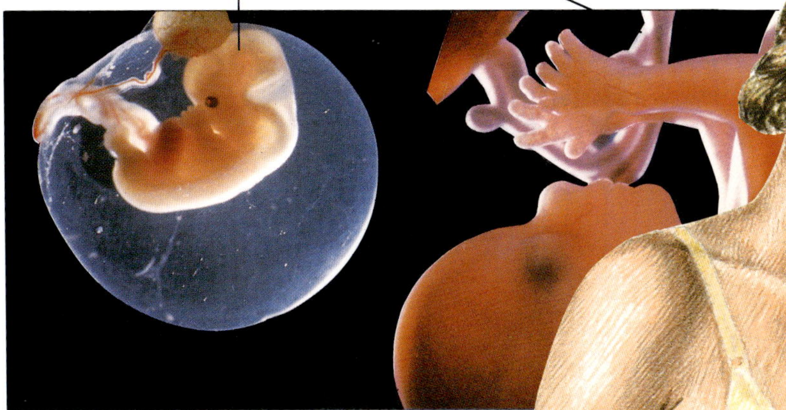

Pregnancy

After fertilisation the egg cell divides, forming a pinhead-sized ball of a hundred or more cells. This settles into the nourishing, blood-rich lining of the womb, and its cells continue to multiply. Gradually the cells become specialised into nerve cells, muscle cells, blood cells and so on, and a tiny baby takes shape. This stage is called the embryo. Two months after fertilisation, the baby is about 25-30 millimetres long. From now until birth, at nine months after fertilisation, it is known as a foetus. At birth the baby passes through the neck of the womb, through the vagina, to the outside world.

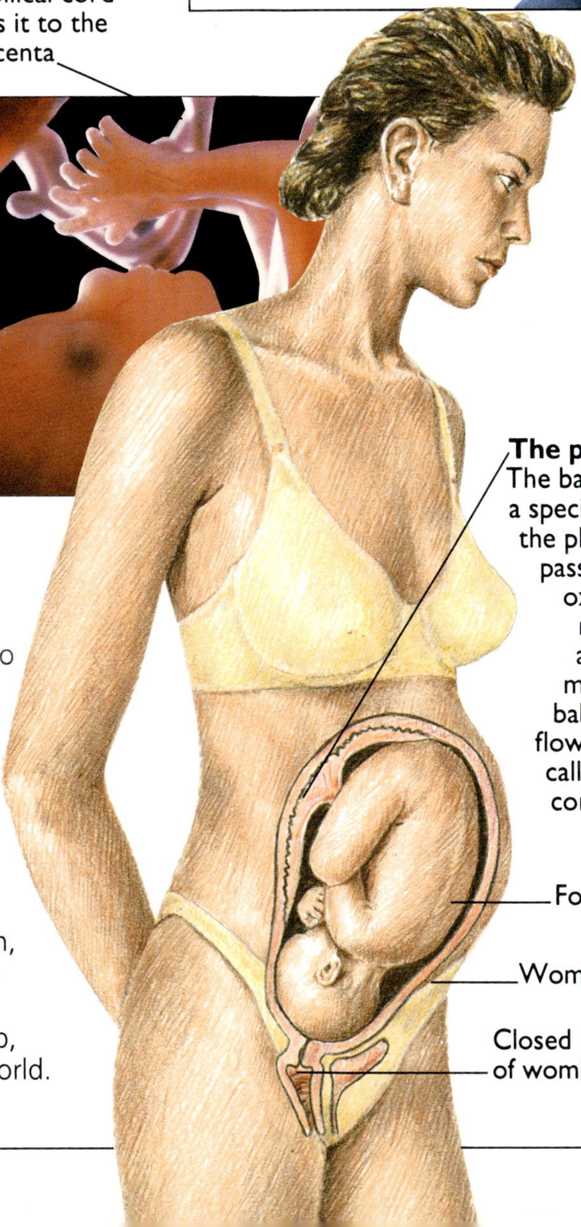

The placenta

The baby is nourished by a special organ called the placenta. This passes nutrients and oxygen from the mother's blood across a thin membrane to the baby's blood, which flows along a "lifeline" called the umbilical cord.

GLOSSARY

Air pressure The weight of the air in the atmosphere pressing down on the surface of the Earth due to the pull of gravity.

Alternating current (A.C.) A current which can reverse the direction of its flow.

Amp The measurement of electrical current.

Anatomy The study of the structure of living things.

Artery A large vessel that carries blood away from the heart to the organs and tissues.

Atmosphere The protective blanket or layer of gases that surrounds a planet.

Atom The smallest part of an element.

Capacitor A pair of electrodes capable of storing small amounts of electricity.

Capillaries A network of very small blood vessels that pass oxygen and nutrients to the surrounding tissues.

Cartilage A smooth, rubbery or gristly substance. It covers the ends of bones in joints, and forms a flexible framework for parts such as the nose and ears.

Catalytic converter A device fitted to the exhaust system of a vehicle which removes most of the engine's harmful gases before they can be released into the air.

Cell The basic building block of living things. An average cell is one-hundredth of a millimetre across and can only be seen with a microscope.

Circuit The unbroken line in which an electric current flows.

Climate The average weather in a place over a long period of time.

Combustible A substance that catches fire easily.

Concave Curving inwards like the inside of a spoon.

Conductor A substance, such as copper, that will allow electricity to flow along it.

Convex Curving outwards, like a ball.

Diaphragm A tough sheet of muscle separating the chest from the abdomen in mammals.

Direct current (D.C.) A current which flows continuously in one direction.

DNA A molecule that contains all the genetic information, which is passed from parents to offspring and tells the body how to develop.

Domains Groups of atoms which are magnetically aligned.

Dynamo A machine which uses magnetism and movement to produce energy.

Electromagnetic radiation Electric and magnetic forces that vibrate at right angles to each other and can travel through space. These include light, radio waves, infra-red and ultraviolet radiation.

Electromagnetic spectrum The complete range of known electromagnetic radiation.

Electromagnetism The relationship between electricity and magnetism.

Electron A tiny particle with a negative charge.

Enzyme A biological substance that speeds up a chemical reaction.

Evaporation The process by which a liquid is heated to become a vapour, or gas.

Fibre optics A way of sending light along very thin glass fibres.

Focus The point at which light rays come together to form a sharp, clear image.

Fossil fuels Fuels, such as coal, oil and gas, which are formed over millions of years from decaying plants and animals.

Frequency The number of sound vibrations per second, measured in hertz.

Fuse A thin wire which melts (fuses), used as a safeguard in an electric circuit.

Gravity The force of attraction between two objects. The size of the force depends on the size of the objects.

Hologram A ghost-like three-dimensional figure normally produced by laser.

Hormone A body substance that acts as a "chemical messenger". Made in an endocrine gland, it circulates in the blood and affects the way some cells and organs work.

Humidity The amount of water vapour in the air.

Hydroelectric power Electricity generated from falling water.

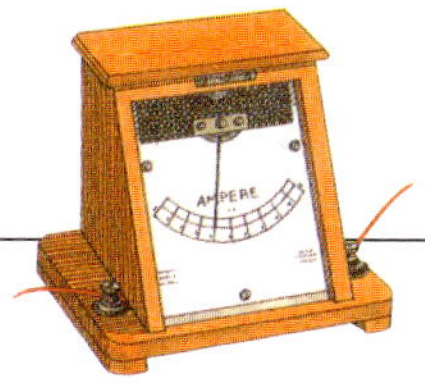

Image The "picture" of an object produced by a mirror or a lens.

Insulator A material that does not conduct electricity.

Laser A machine that can produce a narrow, powerful beam of light of one particular wavelength. The word "laser" stands for Light Amplification by Stimulated Emission of Radiation.

Lens A piece of transparent material with curved surfaces that bend or refract light.

Ligament A strong, slightly stretchy, strap-like part around a joint. Ligaments hold the bones of a joint together, strengthening and stabilising the joint.

Line of force The force of a magnet is exerted along lines of force, which extend from the north to the south pole, all around the magnet. These make up the magnetic field.

Matter Anything that has weight, occupies space and can be seen.

Membrane The thin "skin" over a body cell or larger part.

Molecules Small units which make up any object.

Muscle A body part specialised to contract. Muscles make all the movements of the body.

Nerve A body part specialised to carry messages, in the form of tiny electrical signals or pulses. Nerves control and coordinate most body processes.

Nucleus The central part of an atom, made up of protons and neutrons.

Ohms The unit of measurement of resistance.

Optic nerve A long, string-like structure that carries electrical messages from the eye to the brain.

Ore A natural substance from which metal can be extracted.

Organ A major body part that has a distinct function, such as the heart, lung or brain.

Ozone layer A layer of the gas called ozone in the Earth's atmosphere which absorbs about 90% of the harmful ultraviolet radiation from the Sun.

Particles Tiny parts of a substance.

Photosynthesis A process in which green plants use the energy from water, the sun, minerals and carbon dioxide to make food.

Pigment Any substance that gives colour to plant or animal cells, or can be ground up to a powder to colour paints or dyes.

Prism A solid transparent shape usually made of glass, which can be used to separate the colours in visible light.

Protons Tiny particles with a positive charge.

Radar Tracking the position of an object using reflected radio waves.

Reflection The bouncing back of light from a surface.

Refraction The bending of light when it passes from one medium to another.

Respiration A chemical process which takes place inside the cells of all living things. During respiration food is "burnt" in the presence of oxygen to release energy.

Solar energy The Sun's energy.

Static electricity A non-moving electric charge often produced by creating friction.

Stratosphere The upper layer of the atmosphere, about 10 km above the surface of the Earth.

Tendon A strong, rope-like part at the end of a muscle, that connects the muscle itself to the bone that pulls it.

Tides The rise and fall of sea water twice each day caused by the pull of the Sun and the Moon.

Tissue A group of similar cells that all do the same job, such as muscle or nerve tissue. Collections of different tissues make up major body parts, known as organs.

Transformer A pair of coils on an iron core, used to change the voltage of an alternating current.

Turbines A wheel or motor driven by steam, water or air.

Vacuum A completely empty space with nothing inside it.

Vein A large vessel that carries blood back to the heart, from the organs and tissues.

Volt The measurement of the electric push of a current, measured on a voltmeter.

Watt The measurement of the power of electricity.

Wavelength The length between identical points on two waves next to each other.

INDEX

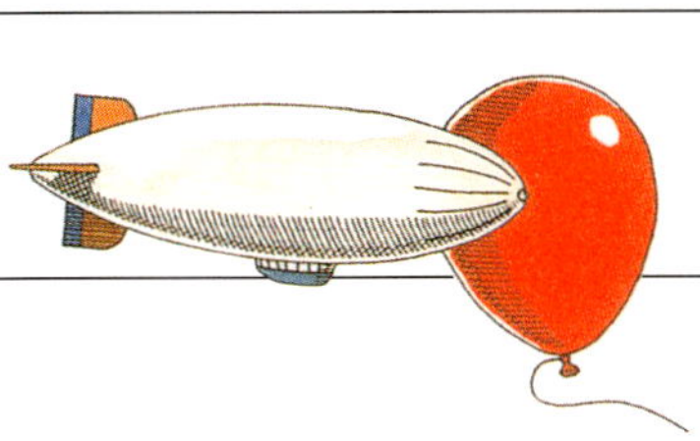

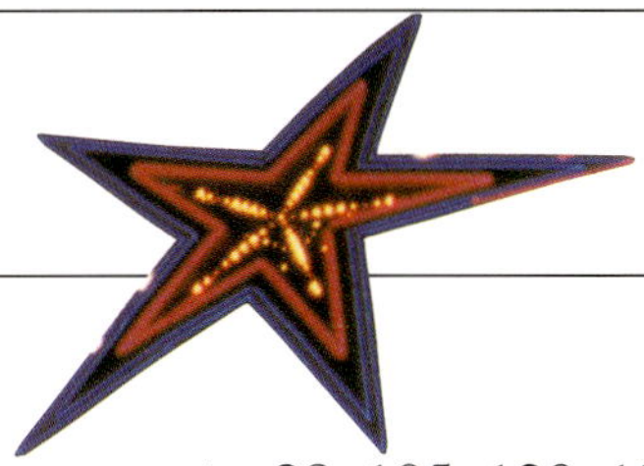